Monetary Policy and Public Finance

Monetary Policy and Public Finance

G. C. Hockley
*Lecturer, Department of Economics,
University College of South Wales and Monmouthshire,
Cardiff*

London Routledge & Kegan Paul

First published 1970
by Routledge & Kegan Paul Ltd
Broadway House, 68-74 Carter Lane
London, E.C.4
Printed in Great Britain by
Northumberland Press Limited
Gateshead

SBN 7100 6691 0

To my Parents

Contents

Part II: Public finance

Acknowledgments

I wish to record my great indebtedness to Professor B. Tew of Nottingham University for comments on 'The Monetary System' Part I of this manuscript, and Mr J. Bates for comments on Parts II and III. Also Professor J. Perrin of Lancaster University and my colleagues Mr J. H. Loosemore, Mr B. L. Jones and Mr J. F. Mackeson for comments on Chapters 12 and 13. Professor Brinley Thomas, Professor Gethin Davies and Mr J. D. Pole have been particularly helpful with advice and encouragement. I received invaluable assistance from the late Professor H. D. Dickinson, who read the whole of the draft manuscript and made many improvements in style and content. Shortcomings and omissions remaining are, of course, my responsibility.

I am indebted to the editors of the *British Tax Review* for permission to use material from my articles 'Taxation and the Employment of Married Women', May/June, 1967, and 'Capital Gains and Inflation', Jan./Feb., 1968 and *The Banker* for 'Incentives under a Value-Added Tax', March, 1968, and to the following for permission to quote from the works listed:

George Allen & Unwin for
 D. R. Denman, *Origins of Ownership*, 1958 and
 R. M. Titmus, *Income Distribution and Social Change*, 1962.
The Bank of England for several issues of the
 Bank of England Quarterly Bulletin.
The *Economic Journal* for
 A. Rubner, 'The Irrelevancy of the British Differential Profits Tax', June, 1964 and
 G. L. S. Shackle, 'Recent Theories concerning the Nature and Role of Interest', June, 1961.
Longmans Green & Co. for
 A. J. Merritt, *Executive Remuneration in the U.K.*, 1968.
Oxford University Press for
 A. T. Peacock and Jack Wiseman, *The Growth of Public Expenditure in the United Kingdom*, 1961.

Prentice-Hall Inc. for
W. J. Schultz and C. L. Harriss, *American Public Finance*, 1965.
C. A. Watts & Co. for
Joan Robinson, *Economic Philosophy*, Pelican, 1962.

As a recent writer on public finance, I must record a general debt to R. A. Musgrave for the stimulation of *The Theory of Public Finance*, McGraw-Hill, 1959.

Finally, as is proper, the last word goes to a woman—my wife—whose help and forbearance greatly eased my task.

University College, Cardiff GRAHAM C. HOCKLEY

Terminology

Since the publication of the *Report of the Committee on the Working of the Monetary System* in 1959, Cmnd. 827 (hereafter referred to as the *Radcliffe Report*, after its Chairman) the following terminology has been widely adopted and will be followed in this book:

Monetary sector is taken to include the Bank of England, the commercial banks, the discount houses, savings banks and the central government.

Monetary authorities are the dominant part of the monetary sector, and comprise the Bank of England and the central government.

The public: all individuals and institutions outside the monetary sector.

Long-term bonds: bonds which have five years or more to run to maturity or are undated.

Short-term bonds: less than five years to run to maturity.

Introduction

This book is intended as an introduction to a university course in public finance and for use of students of professional examinations. Also, I hope, it will be intelligible, and of interest, to the general reader. Taxation and poverty have been two of the most-discussed questions in recent years. In these matters most of us judge from a purely personal standpoint: a good tax is a tax that is paid by somebody else; wise government spending is spending that benefits oneself; correct monetary policy is regulation that protects one's own interests. The multitude of voices raised on almost every aspect of public finance, each claiming right on their side, but frequently each seeking their own ends, tends to drown out general considerations.

Essentially a study of public finance is an attempt to break away from this Babel, to see through arguments based on the interests of this or that group, and attempt to establish rational principles on which policy can be based.

The scope of a public finance course is ill-defined. Government spending and revenue are central to it, but there is considerable overlap with monetary policy. The government can, after all, merely create money to pay for the goods and services it requires, or it can borrow from its citizens as well as taxing them. This book takes the view that it is impossible to have a very realistic understanding of public finance matters without some understanding of the operation of the monetary system.

Part I is therefore devoted to the monetary system. Chapter 1 discusses the nature and attributes of money and then goes on to discuss the value of money—a section that can be omitted at first reading by anyone new to the subject. The following chapters deal respectively with the Bank of England, the discount market and the commercial banks. These institutions have a unique and long-established relationship with each other. Following this is a description of other financial institutions which in recent years have transformed much of the financial scene. Our concern is not so much with the detailed working of these institutions, but with obtaining an understanding of their interrelationships and how they form the monetary system. Chapter 6 draws the previous discussion together in looking at the implications for monetary policy of a Budget surplus or deficit. This chapter therefore provides many of the links between the sphere of public finance and that of money, which will be taken up and developed later in the book.

A description of the monetary system, it will be clear, is a description not of a static framework, but of an evolving structure. The rapidity with which change can take place is indeed one of the remarkable things about the collection of institutions labelled the 'British Monetary System'. As with many rapidly changing things, the spice of controversy is never far away.

Part II introduces the public finance section with four chapters which briefly outline how government expenditure and revenue have changed in this century. This background forms an essential part to understanding the system as it exists today. In this context policy can be discussed from two angles: one approach is to look at reasons for government expenditure and its change over time; the other approach is to concentrate on ways of ensuring that expenditures, given that the decision to spend has been made, are wisely and not wastefully applied. This book has a number of things to say which are relevant to this latter, important question, particularly on simplification of the system of tax and benefits, which could lead to large savings. But the detailed Parliamentary and administrative procedures, and statistical techniques, that attempt to ensure efficiency in this narrow sense have been considered outside the scope of this volume.

Changes up to April, 1969 have been incorporated. Thus the selective employment tax, capital gains tax, land tax, corporation tax, changes in investment allowances and grants, the special charge on investment income, and benefit allowances to individuals are detailed. In addition, a chapter is devoted to looking at a value-added tax, which Britain will have to adopt if she enters the Common Market.

Chapter 11 is a key chapter, setting out the accretion principle of income. This concept is used thereafter as a yardstick to evaluate the current system of taxes and benefits which are detailed in the following chapters. The National Debt raises complex monetary and fiscal issues, and it was decided to include this in Chapter 17, after the monetary and fiscal details have been given. Chapter 18 gathers together previous threads and looks at ways the system can evolve.

Part III, on Policy, does not attempt a detailed assessment of the use of policy in the post-war period: this has been well covered in recent publications; but it outlines the problems of using monetary and fiscal policy to control the economy. The difficulties in control have important fiscal implications which are developed in the final chapter.

Current objectives in society include equity, the full employment of resources, stability of the value of money, a satisfactory balance of payments, and the steady growth of the economy. The heading of 'Growth' covers the effects of monetary and fiscal policy on savings, consumption, investment, prices, output and work effort. All of these aspects are important, but the author is firmly of the opinion that the need for equity in the whole system of taxation and government spending has been very much underplayed, with serious consequences for growth and other objectives.

In a superficial sense, all taxes may be said to have unfavourable effects on growth. The issue is unrealistic. Governments need revenue, and by their investment and other spending policies can make a substantial contribution to growth. The real point at issue is whether an equitable tax and benefit system contributes more to growth and other objectives than an inequitable one. The volume of comment that occurs, almost daily, in the Press and elsewhere on the alleged drawbacks of the current fiscal system is evidence of the concern for this issue. The present system leaves a high-income-earner about 10% of his earned income, 70% of his long-term capital gains, a major part of his gambling winnings and usually all of the sums he receives by way of gifts. This can be put another way. Because of the way income is defined, the majority of employees are taxed on the whole of their spending power, since for most income only comes to them via earnings. They are overtaxed relative to taxpayers with mixed incomes. They are taxed at source, and most of the expenses of earning that income are not allowed to be deducted for tax purposes. It will be argued in Chapter 11 that this is the major flaw in the tax system, all the items mentioned represent purchasing power and a case can be made for taxing them at the same progressive rate. Whether the top rate should be nearer the 30% level of capital gains or the 90% level of surtax then becomes the real question for the community to debate and decide. On the benefit side of the fiscal system even more serious distortions appear: it can almost be described as a system that helps most the richest members of society. Given this situation, the wonder is not that an incomes and prices policy, on which successive governments have pinned so much of their hopes for improvements in the economy, has had so little success, but that it has had any success at all.

Part III also points out that, given the existing state of knowledge, fiscal and monetary changes have only limited ability to achieve the other objectives of society. Excessive concentration on particular taxes or benefits to achieve these ends can distort the impact of the fiscal system as a whole, with serious consequences of the kind mentioned above. A look at the fiscal system as a whole, both from the tax and benefit sides is overdue.

The issue before society is not the stark choice of either/or: of achieving either growth or equity, for example. Inevitable conflicts between objectives will occur and a balance will have to be struck. However, a wide variety of measures are possible, and if equity should be the prime concern of the fiscal system, as is argued here, it is possible that the harmful effects on other objectives can be compensated for in a way that does not seriously distort equity.

To argue for equity is not, it must be stressed, to argue for equality. The concept of equity is treated more fully in Chapter 11. It is composed of two strands: that people in equal positions should be treated equally, and that people in unequal positions should stand in a correct relationship with each other, with regard to the taxes they pay and the benefits they receive. The consensus of opinion in contemporary society seems to be, at its simplest, that a poor person should pay less in tax and receive more in benefits than a rich person. The exact amount of less or more is a matter of choice for the community concerned.

Although no serious commentator on the fiscal system claims that it is an equitable one, opinions differ on the need for, and the urgency of, rectification. Policy since the war has been primarily concerned with 'quantity'. The size of the national income and its rate of growth has been elevated to a prime economic desideratum. Concern for 'quality' and for the distribution of resources has tended to be pushed to one side.

Economists and politicians cannot complain if cynical policies meet with cynical responses. Tax policies that have the effect of helping most those least in need are hardly conducive to the acceptance of an incomes policy. Small taxes on income from gambling and capital gains and zero taxation on gifts, compared with highly progressive taxes on work income, is hardly an inducement to work harder. The pretence that we have a savage rate of estate duty, while it may comfort the wealthy, is likely to exacerbate the feelings of other members.

Better living standards of a community are multi-dimensional. The growth of national product (the amount of resources available) is one dimension; others are the way in which these resources are used (e.g. hospitals or motor-cars) and the way in which these resources are shared amongst the community. Our present fiscal system is inherited from different periods in the past, with many pieces added to patch up this or that particular deficiency. The end-result is less than satisfactory. The adoption of the accretion principle, which is set out in Chapter 11, is important because it helps to turn attention away from special pleading on behalf of interested parties towards more fundamental issues. When income is so defined, it makes sense to discuss the required degree of progression of taxation and benefits.

The belief in the need for growth in the economy is so widely held that it seems necessary to justify the treatment accorded here to equity in rather more detail.

Persuasive arguments are put forward that growth is more important than abstract notions of equity, which can, in any case, never be achieved in practice. Growth, it is argued, provides the means whereby everybody can be better off. This is a comfortable doctrine held, consciously or unconsciously, by many people. Is it possible that by being mesmerized by the concept of growth we have neglected deep-seated currents of human emotion?

In the international field it is generally recognized that the growing disparity between the developed nations and the less-developed nations creates dangerous conflicts and is a serious problem. It is not so much that the less-developed nations are becoming worse off, although in some countries this may be so, as that the developed nations are improving their living standards very much faster than the less-developed. Poverty and wealth are relative concepts. It is curious how little, at the present time, this trend of thought is carried over to standards of living of different sections within a country

Growth, as an aim of society, is seldom made explicit. Growth of what? The measuring-rod of real national product per head is frequently used: it is a crude measure. National product will increase by the same amount if £1,000,000 is spent on hydrogen bombs or if it is spent on hospitals, cars, schools or anything else. There is at least likely to be complete agreement, in that nobody would give equal weight to this collection of things. The further question of how this growth is to be translated into 'better living standards for all' is seldom mentioned. The record is pretty dismal. Britain's national income in real terms has increased considerably since the war: this is not much consolation to the old, the chronic sick, the disabled and the large families who in many cases show little or no improvement. Perhaps the sociologist can explain why the richest nations on earth are so obsessed with getting richer and so little concerned with what it is that is increased, or what happens to it when it has been produced? In any case, this comforting doctrine, that growth will solve the problems of distribution, has received a sharp, bitter shock. Few can doubt that one of the main causes of the rioting, looting, burning and murder which have scarred recent American summers is economic underprivilege of the non-white population. It is irrelevant to the situation that the poor in America may be well off compared to the poor in many other lands. A man compares himself to those around him. Slight improvements in the standard of the underprivileged may exacerbate feelings if this enables them to see more clearly the gap that separates them from the privileged and the nature of the barriers, some of them fiscal, that foster this divide. This is the error of those who define an increase in welfare as a situation where somebody can be made better off without making anyone worse off. Such a situation worsens relative positions, and relative disparities of position can be built up into explosive situations. The desire for fairness, or equity, is a powerful human emotion, but unfortunately, since the desire cannot be measured, it tends to be left out of account.

The idea of growth embodies the important concept that more can be done with a greater output than with a lesser output. Taken as a statement, at this moment of time, this is true, but trite. It does not necessarily follow that a nation, having achieved an increase in national product, will find it any easier to provide more hospitals or more schools. National product is an accounting concept: it shows, in money terms, what was produced in a particular year. If the increase in national product has been achieved by building more hospitals or by making more cars, that is that: the product is not then available for something else. We cannot, as some people would have us believe, have it both ways. Concentrating on growth in the abstract by, for example, suitable fiscal and monetary measures gives an increase of products and services that constitutes the growth. This increase, if it takes the form of consumption goods, will be distributed amongst the community in some way, but it is not then available again to achieve any other social objectives. The point is elementary, but frequently confused.

Growth, then, means more output, which can be planned output of particular things, or growth as dictated by the market-place and distributed by market processes, or some compromise between social and private goods.

The existing fiscal system has therefore grown up piecemeal. Additions and alterations have been made in the past with little thought given to its overall impact on different sectors of the community. Growth, since it is currently fashionable, tends to be the measure by which changes in a fiscal system are now judged. Equity considerations take second place. Lack of facts concerning the impact of the fiscal system might in the past have served as an excuse: this is no longer adequate. The known impact of the fiscal system, on both the tax and expenditure side, for single persons and married persons with and without children is set out in Chapter 18. Paradoxically, it has been pointed out that concentration on growth, to the virtual exclusion of equity, may defeat its own ends by building up resentment in sections of the community. This has probably been at least a contributory cause of the singular lack of success of a prices and incomes policy in the post-war period. The author is sufficient of an optimist to believe that people will work harder to improve a system they believe to be basically fair than they will to continue a system they believe to be basically unfair.

Part I

The monetary system

1
The nature of money

But it is pretty to see what money will do.
SAMUEL PEPYS, March 21st, 1667.

Essential properties of money

To make a comprehensive list of all the items which have been used as money at various times and in various places would be tedious. What have the following items used as money in common: cattle, rice, bark-cloth, women, gold, iron, stone and cigarettes?

These and all items used as money have the common intangible property of *general acceptability*. Within the community concerned, money is accepted because it is confidently believed that it in turn can be passed on for goods and services. The item serving as money in many communities is often scarce, and therefore valuable in its own right, but this is by no means necessary. A look at a £1 note will make this clear. It says: 'Bank of England. I promise to pay the Bearer on Demand the sum of One Pound. Chief Cashier.' It is of itself just a piece of printed paper. If you do demand £1, you can have another £1 note with a different number on it, or two pieces of paper each marked 'ten shillings', or a handful of coins whose intrinsic value—the cost of the metal—is only a few pence. The note is worth having, not because the paper on which it is printed is valuable or because the printing on the note has intrinsic worth, but because it is generally acceptable in Great Britain. That is, whatever goods or services are desired can be obtained by the exchange of a sufficient number of notes. The 'Promise to pay' engraved on the note is a reminder of the origin of banknotes; at one time they were receipts for precious metals deposited with goldsmiths, and it was expected at any time that the note or receipts could be returned and the metal repossessed. It is only in this century that 'backing' for notes, in the form of gold or silver, has been effectively done away with for purposes of transactions internal to a country. Banknotes and coins are not the only form of money in a modern society, for example, the majority of transactions are carried out by means of drawings on current accounts with the commercial banks. More will be said later on the types of assets which should be considered as money, and on the factors which determine the quantity of money in the economy.

Money has been described so far in terms of its function as a *medium of exchange*. The reason why all but the most primitive of societies need a medium of exchange should be self-evident, and is summed up in the phrase, 'the sheer inconvenience of double coincidence of wants'. That is, the need to find a seller of the item you require who at the same time needs what you have to offer.

Money, by its nature, also acts in some degree as a *store of value*. If money were like a day-return ticket on a railway, valueless after the day had ended, nobody would keep it. It is because money is expected to have general acceptability and more or less the same purchasing power the day after, and the day after that, that money is held, and this function is described as a store of value. It is unfortunate that the phrase *store of value* is often taken to mean that the value is constant. What determines the 'value of money'—that is, the amount of goods and services for which it can be exchanged and the problem of its value over time—will be taken up again in this chapter.

Money usually also acts as a *unit of account* and as a *standard of deferred payments*. The unit of account refers to the fact that instead of valuing each and every article and service in terms of all others, it is valued in terms of a common denominator, the medium of exchange. In a similar manner, contracts for future payments are usually made in terms of the medium of exchange, but they can be made in terms of the value of gold, or a foreign currency, or a quantity of goods. It is usual for money to act in both these ways, but is by no means necessary; the guinea today sometimes acts as a unit of account, but it does not circulate as a medium of exchange.

Definitions of money: liquid assets, primary and secondary money

It was a deliberate choice not to start off with a definition of money in our society. This seemingly simple question does not admit of a simple answer. A commonly quoted definition tells us that money is 'anything generally accepted in exchange for goods and services and for settlement of a debt'. This definition, while it is useful, needs further clarification.

The following distinctions will be found useful and can be given empirical content. The first, between *money* and *liquid assets*, is based on the function performed by the asset in question. Money on this definition is used for assets that act both as a medium of exchange and as a store of value, while liquid assets are used for securities which, while acting as a store of value, do not circulate in exchange. Money is liabilities of the Bank of England—that is, coin and notes and bankers' deposits (i.e. deposits of commercial banks at the Bank of England), together with deposits by the public at commercial banks. Liquid assets are such items as deposits at the Post Office Savings Bank, trustee savings banks, building societies, local government and hire purchase companies. These differ from money when the moment for payment arises; they must first be turned into money, rather than exchanged directly for commodities. It should be clear from this distinction that what is money at any particular time is a matter of law and of custom. Deposits at the Post Office Savings Bank could be made transferable by cheque, and these deposits would then fall into the category of money, rather than liquid assets.[1]

There is no hard-and-fast line that can be drawn that enables us to classify an asset into one category or another. For some purposes, it may be desirable to draw the line more widely than has been done above, for other purposes more narrowly. It is important to realize that the presence of a variety of assets with the characteristics of liquidity will affect the demand for money. The determining characteristics of 'liquidity' will be discussed.

Money itself, as defined above, can be split into primary and secondary money. *Primary money* consists of coin, notes and bankers' deposits—often simply referred to as 'cash'. Deposits at commercial banks on both current and deposit accounts are, in this country, what constitutes *secondary money*.

Money should not be confused with legal tender. Only notes, 'silver' coin up to £2, and copper coins up to 1s. are legal tender. In spite of this, the value of payments by cheque are many times the value of payments by cash and notes. The risk of default by banks in Great Britain and most other developed countries is nowadays considered so small, i.e. confidence is so great that transfer of deposits to third persons will be honoured, that deposits are included with notes in the definition of money. In Great Britain also no distinction is usually drawn between current and deposit accounts, because deposit accounts can usually be drawn on with almost as much ease as can current accounts.

[1] After a great deal of procrastination, a decision to set up a giro system was made (*Post Office Giro*, 1965). It started operation in October, 1968. A giro is a means whereby the payer can pay cash into the Post Office (or have his special account debited), and the sum credited or paid to the payee. Facilities for transfer between giro and savings bank accounts are provided. Post Office accounts are therefore now even more close to the money end of the spectrum of assets.

Current accounts, sometimes called 'demand deposits', are subject to cheque and withdrawal on demand. Deposit accounts, often called 'time deposits', formally require seven days' notice before withdrawal, but in practice a cheque would not be dishonoured if it were covered by a balance in a deposit account. An added reason for not distinguishing between these two accounts is that British banks, unlike, for example, American banks, do not have to observe different reserve ratios for each type of account.

Quantity of money and liquid assets

In 1967, in approximate figures, notes and coins outstanding in the economy amounted to £3,250 million, while deposits at commercial banks were three times as large at some £10,000 million. Post Office securities (Savings Certificates, Premium Bonds, Defence Bonds, Post Office and Trustee Savings accounts) amounted to nearly £8,500 million, Treasury bills to nearly £4,000 million. Short-term deposits with local government authorities amounted to over £1,500 million and shares and deposits with building societies to about £7,000 million.

The list of liquid assets is not intended to be a complete one, e.g. for some purposes, deposits with finance houses, accumulated funds in insurance companies, and others may be included. It can be seen that notes and coin are small in relation to bank deposits, and in their turn liquid assets are bigger than bank deposits.

Liquid assets perform some of the functions of money. They act as a store of value and, while they cannot be used directly as a medium of exchange, they affect the demand for money. Coin and notes, together with current account deposits at banks, do not earn interest, deposit accounts earn a small rate of interest, liquid assets, as a rule, rather more. So a change in interest rates may cause the public to switch some money from bank deposits to liquid assets. Alternatively, the public can switch from liquid assets to money by, for example, demanding repayment of some of their Post Office securities. The amount of money in the economy is thus not necessarily a good guide to the spending power of the public. This latter point was very much the concern of the Radcliffe Committee.

Liquidity

The concept of liquidity has unfortunately been used in a number of ways, and come to mean different things to different people. In this book we shall regard it as: *the speed and certainty with which an asset can be turned into money without loss, or into a known amount of money in relation to its face value*. Shares in quoted companies, gilt-edged securities and Treasury bills can all be turned quickly into money: just pick up the telephone and call a stockbroker. Equity shares and gilt-edged would not, however, be classified as liquid assets, for the amount of money obtainable by sale on the market is not known in advance, whereas Treasury bills are highly liquid, for they have only to be held to maturity, at most three months, to be paid face value; or, alternatively, they can be discounted straight away at a rate which is known in relation to Bank Rate. If Bank Rate doubled overnight, a most unlikely occurrence, it will still only inflict a very small capital loss on having to discount a bill, whereas it would severely depress gilt-edged prices.

A second distinction between these assets is that equity shares are the liability of various companies, and therefore there is a possibility of default, whereas government securities are, in most countries, deemed to have a negligible risk of default. In a financial panic, it is better to be holding liquid government assets than liquid private assets.

It is evident that assets can be arranged on a scale: at one end completely liquid, i.e. money; at the other end, illiquid—say, an IOU from me to you or a piece of real property. If liquidity, the ability to exchange an asset quickly for a known sum of money, was the only consideration governing the holding of assets, we should expect to find that the yield on securities would increase as the asset became more illiquid, the better yield being necessary to induce the public to hold the more illiquid securities. It is found that securities do, as a rule, follow roughly this pattern, although a number of other things have to be taken into account. Money, unless it is held in the form of a deposit account at a bank, does not earn interest, while the yield on short-term government securities will normally be lower than the yield on long-term securities. Business fixed-interest securities will normally yield rather more than government securities because of a higher risk of default. Equity shares, since they offer both the attraction of sharing in business profits and the risk of getting nothing, are likely to be more volatile as to yield, depending on the market assessment of their worth.

In the previous paragraph, the terms 'yield' and 'interest' have been used. A fixed-interest security is issued at a particular price and at a particular rate of interest. Say it is issued at £100 at 4%. This means that each year the holder will receive £4 until such time, if the security has a redemption date, it is repaid at £100. The yield on this security is the market price of the security divided into the rate of interest paid. Thus, if the security in our example is sold on the market for £50 the yield is $\frac{100}{50} \times 4$, or 8%. It it fetched £75 the yield would be $\frac{75}{100} \times 4$, or $5\frac{1}{3}$%. The yield on an equity is calculated in the same way, by dividing the market price into the face value of the security and multiplying by the dividend. It is important to grasp this inverse relationship between the price of a security and its yield. If the price of securities goes up, the yield must go down; if the price of securities falls, the yield must increase—in both cases on the assumption that the rate of interest or dividend paid on the security remains unaltered. The stock of liquid assets (stock = assets in existence) is large; in particular, it is large in relation to the flow of new liquid assets. Also the stock of company securities is large in relation to new securities coming on to the market. For this reason a change in the price of existing securities (as we have seen, we are also saying by definition that yields have changed) is likely to affect the terms on which new securities will be taken up by the market. Many of the matters touched on in this section will be taken up later in more detail.

The value of money

This section is more difficult, and can be left until later by those who wish. It has already been established that when we talk about money performing as a 'store of value', this should not be taken to mean that the value of money is constant. In general, we mean by value of money, the amount of goods and services that money will buy, compared to what it would buy, say, last year. The value of money is thus the inverse of the price level. When it is said that the price level has gone up, the same idea could be expressed by saying that the value of money has fallen. In the words of J. Hicks, 'If we have equiproportional changes in all prices, all commodities can be considered as a single composite commodity with price p, where p = the absolute price level.' Putting the matter in this stark form brings out the difficulties of using the terms 'price level' or 'value of money'. If prices do not change in an equiproportional manner, we have no unambiguous measure of the value of money. Everyday habits of talking about the 'cost of living' or 'fall in the value of the £1' may hide, but they do not solve, this problem. They get round it by a more or less arbitrary system of selecting the components to go in the index, and by more or less arbitrary weighting of the components, once these have been selected.

We are faced with a number of variables that interact with one another; we need a general equilibrium system to solve for any variable. A change in the amount of money in the economy is likely to change output and prices in the economy. However, changes in output and prices can occur independently of changes in the amount of money, but they will nevertheless affect the value of money. Talking of a change in the amount of money in the economy, as we have just done, without specifying how the amount of money comes into the economy, can also hide important differences. If the public desire to hold more money, this can come about, for example, by their exchanging some assets for money. If the assets exchanged are Post Office securities, no great effects may be apparent. The net effect is that the government has issued more notes and fewer securities. If the public attempt to obtain the money by selling securities on the market, this does not (unless the monetary authorities themselves buy the securities) increase the amount of money in the economy; the public will be exchanging the same quantity of money and securities amongst themselves, it has the effect of driving down the price of securities, i.e. increasing the yields. The initiative for the increase in money may come from the monetary authorities who buy government securities in the market. If the public's desire for money has not changed, then this increase in money will be spent on securities or goods with probable effects on prices, interest rates and output. When the desire for increased money holdings comes from the public, we should not expect a direct effect on output and prices, the money we have postulated is required by the public to hold, not to spend. When the increase is brought about by the monetary authorities, we may expect direct effects on spending. Increased spending in times of unemployment is likely to result more in increased output than increased prices, while in times of full employment by definition output cannot be increased without changing techniques of production.

The quantity theory of money

There are a number of concepts in economics that, like land-mines, seem to exist for the purpose of trapping the unwary. The quantity theory of money is one of them. In the hands of skilful practitioners, the theory is a useful one in explaining the role of money; in less careful hands it degenerates into a mechanical formula that conceals rather than reveals the truth. The theory is set out very briefly below.

Money has been defined as coin, notes and bank deposits: this (as with any other definition of money) is a *stock* concept. That is, at any particular time there is a certain amount in existence; it has a definite magnitude. Now, money can change hands many times in the course of a year, and we can measure the money value of the annual flow of final purchases of goods and services—the gross national product (G.N.P.). By dividing G.N.P. by the amount of money in existence, we find out the average number of times money turns over in the period, i.e. its velocity of circulation.

In the example above, money was divided into G.N.P. to arrive at the income velocity of money. This concept relates money to final purchases on goods and services. If money is divided into the value of all transactions in the economy, the transactions' velocity of money is arrived at. The latter relates to all purchases in the economy and includes intermediate purchases by firms of raw materials and fabricated parts, whereas the former relates only to finished goods.

Money times its transactions' velocity of circulation or *MV* can be equated with the total flow of the things that are purchased for money, i.e. the volume of trade, *T*, multiplied by the price level, *P*.

So we get $PT \equiv MV$ or $P \equiv \frac{MV}{T}$. This is an identity. That is, the statement is true by definition. The number of transactions times the price level must be equal to the quantity of money times its turnover.

An alternative way of expressing this is the so-called cash balance equation $M \equiv kPT$. Here *k* is the reciprocal of *V* and expresses that fraction of the period's expenditure on goods and services, which on average is held in the form of money. If *V* is 10 in a period, then average money holding is $\frac{1}{10}$th.

These identities can be misleading if figures are substituted and conclusions drawn. Working with $P \equiv \frac{MV}{T}$, it is not legitimate to draw the conclusion that it is always the case that the price level varies proportionally with the quantity of money and its velocity of circulation, and indirectly with the volume of transactions. The reason for this is that we cannot assume that *M*, *V*, *P* and *T*, are independent of each other. For example, it may be that, as has already been pointed out, as *M* is increased *V* decreases because people wish to hold more money. Or the increase in money could go to the company sector, which in depressed times may not want to use it. Or during a depression the increase in *M* may lead not to higher prices, but to more output and sales, i.e. an increase in *T*. It has also been pointed out that prices can increase independently of a change in the money supply or a change in the velocity of circulation.

Summary

The inconvenience of barter has led to nearly all societies using money. Money has taken the form of a very wide variety of items at different times and in different places, having only one thing in common—the intangible property of common acceptability within the community concerned.

The term 'money' is used for assets that act both as a medium of exchange and as a store of value. The term 'liquid' is the name given to assets which, while acting as a store of value, do not circulate in exchange and in addition have the property that they can be turned into money without loss, or into a known amount of money in relation to face value. Examples of liquid assets are Treasury bills and deposits at the Post Office Savings Bank. The distinction between money and liquid assets is not a rigid one, but will depend on law and custom in the society concerned.

In Great Britain the term 'primary money' is used for coin, notes and bankers' deposits at the Bank of England. Secondary money consists of deposits at banks on both current and deposit account. Once again what constitutes secondary money will depend on prevailing law and custom in society.

All economists are agreed in rejecting the crude quantity theory of money that a change in the quantity of money of $x\%$ will necessarily lead to a like change in prices of $x\%$. The effect of changes in the quantity of money on prices is not direct and proportional; there is, in the words of J. M. Keynes, 'many a slip 'twixt the cup and the lip'.

The manner in which a change in the quantity of money may influence prices is a complicated one, which is likely to vary at different levels of employment, according to how the increase comes about, according to the division of the increase between people with different income and wealth, and many other complicating interactions and relationships.

The above remarks are particularly relevant to the short-run, which is our main concern. The long-run relationship between money and prices may have some simpler relationship; Keynes regarded this as a question for historical generalization, rather than pure theory (Keynes, J. M., 1936, 306).[2] Keynes saw the tendency for the long-run course of prices to be nearly always upward as due to the fact that when money is relatively abundant wages rise; and when money is relatively scarce some means is found to increase the effective quantity of money. The latter point has a very Radcliffe ring about it, which we shall be examining.

[2] The custom will be followed of giving an abbreviated reference within the text. A full list of works cited, arranged alphabetically, will be found on pp. 283-6. Books and articles are indexed under the author's name, and anonymous articles and reports under the first substantive word of the title.

2
The Bank of England

A catalogue of changes and developments in the position and character of the Bank of England, over, say, the last forty years, looks impressive; but it cannot conceal the fact that all too often, if not indeed typically, they have failed to match the pace of change in the external situation which they were supposed to meet. . . .

ARTIS, M. J. (1965), *Foundations of British Monetary Policy.*

Today the Bank of England (referred to as the Bank) is one of the partners of the sector termed the 'monetary authorities'.

Starting out as a joint-stock business venture of rather dubious quality in 1694, the Bank soon developed into the Bank of the government and achieved a position of importance in monetary affairs. Since relations between the government and the Bank have grown up as a result of long association, an explanation of these relations is not to be found by examination of legislation. This 'club-like' atmosphere is typical of the British monetary system; rules are obeyed, not because of laws, but because of conventions. It can form a source of strength. Modifications can come about gradually without the need for changes in statutes which may confer on the change a dramatic character it does not warrant. The converse of this is that opportunities for the legislature to have full-scale debates on the institutions are removed.

The organization of the Bank of England

The effective managing body of the Bank now consists of the Governor, the Deputy Governor, and four full-time executive directors. There are a further twelve part-time directors. The Governor and the Deputy Governor are appointed for five years, the directors for four years. All can be reappointed.

The part-time directors are appointed for their expertise in industry, commerce, banking or trade-union affairs, and may be called upon by the Governors for advice on any problem in which they have qualifications. In addition, they attend a weekly meeting—the 'Court', as it is called.

The main work of the Bank is done through committees, of which the principal one is the Committee of Treasury. This committee is the policy-making body of the Bank and receives the reports of all other committees before they are submitted to Court: membership consists of the Governor, his Deputy and five other directors.

No mention has been made of the Bank of England Act, 1946, whereby the State acquired the whole of the capital stock of the bank and brought it into public ownership. Formal powers are written into the Act, whereby the Treasury may from time to time give such directions to the Bank as, after consultation with the Governor of the Bank, they think necessary in the public interest. This provision has not essentially changed the working of the system, which is one based on persuasion and discussion, and one in which the use of coercive powers is considered foreign. The Bank was, under this Act, also endowed with statutory powers to direct the affairs of the commercial banks. Again compulsion is relegated to the background: directives are issued only after consultation with the commercial banks.

Functions of the Bank of England

A look at a simplified statement of the Bank shows up many of its functions.

Bank of England Statement as at December, 1967

Figures in £ million

	Issue Department		
1. Notes in circulation	3,160	6. Government securities	3,199
Notes in banking department	40		
	3,200		3,199
	Banking Department		
2. Bankers' deposits	259	6. Government securities	454
3. Special accounts	213	7. Discounts and Advances	97
4. Public deposits	12	Other	29
5. Other accounts	118	Notes and Coin	41
	602		621

Source: *Bank of England Quarterly Bulletin*, September, 1968, Table 5.

The division between the issue and banking departments is historical. The number of notes in circulation is, as we shall see, whatever the public demands at any time. Notes are *not* issued to finance government expenditure. This matter will be taken up in more detail later. We note here the function of the Bank to maintain a sufficient supply of notes to meet whatever is the demand for them.

The function of the Bank, as banker, is brought out by items 2, 4 and 5 in the statement. The relative smallness of the sums appearing under these items should not mislead one into under-estimating the importance of this function. The Bank is providing for its customers a wide range of services, analogous to those offered by commercial banks to their customers, with the difference that the main customers of the Bank are the government, other banks, both home and foreign, some of the financial intermediaries and international organizations.

Bankers' deposits refer to the accounts of the commercial banks. They form, together with the till money of the commercial banks, their cash reserve. Inter-bank indebtedness will be settled by drawing on bankers' deposits and more important transactions between the commercial banking sector (and their customers) and the government will be reflected in withdrawals or replenishing of these deposits.[1] The cash reserve of the joint-stock banks is kept at a figure of 8% of deposits, so that the figure of bankers' deposits will not show great variation; a surplus of cash is loaned to the discount houses at 'call or short notice', and likewise a deficit is met by calling in some of these loans. This should not be allowed to obscure the importance of bankers' deposits, and the function of the Bank to exercise monetary control over the banks and other financial institutions.

'Public' has been used to denote all individuals and institutions outside the monetary sector. The term 'public deposits', item 4 in the statement, has, however, the meaning of government deposit. Once again the smallness of the account should not be allowed to mislead. The account is deliberately kept to a working balance. The government does not, as a rule, borrow from the Bank, with the minor exception that small sums may be borrowed overnight by way of 'Ways and Means Advances', to meet residual requirements. A deficit will be made up by the issue of government securities, either Treasury bills or bonds, and likewise a surplus will be used to buy securities, i.e. fewer securities will be offered on the market. The Bank itself

[1] For example, if Smith pays the Inland Revenue a £100 cheque for tax owed, the joint-stock bank will debit Smith's account, and the joint-stock bank, in turn, will have its bankers' deposits account, at the Bank of England, debited in favour of the Exchequer.

manages the sale or purchases of these securities on behalf of the government.

Special deposits (item 3) are also deposits by the joint-stock banks, but in this case they are not allowed to treat these deposits as cash or as liquid assets. This is a recent form of monetary control which will be dealt with more fully later on.

Other accounts (item 5) covers the accounts of discount and acceptance houses, of overseas central banks and of such bodies as the International Monetary Fund. In addition, the Bank keeps accounts for a few individuals, amongst them its staff, and for a few private and public companies—a legacy from the days when the Bank was active in general banking.

Item 7, discounts and advances, points the way to one of the Bank's crucial functions, that of lender of last resort. This means that any institution with the privilege of access to the Discount Office of the Bank with 'eligible paper' (e.g. Treasury bills) knows that the Bank will re-discount them. Bank Rate is the rate at which the Bank normally lends at last resort; it is announced by the Court of Directors, customarily on Thursday mornings, after the Governor has consulted with the Treasury and the Chancellor of the Exchequer. Bank Rate is a key rate among short-term rates, because it exercises a powerful influence on other rates. It will be shown that the rate on Treasury bills moves in sympathy with Bank Rate; commercial banks' rates are geared by convention to it. With these important rates changed as a result of a change in Bank Rate, market influences spread the impact through to other rates. In practice, rates given by local authorities on short-term borrowing change overnight, and financial institutions and intermediaries change their rates with different time-lags, as the effect of higher rates to be obtained in the markets mentioned draws funds away from them.[2]

Although Bank Rate is the usual rate at which the Bank will lend at last resort, this is at the discretion of the Bank. In recent years, on occasions, the discount houses have been charged more than Bank Rate, and they can always be assisted by the Bank buying bills in the market—so called 'open-market operations'.

Interest rates are also influenced by the activities of the government broker—one of the discount houses, which acts under instructions from the Bank. 'The prices he [the government broker] bids in response to an offer are therefore seen as the expression of the Bank's current policy, and are closely watched by the jobbers for any sign

[2] In Chapter 6 we shall look at a proposal that commercial banks should drop the convention whereby they maintain fixed differentials with respect to Bank Rate, and instead leave themselves free to compete with each other, and with other institutions for deposits.

of a change of emphasis in the policy, such as might lead the market to expect new movements in prices' ('Official Transactions in the Gilt-edged Market', June, 1966).

The Bank also acts as an agent for the government in administering exchange control; it manages the Exchange Equalization Account—which holds the reserves of gold and foreign exchange; and acts as registrar of government stocks, stocks of nationalized industries and of some local authorities, public boards and Commonwealth governments.

The final function of the Bank is one that is not apparent from the statement: that of financial adviser to the government. Its leading position in the financial structure of Great Britain and activities and contacts abroad means that the Bank is in an unrivalled position to tender advice.

Relations between the Bank of England and the government

The relation between a central bank and the executive is always a tricky one. Checks and counterchecks are needed to ensure, on the one hand, that the government does not resort to the printing of notes to solve its fiscal problems, and, on the other, that the management of the monetary side of the economy, in so far as it is within the control of the central bank, shall be in accordance with the wishes of the government. The personalities of the Governor of the Bank, together with that of his opposite number in the Treasury and the Chancellor of the Exchequer, is probably as good a guide as any to their influence at any one time.

Enough has been said to make it clear that the relations between the Bank and the government are subject to change. One recent example to illustrate what has been said will be given. In the words of a former Governor, the Bank has 'the unique right to offer advice and to press such advice even to the point of nagging; but always, of course, subject to the supreme authority of the government'.

What is not as yet clear is whether this right to offer advice should be confined within the circle of discussion of the monetary authorities, or whether the Bank should be free to make its disagreements known. The American practice in these respects is to have much fuller public discussion and to publish dissenting views. There is less search for a viewpoint on which all can agree.[3]

Britain seems to get the worst of both worlds, in that the few times the Bank is moved to make their disagreements public may help to make the situation (it is usually one of confidence in the £1) worse,

[3] Contrast the *Radcliffe Report* and the *American Report of the Commission on Money and Credit.*

and in addition has all the appearance of trying to coerce the government to its point of view. Either the adoption of the convention that disagreements are fought out in private or much fuller publication of information and views would seem to be a better solution. The Bank, until the publication since December, 1960, of its *Quarterly Bulletin*, was notorious for the secrecy with which it conducted its operations. The *Bulletin* has done much to enable an informed discussion of monetary issues to take place.

This section deals with contentious matters that largely lie outside the scope of this volume. It has been stressed in this chapter that the monetary system, and within it the Bank, is not subject to formal regulations. It has changed a great deal over the last forty years. Inevitably it has not changed, as the quotation that heads this chapter indicates, as fast or in as radical a manner as some of its critics would like.

Summary

The effective management of the Bank is in the hands of a small group: the Governor and his Deputy, who are appointed for five years, and four full-time directors appointed for four years. They are assisted by twelve part-time directors.

The Bank manages the note issue, acts as banker to the government, other banks and many financial intermediaries and international organizations. It exercises monetary control as agreed by the monetary authorities, of which the Bank itself forms an important part. One of its crucial functions is that of lender of last resort to the discount houses, which gives the Bank influence over short-term interest rates. The Bank manages the Exchange Equalization Account and acts as registrar of government, nationalized industries and a number of public authority stock issues.

Finally, the Bank, because of its leading position in the financial structure of Great Britain and activities and contacts abroad, tenders advice to the government on economic matters.

3
The discount market

Because that is the way the market has always been, going back a long way.
Verbal evidence of the London Discount Market Association to the Radcliffe Committee.

It is easy to imagine the despair of people when they attempt to understand the English monetary system. Because it has grown up over so many years, it appears haphazard, full of illogicalities. If the system were being constructed afresh, the monetary system would probably appear simpler and more tidy. For example, the functions performed by the discount houses could be performed in other ways; it was, however, the considered opinion of the *Radcliffe Report* that they performed effectively and efficiently, and it seemed unlikely that savings in cost or manpower would result from a change. With these preliminaries in mind, we will consider the organization and functions of the discount houses.

Structure of the London discount market

The London discount market now consists of twelve major discount houses. They stand as an intermediary between the government and the Bank of England in the sense that we have seen that the government borrows (other than overnight), not from the Bank, but by issuing securities which are chiefly channelled through the discount houses. In a similar manner, the discount houses stand as an intermediary between the Bank of England and the commercial banks; funds required by the latter are channelled through the discount market rather than by the commercial banks borrowing directly from the Bank.

The discount houses are commercial bodies and, like banks, they aim to make a profit by borrowing money more cheaply than they lend it. They operate for the most part in the short end of the market, and operate almost entirely on money which is borrowed on even shorter terms than they lend. They are able to do this in safety because the discount houses enjoy access to the Bank as lender of last resort.

Source of funds

Normally the cheapest source of funds for the discount houses is provided by borrowing 'money at call and short notice' from the commercial banks. This money, as the name implies, can be recalled by the banks either immediately or at very short notice. The cost of this money to the discount houses is related to Bank Rate and will be, at best, 1⅝% below the existing level of Bank Rate.[1] We can now see how the commercial banks are able to maintain a rigid cash ratio of 8% in spite of differences, day to day, in the calls for cash. Any cash above the 8% level can be loaned overnight to the discount houses; a shortfall can be met by recalling funds. A surplus, or deficit, which continued for any length of time will call for more fundamental action by the commercial banks, but temporary departures from the 8% ratio are taken care of by the buffer provided by the discount houses.

The money at call and short notice is the cheapest source of borrowed capital of the discount houses. They also borrow at slightly higher rates of interest from acceptance houses and foreign banks with surplus funds in London, and minor amounts from other sources. They also, as we have noted, have access to the Bank of England; funds borrowed from the Bank will normally be charged at the same rate as Bank Rate, which, as we shall see, is a penal rate for the discount houses. However, if the Bank wishes to influence the money market in a particular way, the Bank can accommodate the discount houses at less than Bank Rate, and in recent years has on occasion charged more than Bank Rate.

Functions of the London discount market

The discount houses, for their part, undertake to 'cover the tender' of Treasury bills issued weekly by the government. This means that, however many Treasury bills the government decides to issue, they can be sure that, failing other buyers offering better terms, the discount houses will take them up. In turn, the discount houses sell the bills to commercial banks in suitable maturities and to the Bank and other holders. The discount houses are able to give this undertaking

[1] Part, so termed 'regular money' is borrowed at the rate 1⅝% below Bank Rate. Other call money is loaned at rates which vary from day to day, but will approximate to the less favourable rates the discount houses have to pay from other sources.

to cover the tender only because they know that, if they are unable to borrow funds from other sources, they can borrow from the Bank. The discount houses do not normally keep the bills they buy until they mature, but sell them, chiefly to the commercial banks, as and when the banks require them. The commercial banks could tender directly for bills, but prefer to keep to the custom whereby they buy from the discount houses the bills in the quantities and maturities that suit them best.

The discount houses, as well as channelling finance to the government, provide finance to the private sector by discounting bills of exchange. They also act as jobbers in short-term government bonds. Historically, commercial bills should be mentioned first, because the discount houses grew up to provide discount for them. It was not until the 1880s that the Treasury bill came into existence and much later before it came into widespread use.

The bill of exchange is an old device whereby the seller of goods draws on the purchaser of the goods an order for the sum of money involved to be paid on demand or at a fixed time in the future. Once the purchaser 'accepts' the bill by signing on the face of it, the seller is able, if the acceptor is sufficiently well known, to rediscount the bill through the money market. The purchaser doesn't have to pay for the goods before receipt, and the seller, for a small discount, can obtain his money as soon as the goods are sold. The convenience of this in times past, when delivery of goods, particularly between countries, took months, is obvious. Hence also the growth of acceptance houses, who specialized in accepting bills—that is, adding their names to a bill and so making themselves liable to pay the bill if the original acceptor defaulted. Once a bill had been accepted by a reputable house it became an easily negotiable instrument.

So convenient a device has been widely adopted by governments by means of Treasury bills. These have no counterpart in the dispatch of goods, but otherwise are similar to bills of exchange, being promises to pay a stated amount, usually ninety-one days from the time of issue. In amount the Treasury bill outweighs the commercial bill in importance. The amount of the former outstanding at any one time can rise to £500 million or more. Paradoxically, the commercial bill becomes important during a credit squeeze. An obvious source of funds to certain traders if they are denied bank credit is to make more use of bills of exchange; that this is done shows clearly in the figures of amounts of bills outstanding. Recently directives to the joint-stock banks on restricting credit have also included bills of exchange.

The Treasury bill market

It remains to outline briefly the market structure for Treasury bills. These are issued weekly. Tenders (minimum sum £10,000) are invited every Friday for the bills to be issued in the following week. In general, the highest tenders, i.e. those offering the nearest to the face value of the bills, will receive the bills. The difference between the tender price and the face value of the bill represents the rate of interest the government pays for borrowing money. The quantity coming on to the market depends on two factors: the requirements of government finance, which will be considered later, and the amount of surplus funds held by government departments. These surplus funds are used for Treasury bills—the so-called 'tap issue'—and the remaining bills are offered on tender.

The discount houses submit a 'syndicated bid'—that is, they submit a common tender price between them. This 'price' or discount at which they will take bills is fixed somewhere between the cost of their cheapest and dearest source of borrowed funds. That is somewhere between the cost of funds borrowed from the commercial banks and the cost of borrowing from the Bank of England at penal rate. Since the cost of borrowing from commercial banks is at best 1⅝% below Bank Rate, the discount houses' bid will normally be below Bank Rate by a slightly smaller percentage, to cover the cost of dearer money and allow for a small turn of profit. Other tenderers must normally submit better terms than this to secure an allocation of bills.

The structure of interest rates

The Bank, because of its key position as issuer of the securities and as lender on its own terms, can normally get the bill rate to the level it requires. Important implications follow from this. The cost of funds to the discount houses moves in the same way as Bank Rate. The commercial banks automatically change the rates at which they lend so as to maintain the customary differentials with Bank Rate, and rates from other sources are likely to move in the same direction as Bank Rate. Thus, the rate (or discount) on Treasury bills will move with Bank Rate. In practice, if the discount houses have correctly judged the state of the market, the change in the rate on Treasury bills will precede the change in Bank Rate. Thus, if the rate on Treasury bills is increased slightly for a number of weeks, this is an indication that the discount houses expect an increase in Bank Rate, and vice versa. This is because the discount houses try to anticipate the course of Bank Rate (and hence the cost of funds to them) over the life of the Treasury bills for which they are tendering.

The following picture thus emerges: because Treasury bills overshadow in quantity any other kind of short-term paper, the rate on Treasury bills is of key importance in influencing the structure of interest rates throughout the short end of the market. And the rate on longer-term securities will also tend to move in sympathy with short-term rates. Thus, the level of interest rates in the economy is under the control of the monetary authorities in the sense that changes in Bank Rate will influence most other rates. The monetary authorities can also, as we have seen, reinforce their influence on the key Treasury bill rate by lending money to the discount houses above Bank Rate (if they wish to keep interest rates up), or below Bank Rate in the reverse situation. The monetary authorities can also, in a way to be explained, ensure that the discount houses are forced to borrow from the Bank; that in the terminology 'money is tight'.

The reservation above that, 'the level of interest rates in the economy is under the control of the monetary authorities *in the sense that* changes in Bank Rate will influence most other rates', must not be taken to imply that Bank Rate can be manipulated at will by the monetary authorities. There are a number of constraints which the monetary authorities have to consider when setting the level of rates. The most important of these is the level of interest rates abroad and the state of the home economy. The much-quoted reason that the cost to the Exchequer of servicing the National Debt must also be taken into account is, as we shall see in the public finance section, important, but of less significance. Also, we must not prejudge the significance of high- or low-interest rates in affecting the economy.

It will be seen from the above account that the discount houses operate on an extremely narrow margin between the cost of the funds they borrow and the return on the funds they lend by buying securities. It may also be noticed that they are in a 'monopolistic' type of position where, because they bid collectively, they could manipulate the market to their own advantage. The narrow margin on dealing in bills is taken care of by the huge volume of bills that are dealt in. The second point can be met by saying that there seems to be sufficient counter-checks in the system to ensure that the market is not so manipulated. The commercial banks can vary the terms on which they lend and so can the Bank of England. The discount houses' position is thus very dependent on the goodwill of the other partners. Para. 590 of the *Radcliffe Report* does complain about the practice at one time of the 'syndicated bid' being jumped up and down in order to discourage outside tenderers. The 'frown' on the face of the monetary authorities seems to have been sufficient to stop this practice.

Summary

The discount houses were originally set up to discount commercial bills. Today Treasury bills form the major part of their business. There are now twelve major discount houses enjoying access to the Bank as lender of last resort. This access enables them to act as an intermediary between the government and the Bank in the sense that the government normally borrows not directly from the Bank, but by the issue of securities which are channelled through the discount market. The discount houses also stand as an intermediary between the commercial banks and the Bank. The commercial banks replenish cash not by borrowing from the Bank, but by calling in their loans to the discount houses.

The discount houses operate almost entirely on money borrowed at call and short notice. Their cheapest source of funds will normally be the commercial banks and the rates at which they borrow will be linked to Bank Rate. The discount houses try to anticipate changes in Bank Rate, so that movements in the Treasury bill rate will normally anticipate a change in Bank Rate.

Because of the volume of Treasury bills, the rate on these is important in influencing other short-term rates: since the rate on Treasury bills is linked to (though it may anticipate) changes in Bank Rate, we can say that the level of short-term interest rates is under the control of the monetary authorities, although this must not be taken to imply that Bank Rate can be manipulated at will by them. The most important constraint on the monetary authorities is the need to take account of the level of interest rates abroad.

4
The commercial banks

> We consider that the banks can in fact successfully take such initiatives (to stem this decline in their relative importance) and that the contrary view implicitly rests upon an assumption that the volume of bank deposits is arbitrarily determined at some level by the monetary authorities. It is, of course, true that the actions of the monetary authorities play a crucial role in determining the volume of bank deposits, but they do so in the context provided by the preferences of the public (including financial institutions) about the kinds of assets it wishes to hold and the ways in which it wishes to borrow. The actions taken by the monetary authorities —for example, in buying and selling bonds or in making calls for, or releases from, special deposits—will be taken with the ultimate aim of securing the stability of the economy, and are directed at such variables as the level (and pattern) of interest rates, the flow of lending and the general state of liquidity. This being so, it seems to us that the volume of bank deposits can be greater—consistent with the monetary authorities realizing their aims—the more attractive are bank deposits and the less inclined is the public to shift funds into other liquid claims.
>
> *Bank Charges* (1967), Report No. 34, National Board for Prices and Incomes.

This chapter is concerned with the domestic banks, known as the London clearing banks. The term 'clearing banks' comes from the mechanism that has been developed for settlement of inter-bank indebtedness.[1] Merchant banks or accepting houses, and overseas banks, are important and will be looked at in the next chapter. The clearing banks will hereafter be referred to as commercial banks.

[1] Strictly, an account of domestic banks should give a separate account of the Scottish banks, as there are minor differences between them and the clearing banks. For example, they have limited power to issue notes and slightly different reserve requirements. In practice, the Scottish banks are not sufficiently large enough, or different in operation, to distort the picture, and most of what is said about the clearing banks applies to the Scottish banks. For details of the Scottish banks, see *Radcliffe Report*, paras. 149-61.

Structure of the commercial banks

The structure of British banking had been stable, apart from regrouping amongst some of the smaller banks, since the 1930s: a system of eleven clearing banks, dominated by the 'Big Five'—Barclays, Midlands, Lloyds, Westminster and National Provincial—with Martins Bank coming next in size of total deposits. This stability was broken early in 1968 when a merger was announced between the Westminster and National Provincial, the smaller two of the 'Big Five', which would put them at, or near, the top in size. Shortly afterwards Barclays, Lloyds and Martins announced their intention to merge.[2] The merger would have made, ranked by deposits, the second biggest bank in the world, exceeded only by the San Francisco's Bank of America. This triple merger was referred to the Monopolies Commission and advised against by a majority of six to four.

In spite of this decision, a period of change in the structure of the commercial banks is likely for several reasons. One is the success of other types of financial intermediary and foreign banks in attracting deposits. Another is the possibility of economies in staff at headquarters and the possibility of some reduction in the number of branches where these duplicate each other. If branch reductions on a sufficient scale turn out to be possible, considerable capital could be realized from the sale of sites and premises. Of more immediate importance are the greater financial resources, which would enable the groups to meet the needs, at home and abroad, of the largest industrial organizations. Also, the banks are at present engaged in expensive installations of computing equipment, and financial economies could be expected from this source.

On the wider issue, of whether these mergers would result in better service to the public, the answer depends so much on the way the proposed groups would operate. The reader will be in a better position to judge this issue for himself after he has read this section of the book and taken in the criticisms that have been made of the current structure of banking.

Commercial bank operations

The clearing banks are profit-making institutions, drawing their revenue from the difference in rates which they pay for borrowed money (nil in the case of demand deposits) and the return they obtain by lending or investing in financial securities of various kinds. The

[2] Two Scottish banks, the Royal Bank of Scotland and the National Commercial Bank of Scotland, also announced their intention to merge at this time.

commercial banks maintain an interest-rate structure geared to Bank Rate. Loan and overdraft rates vary with the class of borrowing, but follow a set pattern. The rate for most industrial, commercial and private customers is usually 1% above Bank Rate, with a minimum rate of 4½% or 5%. Local authorities, building societies, insurance companies and other first-class industrial and commercial borrowers pay ½% below Bank Rate. Nationalized industries are normally charged Bank Rate. Rates paid on deposit accounts are 2% below Bank Rate. Corresponding levels are maintained on such other rates as loans at call and short notice. The result is that the commercial banks do not compete with each other by means of rate differentials, and, a more important point, they do not compete with other institutions who adopt flexible interest-rate policies.[3] In Chapter 1 it has already been explained that deposits both in current and deposit accounts are counted as money.

Banks are not confined to lending out only the money which is deposited with them; they can 'create money' by creating claims on themselves, e.g. allowing a customer to overdraw his account. A clear knowledge of the process by which banks create credit, the limits to this process, the influence and limitations of the monetary authorities in controlling it, and the similarities and differences of other financial intermediaries in creating credit are essential and form our chief concern in this and the next two chapters.

Creation of credit

In order to make this process clear, we start with a very simplified system. When this is understood, it is relatively easy to bring in real-life complications. Let us assume an economy with only one bank, where any money lent by the bank is redeposited back in the bank. Further, it is assumed that this bank has found from experience that it need only keep 20% of whatever sum is deposited with it as a reserve, in case cash is demanded back by its customers. (20% has been chosen to make it quite clear that our system is not intended to be a replica of the current banking system.)

Stage 1 starts, we will assume, with the deposit of £1,000 in the bank. Of this the bank needs to keep only £200 (20%) as a reserve.

Stage 2 is the process whereby the bank lends out the remaining £800, or, what amounts to the same thing, purchases securities for this amount. (Our assumption is that the whole of this £800 is

[3] Except indirectly in the sense that commercial banks have set up a number of subsidiary or affiliated companies who are chiefly concerned with hire-purchase financing. These companies do compete for deposits. For details refer to 'How the Banks compete for Deposits' (July, 1967) 582-7.

redeposited back in the bank.) If we assume that Holder A obtained an overdraft of £800 and paid this to Holder B by cheque, then the bank makes a simple book entry. Holder A is indebted to the bank for this sum, his liability has not decreased, while the deposit account of Holder B has increased by £800.

Stage 3 is a repetition of Stage 2, with the bank free to lend or buy securities to the value of £640, keeping the remaining £160 as a reserve, and so on. The ultimate value of the credit created is given by the formula:

$$\text{Total deposits created} = \frac{\text{new reserves}}{\text{percentage reserve ratio}}$$

which in our example is $\frac{1{,}000 \times 100}{20} = £5{,}000$. An initial deposit of £1,000 has led to a 'multiplier' process, whereby total deposits have increased by £5,000.

Table 1 sets out the process in detail.

Table 1

Hypothetical example of the creation of bank credit

Stage	Loans and Investments made	Total	Deposits created	Total	Reserves required for Deposits created	Total
	£	£	£	£	£	£
1.	—	—	1,000	1,000	200	200
2.	800	800	800	1,800	160	360
3.	640	1,440	640	2,440	128	488
4.	512	1,952	512	2,952	62⅖	550⅖
Final	—	4,000	—	5,000	—	1,000

From Table 1 we see that Stage 1 is the deposit of £1,000, of which the bank needs only £200 as a deposit. Stage 2 records that a loan or investment is made by the bank of the remaining £800. This results in a return of the £800 to the bank as a deposit by another party. The bank needs to keep £160 of this as a reserve and can therefore in Stage 3 make loans or investments of £640. The final result of this process is recorded in the bottom line, where we see that total loans and investments made by the bank come to £4,000; so deposits are up by £5,000, £1,000 of which must be kept as a reserve.

The assumption of our model, that there is only one bank, does not alter our argument in any essential way. A number of banks must make sure that they keep in step in their credit-creation, otherwise one bank would lose deposits to another.

The fact that the banking system is not a completely closed system of payments leads, as we shall see, to an ability to create credit which is much below that indicated by this simple model. Before examining this point, the reserve ratios of the commercial banks are described.

Cash and liquid asset ratios

It was mentioned in the beginning that commercial banks are profit-making institutions, but they must conduct their activities so as to maintain the confidence of the public. The history of banking is a long and fascinating one that we cannot go into. It is sufficient for our purpose to know that the banks now maintain a cash ratio equal to 8% of deposits. As we have seen, 'cash' consists of money in the tills of the banks and their deposits with the Bank of England, and this ratio can be strictly maintained at 8%, because the banks are able to call in money they have lent to the discount market to meet a shortfall, and likewise to lend any surplus funds to the discount houses. This ratio is also buttressed by keeping a quantity of liquid assets. It is now the rule that joint-stock banks must keep liquid assets equal to at least 28% of deposits. The Bank of England lays down what constitutes the assets which the banks are allowed to count in their liquid-asset ratio. Cash itself will form 8% of them; Treasury bills and commercial bills the bulk of the remainder. Commercial bills which have been accepted by a British bank or by an acceptance house, if it has one other British name on it, are eligible paper. In addition a number of miscellaneous items may be included. For example, in order to encourage banks to make certain loans to help exporters, these loans in the last eighteen months before maturity were declared eligible paper.

In terms of the simple model set up in the beginning of this chapter, we could arrive at two versions of the credit multiplier. One would be the reciprocal of the cash ratio—that is, 12½ times the increase in deposits. The other would be the reciprocal of the liquid-asset ratio, or 3·9 times. Which ratio would depend on whether the monetary authorities control the cash or the liquid assets of the banks. It will be argued that this attempt to decide the ability of the banks to create credit by some mechanical formula relating to the reserve ratios of the banks is a misleading one. Expansion of deposits is in most circumstances not likely to exceed two times the initial sum. Contraction of deposits, for reasons which will be outlined, is even more circumscribed. The advantage of setting out the credit multiplier, as we have done, is so that the process whereby credit is created in the economy may be clearly understood, it should not be used to derive a ratio. A better understanding is obtained by an analysis of leakages in the flow of money in the banking system, to which we now turn.[4]

The limits to the process of creating credit

In the simplified example used, the multiplier, or limit to credit creation, is simply determined by the formula:

$$\frac{\text{new reserves}}{\text{\%age reserve ratio}}$$

The higher the reserve ratio the lower will be the amount of credit that can be created. The actual reserve ratios kept by the joint-stock banks will give us the upper limit of the bank's power to create credit. This limit is of theoretical interest only for the assumption of our simplified model—namely, that any money lent by the bank is redeposited back in the system—must be subject to important qualifications. The circular flow of money from bank to A, A to B and B back to the bank which we envisaged in our simple model is subject to 'leakages'.

Given below are some important leakages:

Firstly, some receivers of bank money will require cash; for them a deposit at a commercial bank is not an acceptable means of payment. The bank has no option but to 'pay for' the asset in cash—that is, to run down its deposit with the central bank. From an aggregate viewpoint, the more cash the public wish to hold the less will be the amount of bank deposits.

Secondly, and more importantly, transactions between banks or members of the public (using their bank accounts) and the government result in equal and opposite movements of bankers' deposits. This is so, as indicated earlier, because the government do not bank with the commercial banks. Thus the purchase of bonds from the government by banks or purchases from the government by the public reduce bankers' deposits. Purchases of bonds from the banks or the public by the government increase bankers' deposits. In a

[4] The economic journals have for some years contained a recondite debate over the cash and liquid-asset ratios of the banks. For example, Newlyn, W. T. (June, 1964), Crouch, R. L. (December, 1964 and August, 1965). A criticism of points of view expressed in these articles is given by Cramp, A. B. (June, 1966 and October, 1967). For a discussion of the value of the multiplier see Cramp, A. B. (February, 1963).

similar manner, all payments to the government—for example, tax payments—reduce bankers' deposits, and payments by the government to the public increase them.

Thirdly, we have so far been implicitly talking about a closed system. As soon as we admit the possibility of payments to foreigners we get another leakage, as these holders are unlikely to bank with the commercial banks.

Fourthly, there are a large number of foreign banks with branches in Britain. Sums that find their way to these banks represent a leakage from the commercial banking system. From a monetary viewpoint, this transfer of assets to foreign branch banks is, however, merely a transfer of the power to create credit from the commercial banks to these foreign banks. This important difference will be taken up in the next chapter.

As a simple illustration of the difference between flows of money between the banks and the public and flows between banks and the government, let us take the balance-sheet entries for the banks: firstly, when they extend a loan to a customer of £100, and, secondly, when they purchase £100 worth of securities from the government:

Result of commercial banks making a loan of £100 to a customer

Liabilities		*Assets*	
Deposits (i.e. credit balances of customers represent a liability to pay by the bank)	+£100	Loans (liability on the customer to repay, i.e. an asset of the bank)	+£100

Deposits created for the public are not lost to the banking system as a whole, since members of the public bank with the commercial banks. A, who has the added deposit originally writes a cheque to B. This is from the bank's point a transfer of ownership, deposits and loans still remain at +£100, and the bank can extend further credit, subject to the need for sufficient reserves and no leakages.

Results of commercial banks acquiring assets from the government

Liabilities	*Assets*	
No change	Cash (i.e. bankers' deposits at Bank of England)	−£100
	Securities	+£100

Table 2

London Clearing Banks: averages of monthly figures

Year	Total Gross Deposits £ million	Of which Advances £ million	Assets as a percentage of total Deposits: Liquid Assets	Special Deposits	Investments	Advances to Customers
1958	6,636	1,923	34	—	32	29
1959	6,935	2,522	33	—	27	36
1960	7,236	3,123	32	1·0	20	43
1961	7,395	3,357	33	2·4	15	45
1962	7,611	3,408	33	2·1	16	45
1963	7,971	3,880	32	—	16	49
1964	8,550	4,328	30	—	14	51
1965	8,989	4,653	31	1·0	12	52
1966	9,376	4,732	31	1·5	12	51
1967	9,772	4,725	31	2·0	14	48

Composition of liquid assets — *£ million*

	Cash	Money at Call	Treasury Bills	U.K. and Other Bills	Investments
1958	543	435	1,167	110	2,149
1959	565	489	1,089	135	1,836
1960	588	562	1,007	142	1,407
1961	607	606	992	233	1,122
1962	623	718	933	272	1,194
1963	647	748	842	297	1,244
1964	696	738	790	365	1,220
1965	739	910	653	461	1,087
1966	767	1,006	689	446	1,137
1967	798	1,136	564	492	1,340

Source: *Financial Statistics*, No. 61, Table 37, May, 1967, and No. 76, Table 35, August, 1968.

The purchase of a security from the government results in no change in bank liabilities, but a rearrangement of assets. Cash is down while there is a corresponding increase in securities.

When a member of the public purchases securities from the government with a cheque drawn on his account, bank liabilities are down by this amount with no corresponding increase in assets of the bank, a process described earlier as a leakage.

The conclusion of this section is that an initial increase in deposits of the commercial banks as a whole sets in motion an expansion of the credit structure. The banks know from experience that the bulk of this increase can be used to purchase financial instruments (investments or advances) giving a positive yield. It is not possible to deduce the size of the ultimate increase in credit by a look at either the cash or the liquid-asset ratios of the banks. The expansion is limited in a number of ways, in particular by the whole complex of operations between the government, the banks and the public sector. Chapter 6 takes up the story at this point.

Reversibility of bank expansion

So far the analysis has been conducted in terms of an expansion of bank deposits. Similar reasoning applies to a contraction of deposits.

Table 2 shows the composition of commercial banks' assets from 1958 to 1967. In spite of this period being one of 'stop-go', with a variety of credit squeezes in force, total deposits and advances which form part of total deposits show an upward trend. This trend should not cause too much surprise. It has been indicated that the multiplier in credit-creation is not large, and it will be found that there are several ways in which the commercial banks can resist making a reduction in deposits and advances.

Let us enter the picture with the monetary authorities trying to squeeze the liquid assets of the joint-stock banks (see 'Bank Liquidity in the United Kingdom', December, 1962).

This will normally take the form of attempts, termed 'open-market operations', to increase the amount of government debt held outside the banking system. This pressure can be applied, as we have seen, by trying to induce the non-bank public to take up Treasury bills or, better still, long-term debt. Or the authorities can try to increase the public's holding of non-marketable debt by, for example, offering a better return on National Savings. Such sales reduce bankers' deposits, as they are transferred to the government's account. As the cash ratio must be maintained, this will initially cause a reduction in liquid assets and the liquidity ratio. The reactions of the banks firstly in the short run and then in the longer run to this reduction in their liquidity is outlined below.

THE SHORT RUN

The commercial banks do not borrow directly from the Bank of England. If they wish to replenish cash, they will first of all recall some of the money at call and short notice from the discount houses.

The discount houses, provided that they cannot get the money from elsewhere, e.g. from foreign banks with funds in London, will go to the Bank of England. The Treasury bill rate is, as we have seen always below Bank Rate and the commercial banks provide the cheapest source of funds for the discount houses. The effect of this borrowing from the Bank on the discount houses is therefore to reduce their profits.

The discount houses can wriggle out of this in two ways: borrowing more from outside the banking system by offering better rates or raising their rate on Treasury bills so that more will go to outside tenderers. The result is the same: a tendency for the Treasury bill rate to increase and for other short-term rates to follow, by the market mechanism of funds seeking, other things being equal, the highest return.

If the monetary authorities do not wish market rates to rise, they can stop the process right at the start by accommodating the discount houses at market rate. The 'Special Buyer' (one of the discount houses acting for the Bank of England) will be instructed to buy Treasury bills on the market and so release cash into the system.

The implications should be quite clear: the monetary authorities can operate on either the rate of interest or the quantity of money. Only fortuitous circumstances will enable both to be achieved at the same time. The authorities' policy has been to seek to establish the rate structure they would like.

The above account details the short-term reactions of the commercial banks and the discount houses to a squeeze. Below are detailed the longer-term reactions.

THE LONG TERM

A look at Table 2 will show ways in which the banks reacted in the years 1958-67. The simplest method is, if their liquid assets are above the minimum level, merely to acquiesce in the reduction of their liquid assets. Thus from the table it will be seen that while liquid assets comprised 34% of total deposits in 1958, this figure was down to 31% in 1967, and in 1964 it was 30%.

Another method open to the banks is to try to replenish their liquid assets by running down their other investments. This process is also in evidence during this period. Table 2 shows investments accounted for 32% of deposits in 1958, but only 12% in 1966; they had increased slightly to 14% in 1967.

Attempts by the monetary authorities to reduce the number of Treasury bills (a policy successfully undertaken in this period) can be overcome by the banks if they are able to substitute alternative liquid assets. Table 2 shows that a drop in the banks' holding of Treasury bills of £603 million was partly compensated for by an increase in 'U.K. and other bills' of £382 million.[5]

The above account is far removed from a mechanical formula which can be applied to give us the final adjustment which a bank has to make in order to compensate for a change in deposits. The process described above whereby the banks can compensate by running down their other investments is a complicated process which can have different results in different circumstances. In order to understand this, it must be borne in mind that these portfolios are largely gilt-edged holdings in short-dated stocks with less than five years to run to maturity. These stocks can normally be realized without substantial loss. The simplest, but slowest, way to reduce these portfolios is for the banks not to renew the securities as they come up for redemption. The effect of actual sale of the stocks before maturity will vary with the identity of the other parties to the transactions:

1. If the banks' sales are taken up by the monetary authorities (they may not wish to see the established pattern of interest rates disturbed), such sales will increase the banks' liquid assets by the proceeds of the sale, leaving deposits unchanged, but, of course, the banks more liquid.

2. The sales may be made to the discount market. The discount market can finance these holdings either by selling Treasury bills to the banks or by borrowing more call money. The effect is the same as before. There is, however, a limit to the amount of stock that the discount houses are able, or willing, to hold.

3. Lastly, the banks may sell to the general public. This reduces bank deposits and leaves liquid assets unchanged and so improves the liquid-asset ratio. From the banks' point of view (but not from the point of view of monetary control), it is a less satisfactory method

[5] The increase in commercial bills is due to a number of factors: the replacement of the *ad valorem* duty of 1s.% by a flat duty of 2*d*. per bill in 1961, the increase in international trade, the growing use of bills to finance hire-purchase transactions, and the resort to bill finance by firms during a time of restrictions on bank-lending. For greater detail see 'London Money Market' (May, 1966).

than the other two ways. Even so, however, if the public finances its purchases of stock from the banks by holding less Treasury bills or non-marketable government debt, its deposits will be unchanged, and the final effect will be the same as if the banks had sold the stock direct to the authorities.

The fact that banks in recent years have run down their liquid assets nearer to the minimum levels, and also have greatly reduced their investment portfolios, means that these methods of replenishing their liquid assets in future are more circumscribed.

The conclusion to this section is that attempts to control the cash and liquid assets of the banks is subject to important qualifications. It depends in particular on the attitude of the public to holding cash and government debt, the willingness of the banks to substitute assets, and the fiscal policy being pursued by the government. Many of the factors noted that tend to offset monetary control may only operate at certain times and be of limited duration. But time is often the essence of the problem in monetary matters. It is not surprising that other methods of control have been devised to supplement control over cash and liquid assets. To these we now turn.

Other methods of bank control

BANK RATE

The use of Bank Rate was for a long time considered as the proper means of controlling the banks. An increase was supposed to deter borrowing from the banks since their rates are, by convention, tied to Bank Rate. Similarly, a decrease was supposed to encourage borrowing.[6]

The effects of changes in interest rates will be examined in more detail in the section on policy. It is sufficient to say now that at least in the circumstances of mild inflation which have prevailed since the war, this effect seems so weak in most sectors of the economy as not to be an effective constraint. It has always been recognized in Keynesian literature that low rates, while helpful, were not sufficient to generate business confidence in a depression. It also seems that high rates, by themselves, may not be sufficient to deter expansion in inflationary conditions—at least, within the acceptable range of movements of Bank Rate. The above remarks apply to the dearness

[6] It is worth noting that since the commercial banks do not pay interest on current accounts, an increase in Bank Rate, and therefore an increase in rates at which they lend, means greater profit for the banks. The term 'endowment' has been coined by the report on *Bank Charges* (1967) to cover this element in bank profit.

of money, not to its scarcity—a point which is frequently confused. If borrowing can be made more difficult, the effects are immediate. However, the act of changing Bank Rate has little effect on the scarcity of money. The classical theory of the monetary system tacitly identified dearness of money with scarcity. It assumed that high-interest rates automatically reduced the supply of money. This effect could come about if high-interest rates caused depositors to switch from bank deposits to government securities, an effect which has not been very much in evidence in the post-war period. The only other way in which changing Bank Rate can affect the scarcity of money is if there is a 'liquidity effect'. This effect refers to the fact that banks and other institutions may be deterred from selling securities by an increase in Bank Rate, which, if it affects other rates, will move security prices down. It is argued that the fear of having book losses will deter, in particular, banks from realizing investments and so recouping their liquid assets. From Table 2 we have seen that there is no indication that this has happened in recent years. Banks have dramatically run down their investments in spite of historically high levels of Bank Rate. This is not surprising, as we have seen, because banks' investments are in securities with less than five years to run to maturity, and in any case banks are allowed (rather controversially) to present balance sheets which obscure the detailed working of their operations.

SPECIAL DEPOSITS

Special deposits came into being on the recommendation of the Radcliffe Committee. If the monetary authorities call for special deposits, the banks are required to place a proportion of deposits at the Bank. These, unlike ordinary bankers' deposits, do not count towards either the cash or liquid-asset ratios of the banks. These deposits earn interest $\frac{1}{16}$th nearest to the average Treasury bill rate.[7] Thus, if banks are unduly liquid and the monetary authorities wish to limit credit, they can call for special deposits. As with pressure on the liquid-asset ratio by open-market operations, the banks may be able to overcome the effect of this type of squeeze in exactly the same way—namely, selling securities or substituting other assets. Like other pressures on the banks, it gives them a lever, if they wish to use it, to politely refuse advances.

Special deposits have been used only in a half-hearted manner, although it has been announced that they will be used more flexibly

[7] In May, 1969 the Bank announced that the rate of interest would be halved on these deposits until such time as the banks had conformed to the Request that lending should not exceed 98% of the November 1967 level.

in the future. The arguments used by the Radcliffe Committee to justify special deposits are not very convincing. The adoption of a variable liquidity ratio, as in some countries, whereby the authorities would announce from time to time the level of liquid assets the banks should hold, would seem to be a better device.

DIRECTIVES, REQUESTS OR EAR-STROKING

During the war and until 1951 the banks were obliged to hold Treasury deposit receipts. This at one stage amounted to 40% of their deposits and were a method by which the assets of the banks could be maintained in a manner desired by the monetary authorities. A process of 'forced funding' has been used on one occasion in 1951. For details refer to the *Radcliffe Report,* para. 406. In effect, the banks had to exchange £500 million of Treasury bills for the equivalent of short-term bonds.

Control of the banks by requiring them to hold specific assets, as outlined above, is regarded as an exceptional measure: the process is disliked by both the central and commercial banks. Instead, a process has grown up whereby the Bank of England makes requests to the banks. The procedure is sometimes called issuing directives or, more familiarly, 'ear-stroking'. These 'requests', as they will be called, are conventions which the banks observe even though they have not the force of law. The legal powers which were given to the Bank of England under the Nationalization Act could be used for the same purpose, but the use of such powers is not the way the system is operated. The Bank of England has said that if it had to use force to coerce the commercial banks it would regard this as a breakdown of the monetary system. For our purpose, the distinction is a fine one that need not trouble us; what matters is that requests are carried out.

These requests must take a general form, such as 'Do not lend more than last year' or 'Do not lend more to hire-purchase companies'. They cannot take the form of specific requests not to lend to a particular person or company. The banks are given guidance on the amount of lending: within this constraint they are free to select the happy or unhappy customers who get or do not get the loans.

Summary

The structure in Great Britain of commercial banking—eleven banks dominated by the 'Big Five'—was stable for many years, but is currently undergoing reappraisal. The need for this has been partly brought about by the success of other types of financial intermediaries and foreign banks in attracting deposits, partly by the introduction of a Post Office Giro system, and partly because of the wish to make internal economies and rationalization, both in the number of branches and use of expensive computing and other equipment.

Banks as a whole are able to create credit because, when they relend money that has been deposited with them, a portion of this money finds its way back into the banking system and can in its turn be used to make new investments or advances. The credit-multiplier is not large; it depends in particular on the whole complex of operations between the government, the banks and the public.

It has been shown that there are a variety of methods by which the monetary authorities influence the commercial banks. These are open-market operations, special deposits and requests. Bank Rate is no longer regarded as a direct method of control, although it may be used as a signal by the authorities to indicate their wish for tighter or easier money. The ease with which money control can be exercised depends intimately on the whole fiscal framework, and we pursue this point in Chapter 6.

Commercial banks form only a part of the monetary system, so that control of the banks may not mean control over the monetary system as a whole. In the next chapter we describe other financial institutions that form part of the monetary system and look at some of the implications for monetary policy.

5
Other financial institutions and financial intermediaries

Above all, the maintenance in the primary market generally and by the clearing banks of long-established arrangements on interest rates, following a rigid pattern, left wide-open opportunities which the new markets, with their uninhibited flexibility, were not slow to fill.

Midland Bank Review, August, 1966.

In this chapter financial institutions other than the commercial banks discussed in the previous chapter are dealt with. Firstly, we look at local authority borrowing, because it is their debt which is often held by the other institutions discussed in this chapter. Next we look at acceptance houses and overseas banks. The important growth in these institutions has largely taken place since the *Radcliffe Report*. It coincided with the granting of convertibility to external holders of currently earned sterling in 1958, and has benefited from the general relaxation of monetary restrictions which has taken place since. Then we look at a group of institutions performing various functions which usually go under the title of 'financial intermediaries'. After a brief description of these intermediaries, their implications for monetary policy are taken up, their impact on liquidity and finally their influence on financial markets.

Local authorities

Local authorities have not been included as financial intermediaries, although a case can be made out for doing so. Local authorities are large borrowers on the market, especially on short-term, and in considering financial flows they rank large in the picture. To the extent that local authorities relend for house-purchase and house-improvements, they act in a similar way to other financial intermediaries, but their borrowing is linked to their own needs for finance and not directly to their lending activities, and they are best treated separately.

Until 1955 local authorities had to meet their needs for borrowing by going to the Public Works Loan Board (P.W.L.B.). In 1955, a change of government policy occurred and local authorities were required to meet their needs in the market if they could. Access to government funds through P.W.L.B. was to be available only if funds could not be raised from the market. They were so successful in this policy that at times they embarrassed the monetary authorities, who found that their efforts to reduce liquidity in the economy were being nullified by the increase in short-term borrowing by the local authorities. In recent years this policy has been eased and local authorities now have easier access to the P.W.L.B.

Table 1

Growth of Local Authority temporary borrowing

(£ million)

Year	Up to 7 Days	7 Days to 3 Months	3 Months to 12 Months	Total[1]
1955	—	—	—	169
1961	558	229	146	933
1962	711	359	167	1,237
1963	693	284	291	1,268
1964	878	289	351	1,518
1965	1,239	315	293	1,847
1966	1,188	329	211	1,728
1967	1,238	229	253	1,720
1968	1,545	311	217	2,073

Source: *Financial Statistics*, Table 26, No. 61, May, 1967, and No. 76, August, 1968.

Table 1 shows the growth of local-authority temporary borrowing. From a figure of £169 million in 1955, it has grown to £2,073 million in 1968. The bulk of this money was recallable by the lender within seven days, as the breakdown for the years 1961-8 shows. These funds were drawn from a wide market, including the commercial banks, acceptance houses, overseas banks, other financial intermediaries, individuals and overseas. A detailed analysis of holders for the years 1955 and 1958 is given by Revell, J. R. S. and Hockley, G. C. (July and December, 1960). From 1961 refer to *Financial Statistics* (monthly publication).

In addition to temporary borrowing, local authorities also borrow on a smaller scale by way of mortgages for periods of one or more

[1] Total includes inter-authority borrowing. In 1968 this amounted to £66 million.

years, by the issue of stocks, and more recently by the issue of one- or two-year bonds.

The period since 1955 has therefore seen the rapid growth of a local-authority short-term money market. Local authorities have to pay rates marginally higher than the government for equivalent dated securities. They also pay ½% more than nationalized industries (with Treasury guarantee) for bank loans.

The fact that local authorities have to pay rather more when borrowing on their own account has long been a matter of dispute between them and the government. The Radcliffe Committee gave this and the difficulties it created for monetary control as the chief reasons why the local authorities should be given freer access to the P.W.L.B. The National Board for Prices and Incomes in *Bank Charges* (1967), paras. 90-2, has come out in substantial agreement with the Radcliffe recommendations. As an alternative suggestion, they put up the idea that a new co-operative financial institution, guaranteed by the Treasury, be set up for local-authority borrowing. Our interest is rather that a sophisticated short-term money market has grown up. Since local authority borrowing is secured on the local rateable value of property, their debt has almost the same market standing as government debt, and rates obtainable in this market will exercise a powerful effect on the rates which financial intermediaries need to give in order to attract deposits.

Acceptance houses and overseas banks in the United Kingdom

Acceptance houses and overseas banks are treated together because both are concerned with deposits of British and of foreign residents. First, an outline is given of the functions performed by these two sectors. This section draws on the *Radcliffe Report*, paras. 185-9 and 197-201, and 'Overseas and Foreign Banks in London' (September, 1961, and June, 1968) to which the reader is referred for greater detail.

ACCEPTANCE HOUSES

A wide variety of city institutions are known as 'merchant banks'. This name reflects their origin in the trading of goods. Today they undertake a wide variety of financial services. Eighteen of them belong to the Accepting Houses Committee: to these the term 'acceptance house' can properly be applied. They have always had close associations with the Bank of England, and at one time a merchant-banking background was necessary to obtain a Governorship at the Bank of England. The acceptance of bills of exchange (at a discount plus an acceptance commission) is an important part of their business.

A bill of exchange by a British bank or by one of the eighteen accepting houses is, if it has one other British name on it, 'eligible paper' at the Bank of England, and has therefore the highest degree of liquidity, shared only by Treasury Bills and short-dated Government bonds. Having this maximum of liquidity and the complete assurance of payment (on which of course the liquidity depends), it commands the lowest rate of discount available for any non-Government paper. An acceptance house thus, when accepting a bill, confers on the drawer of the bill (and on anyone who discounts it for him) the certainty of being able to get sterling in exchange for it from a bank or discount house in London, at the least possible sacrifice in discount (*Radcliffe Report*, para. 186).

Besides acceptances, these houses carry out a wide range of other services; in raising loans, dealing in foreign exchange, financial advice (which includes advice to firms contemplating take-over bids, or are themselves the subject of take-over offers) and a wide range of other activities.

OVERSEAS BANKS IN THE UNITED KINGDOM

Statistics of overseas banks now cover over 100 institutions are collected under four headings. These are:

British overseas and Commonwealth banks.
American banks.
Foreign banks and affiliates.
Other banks. These are distinguished because they were not included in the statistics until 1962.

It will be seen from this list that the category 'overseas banks' covers diverse institutions. Some are head offices of British banking concerns overseas, while others are branches of banks whose head offices are abroad.

These banks:
operate as exchange dealers, particularly on the Euro-dollar market;
finance the movement of goods between countries which will include acceptance credits giving rise to bills of exchange which can be negotiated in the discount market;
accept and deploy funds moving to London from abroad.

Regarding their activities in the United Kingdom, the Radcliffe Committee were able to say:

This domestic business is negligible in comparison with the activity of the clearing banks. It is as holders of Government bonds and as operators in the discount market that the overseas banks have their main relevance to the liquidity structure of the economy (para. 201).

Since the publication of the *Radcliffe Report*, this situation has been transformed. While still important in the fields quoted, these banks have greatly extended 'domestic business'.

While the total gross deposits of the commercial banks have increased from £6,636 million in 1958 to £9,772 million in 1967 (see p. 31), the corresponding figures for acceptance houses and overseas banks have increased from £1,085 million to £9,300 million (see Table 2), an increase of 47% in the former case and of 757% in the latter case. Allowing for the fact that this slightly overstates the position because

Table 2

Acceptance houses and overseas banks in U.K.: Deposits at Dec.

£ million

Year	U.K. Banks	*Other U.K. Residents* Sterling Balances	*Other U.K. Residents* Other Currency Balances	*Overseas Residents* Sterling Balances	*Overseas Residents* Other Currency Balances	Certificates of Deposits[2]	Total Deposits
1958	—	—	—	—	—	—	1,085
1959	—	—	—	—	—	—	1,327
1960	—	—	—	—	—	—	1,891
1961	—	—	—	—	—	—	2,013
1962	460	431	76	1,096	959	—	3,022[3]
1963	622	655	83	1,208	1,166	—	3,734
1964	760	815	79	1,283	1,752	—	4,689
1965	1,050	1,046	90	1,356	2,042	—	5,584
1966	1,403	1,158	121	1,250	2,793	81	6,807
1967	2,245	1,399	211	1,167	4,030	248	9,300[4]

Source: *Financial Statistics*, No. 76, August, 1968, and *Bank of England Quarterly*, September, 1964.

[2] These certificates, minimum amount £25,000, are in effect deposits mostly for terms up to one year, but since they are negotiable instruments they are more liquid than fixed term deposits and earn only slightly less in interest.

[3] Figures before 1962 exclude 'Other overseas banks' as data are not available. These banks in 1962 account for total deposits of £409 million.

[4] In 1967 a further £298 million can be added to total deposits in respect of institutions included for the first time. These new institutions have not been included in any of the figures shown.

the figures for 1958 excluded a number of overseas banks which were not included until 1962 and the fact that about one-quarter of deposits represents inter-bank balances (mostly with each other) there must still be an impressive increase in the deposits of this sector compared to the commercial banks.

Taking the period from 1962 to 1967, gross deposits of the commercial banks increased from £7,611 million to £9,772 million, or 28%. Acceptance houses and overseas banks increased their deposits from £3,022 million to £9,300 million, or 207%. Of this increase United Kingdom residents, other than banks, increased their sterling holdings by 225%, while overseas residents increased their balances in other currencies by 320%.

Our concern at the moment is with the sterling holdings of the acceptance houses and overseas banks. Overseas holdings will be taken up in the next chapter. It is clear that in this period they were able to compete very successfully with the commercial banks for deposits. First, the reasons for this will be examined and then the implications for monetary policy looked at.

The acceptance houses and overseas banks are subject to some of the restraints that affect commercial banks. They are, for example, now subject to Requests from the Bank of England on their domestic business, but in general they are freer from restrictions. In particular, in much of this period they were not subject to the cash or liquid-asset requirements of the commercial banks, nor do they follow the interest-rate structure of the commercial banks.

The effect of not being subject to a cash ratio is that:

> Their individual cash positions can vary substantially day by day, from the nature of their business, and it is to their advantage to employ to the utmost channels in which they can earn interest on money that is recallable within twenty-four hours. The existence of the discount market, through which they can smooth out the irregularities of their cash position while maximizing their earning capacity, is a great advantage to such banks, and is indeed one of the attractions which have brought many overseas and foreign banks to London and keep them there (*Radcliffe Report*, para. 177).

One explanation of the faster growth of acceptance houses and overseas banks is thus that they have greater freedom to manipulate their funds *vis-à-vis* the commercial banks.

The second reason referred to, their freedom on interest rates, is probably of more importance in explaining their rise in domestic deposits. They are able to offer, in particular to the institution or business with large funds at its disposal, more attractive rates of interest on deposits than the commercial banks. The commercial banks have reacted recently by setting up special subsidiaries offering higher rates for deposits.

The implications for monetary policy of the growth of acceptance houses and overseas banks is that control of the commercial banks is not sufficient to ensure control of the monetary system. The evidence points to the fact that commercial banks have been unduly penalized (or have penalized themselves) by efforts at monetary control. Restrictions on commercial banks are at least partly overcome by expansion on the part of acceptance houses and overseas banks.

Financial intermediaries

One characteristic of a developed economy is the presence of a wide variety of financial intermediaries. This is in contrast to many underdeveloped countries, where an individual who does not wish to spend the whole of his income has little choice but to hold currency or precious metals, deposit the money in a bank, or lend the money directly to an individual or to a business. A developed country has a great variety of institutions interposed between the owner of funds

Table 3

Main financial intermediaries

(£ *million*)

	Stock of Assets *at the end of* 1963	Assets *acquired in* 1963
Insurance Co's: life funds	7,425	577
non-life funds	972	3
Pension and superannuation funds	4,652	362
Building societies	4,359	518
Investment trusts	2,848	68
H.P. finance houses	796	71
Trustee Savings Banks (Special Investment Depts)	755	133
Unit trusts	350	54
Special finance agencies	215	23
	22,372	1,809

Source: *Bank of England Quarterly*, June, 1965.

and the user of funds. Lending can still take place directly, but usually it takes place by means of the intermediaries. The intermediaries receive money from a variety of sources and employ or invest it in a variety of ways.

Financial intermediaries should be clearly distinguished from brokers, who merely act on behalf of their client to arrange a transaction and then drop out of the picture. Financial intermediaries accept claims on other people, and in exchange offer their liabilities, i.e. claims against themselves. If their claims were widely accepted in payment of debts, as bank deposits are, they would be on the same basis as banks. They are inferior in this respect, e.g. a deposit with a building society must first be turned into money to pay off a debt, whereas a bank deposit can be transferred directly. However, these claims do act as a store of value (which can economize in the use of money) and the intermediaries are a source of credit.

Table 3 lists the main financial intermediaries in order of size of their assets at the end of 1963. (This is not necessarily the same as their economic importance.) The figures are a mixture of market, book and nominal values, and so should be treated with caution.

These intermediaries differ widely from each other. In particular, insurance company life funds, pension and superannuation funds and the special finance agencies are on a different footing from the other intermediaries listed. Special finance agencies will be looked at below. Insurance and pension companies, because of the size of their assets and the annual flow of funds to them, have important repercussions on financial markets in a way which will be outlined at the end of this chapter. In general, however, their liabilities to the public are less liquid than those of the other financial intermediaries. Funds in pension and superannuation schemes are not usually available to the beneficiary before retirement. Insurance life policies are in an intermediate category from a holder's viewpoint: encashment before the policy matures usually involves financial loss, particularly in the early years of the policy. However, a policy can frequently be used as collateral for a loan from the insurance company concerned, a bank or other lender.

Deposits in building societies, hire purchase companies and trustee savings banks are liquid, since deposits can usually be withdrawn on demand or at short notice with no capital loss. Investment trusts and unit trusts differ in that the capital subscribed is usually by way of taking up shares or units in the trust. The funds so subscribed are in turn invested by the trusts in company shares and other assets. The value of these assets will in turn determine the market value of the shares or units of the investment or unit trust. These assets are therefore less liquid than deposits, since their capital value is uncertain.

The special finance agencies include four institutions: the Agricultural Mortgage Corporation, the Finance Corporation for Industry, the Industrial and Commercial Finance Corporation and the Commonwealth Development Finance Company. In general, the capital of these institutions comes from the Bank of England and the commercial banks, with, in the case of C.D.F.C., some being subscribed by a number of Commonwealth central banks. These agencies are government-inspired to meet the needs of agriculture and business for medium- and long-term funds, and in particular to meet legitimate needs where the enterprises find difficulty in raising funds from the normal market sources.

The presence of a host of financial intermediaries raises a number of points.

Power to create credit

From a monetary management point of view, one of the major questions is: supposing the banks are controlled, will the presence of financial intermediaries thwart their attempts at credit control?

If the section on how a bank creates credit has been understood it is easy to see that financial intermediaries differ only in degree in their ability to create credit. A bank can create credit because people deposit notes and coin at a bank in the belief that they can always reclaim deposits in notes and coin. In practice banks find that claims on money are accepted in lieu of notes and coin, i.e. most of the payments in the economy take the form, not of exchange of notes and coin (primary money), but of bank deposits (secondary money). This means a large part of initial deposits can be reloaned, subject only to the need to keep adequate reserves. There was a theoretical stalemate at this point for about 100 years *on whether banks created credit or just loaned out part of existing deposits.* This has been sorted out by considering the flow of income. So long as deposits do not leave the banking system, the process of lending by the banks or of the banks buying securities can repeat itself many times. The process comes to an end because of the need to keep a proportion in reserve at each 'round' of lending and because of leakages from the banking system.

An analogous picture can be drawn for financial intermediaries. A building society will be used as an example. It will find that a certain proportion of money that it lends out will be redeposited with it. This money can be relent, subject only to the need to keep a reserve for that proportion of depositors who demand the return of their money. If we postulate the same sort of closed system of circulation of money, as was done for the banking system, e.g. a house-builder who receives the sum of money loaned by the society deposits this sum back in the building society, then it is clear that the building society can reloan this money, less a proportion to build up its reserves.

The difference between banks and financial intermediaries is thus only one of degree, not of difference in kind. Because financial intermediaries' liabilities are not counted as money, they are likely to have to keep a greater proportion of money as a reserve, or, what amounts to the same thing, see that they secure an adequate flow of new deposits. Also the flow of funds back to the building society is likely to be much less than the flow of funds back to the banking system.

As was the case when considering the banking system, it is necessary to distinguish between a single financial intermediary and financial intermediaries considered as a whole. Although lending by, say, a building society may not lead to very much money being deposited back in the building society, collectively financial intermediaries may be taking in each other's loans, and so be able to expand collectively in a way analogous to the banking system considered as a whole.

Credit creation need not be at the expense of the banking system

It is important to realize that the ability of the financial intermediaries to create credit does not necessarily affect the commercial banks, unlike, for example, the purchase of government securities.

Let us take the case where £1,000 is withdrawn from a bank and is deposited in a building society. From the point of view of the banking system, all that has happened at this stage is that an individual's account is debited by £1,000, while the building society's account is credited by a corresponding amount. The total of bank deposits is unchanged, but the total of financial claims has increased by £1,000 the increase in the deposit at the building society (i.e. a liability of the building society to repay this sum).

Whether, and to what extent, the banks are affected at the next stage depends on the use to which the building society and subsequent holders put this money. Let us assume for simplicity that the whole of this £1,000 is lent by the building society to a borrower, who pays it over to a builder for a house. If the builder deposits the money back in the banking system, once again all that has happened from the banks' point of view is that the ownership of deposits has changed once more. It is clear that the banks will only be affected if there is a 'leakage' in the flow of income: from *their* point of view, a cheque drawn in favour of a financial intermediary is no different from a cheque drawn in favour of an individual. This is so because financial intermediaries bank with the banking system. Commercial banks are affected, as we saw, if the money is deposited with an acceptance house or overseas bank.

Implications for monetary policy

From the point of view of the monetary authorities, a transaction as outlined above is not neutral. The transfer of £1,000 to a building society did not alter the total of bank deposits; it did, however, enable the building society to lend more. We see why the presence of financial intermediaries is so essential to a developed economy and at the same time poses problems for monetary management. The financial intermediaries provide a channel for finance to get to ultimate borrowers. Individuals are not likely to lend substantial sums directly for house-purchase, but are likely to lend to a building society, which in turn lends for house-purchase. This aspect will be taken up in the next section. The problem comes if the monetary authorities are trying to control the amount of credit in the economy by limiting the banks' power to lend. If deposits flow to the financial intermediaries (merely a change of ownership of deposits from the banks' point of view), the financial intermediaries can extend the credit instead of the banking system.

The *Radcliffe Report* went to some length to spell out the implications touched on in this section. It might be supposed that in the circumstances the logic of the situation would dictate that controls over the financial intermediaries be recommended and discussed in some detail, to correspond to existing control over the banking system. In fact, this was not the case, and the position was left rather ambiguous:

> Since we envisage the use of monetary measures as not in ordinary times playing other than a subordinate part in guiding the development of the economy, we do not consider such an elaborate extension of compulsory powers to be justified in the conditions immediately before us. In times of emergency we believe that the rough justice of the blunter measures we propose in paragraphs 524 and 528 would be appropriate.[5]
>
> But it is not impossible that there may be longer periods, not amounting to emergencies, in which excessive liquidity persistently embarrasses the authorities in their conduct of economy policy. In such circumstances an extension of direct control over credit-giving to cover other groups of financial institutions besides the banks would reinforce the efficiency of the restraints imposed on the banks, as well as having the appeal of equity,

[5] The measures recommended were a combination of controls of capital issues, bank advances and consumer credit, aimed to contain private borrowing, and so spending, coupled with a critical review of government spending.

and it might therefore be necessary to accept the degree of interference with business, and to overcome the practical difficulties which such a wide-ranging scheme of registration and direction would entail (para. 511).[6]

In practice, informal control, or Requests, by the Bank of England have been extended from the commercial banks to many of the financial intermediaries. Thus on February 1st, 1965, the Bank wrote to the Chairman of the Committee of London Clearing Bankers requesting that bank advances to the private sector should not increase at an annual rate of more than 5%, and that the banks should apply a similar limitation to both their provision of acceptance facilities and their purchase of commercial bills.

The Governor also wrote to the Accepting Houses Committee and to the organizations of overseas banks in London asking that these banks should similarly limit their sterling advances, acceptances and commercial bill holdings. The London Discount Market Association and the leading associations of hire-purchase finance houses were asked to observe a comparable degree of restraint: and members of the British Insurance Association, the National Association of Pension Funds and the Building Societies Association were also requested to co-operate in maintaining restraint—in particular in relation to the finance of building and property development, other than housing for the owner-occupier (*Commentary*, March, 1966, 3).

In 1968 the Bank announced that a 'new, and to some extent experimental' form of control had been agreed with overseas and foreign banks, to be known as the Cash Deposits Scheme. See 'Control of Bank Lending: the Cash Deposits Scheme' (June, 1968), on which this section draws.

The diversity of these banks precluded bringing them within the system of special deposits. Instead, these banks may be required to make cash deposits with the Bank, calculated as a percentage of certain of their deposit liabilities in sterling. The scheme is not intended to affect the banks' business in foreign currencies. The percentage called will normally be the same for all banks, although the right is reserved, in exceptional circumstances, to treat banks individually. The Bank will pay a Treasury bill rate of interest on the cash deposits, but reserve the right to pay a lower rate than this. The Treasury bill rate will often be less than the banks would otherwise have earned.

The Bank has therefore two methods of control over overseas and foreign banks: strict quantitative controls brought about by

[6] This paragraph has the signs of being the result of compromise between different opinions in pursuit of the British passion for unanimous reports. Would it not be better to have stronger majority recommendations with dissenting opinions?

Requests and the less rigid form of control in the new system of cash deposits.

Thus since the time of publication of the *Radcliffe Report* informal control has been extended to embrace the financial intermediaries. We have not yet been told very much about how the Bank's directives are made known to the financial institutions concerned, to what extent they are effective, and, if so, how they are made effective. It is likely that further evolution will take place. It is now clear that in the absence of restraint the financial intermediaries can, at least in some circumstances, frustrate or partially frustrate a credit squeeze, so that control by informal or formal means is essential if credit restriction is to be successful.

Increase in liquidity

In the previous section we dealt with the ability of the financial intermediaries to create credit. Another aspect of a well-developed sector of this kind was touched on: the increase in liquid assets which they bring about. In general, the financial intermediaries enable long- and medium-term investment to be financed, although the securities which they issue in exchange for deposits are often liquid, i.e. quickly convertible into a known amount of cash. One result of this is that medium- and long-term interest rates are lower than they would otherwise be.[7] This is one of the reasons why interest rates are likely to be higher in underdeveloped countries.

The ability to lend money for a longer period of time than the funds borrowed is an important function in a modern economy. Banks have, of course, long cultivated this art. At the root of this process lies the confidence which must be built up between the depositor and the institution accepting the deposit. The early history of banking, and the bank failures that have occurred in some countries in recent times, are evidence of this. The problem of a country trying to establish a financial sector is not merely that of duplicating the institutions of a developed economy, but of engendering confidence in them once they have been set up. In Britain confidence in the financial sector and the financial intermediaries in particular is

[7] It is sometimes asserted that the movement of funds into institutional hands means that they, as opposed to individuals, are less inclined to invest in newer and riskier projects. The special finance agencies must be exempted from this conjecture, as they were set up expressly to provide finance in this field. A counter-argument is used: that we might expect institutions to exercise their responsibilities of share-ownership more effectively. Either of these conjectures could be important, but there is little satisfactory evidence on either side and it is easy to exaggerate both points of view.

achieved in numerous ways. The various parts are linked together in many ways as a result of formal and informal ties, many of the institutions are subject to legal restrictions governing their reserves and other matters, and most are subject to regulation from their own professional associations.

As an illustration of lending longer than borrowing, we can continue with our example of building societies. It might be questioned how, if building societies lend money for from twenty to twenty-five years on the purchase of houses, they can afford to let depositors have their money back on demand or at short notice. The fundamental point has already been made that because there is general confidence in the way societies are run withdrawals are not likely to be panic measures of a kind that would force any financial institution to close its doors. The building societies, like banks, keep reserves to meet normal withdrawal demands, but, apart from this, their lending is not as long as it seems.

Most mortgages are being repaid over the course of the loan, so that a continual flow of capital is coming into the building society's hands: together with early redemptions, this results in a fairly liquid position.

Building societies are also, to some extent, able to influence the flow of deposits into and out of their accounts by changing the rate of interest they are offering. Here we are not considering the general level of interest rates prevailing in the economy, which will be taken up in a later chapter, but the differential effect of particular interest rates. It is well known that building societies do not follow Bank Rate up or down immediately, unlike, for example, the commercial banks. However, if Bank Rate changes for a considerable length of time, they are forced to follow suit. In the case of an increase in Bank Rate, they find funds flowing from them to institutions who have raised rates, e.g. local authorities and finance companies, and existing deposits may be withdrawn for the same purpose. In this circumstance, building societies are forced to increase their rates in order to protect themselves. In a similar way, societies reduce their rates after a decrease in Bank Rate, when their reserves are sufficiently built up.[8]

The argument in this sector is that financial intermediaries increase liquidity, and that this is an important function in a modern economy.

[8] This example of how an institution is able to make loans for periods in excess of twenty years, and yet let its depositors have their money at call or short notice, illustrates the weakness of the case of the commercial banks, who frequently protest that making long-term loans would endanger their financial security. For a critical look at commercial bank practices see *Bank Charges* (1957).

In essence, financial intermediaries lend or invest long while frequently borrowing short. Long-term lending is more hazardous than short-term lending, and they remove much of this uncertainty for the investor *vis-à-vis* his position had he lent direct to the final borrower.

Impact on financial markets

The final aspect of financial intermediaries that we wish to stress is their impact on financial markets. This impact can come about in two ways. Firstly, from the existing flow of funds and, secondly, from switching of existing assets. From Table 3 it will be seen, for example, that insurance company life funds acquired assets of £577 million during 1963. Of this sum 23% went into gilt-edged or local authority stocks, 29% in company fixed-interest stocks and 21% in ordinary company shares, 16% was used for loans and mortgages and the remaining 10% for land property and ground rents.

The size of the financial intermediaries and the size of the flow of funds to them make these institutions of prime importance. We do not know at present how much of this money is channelled into buying old assets and how much into new assets, but the impact on both markets is likely to be very considerable. The Bank of England estimates that the institutional share of turnover in United Kingdom equities in 1963 was about a quarter of the whole, and that they accounted for rather more than three-fifths of the turnover in fixed-interest stocks.

It is clear that if the authorities can keep these institutional investors happy these financial markets are likely to be orderly.

Summary

The commercial banks form an important part of the monetary system, but in recent years acceptance houses, overseas banks and financial intermediaries have been growing much faster. They are important, not only because, like commercial banks, they can create credit, but because they increase liquidity and have a marked impact on financial markets. The fact that the Bank of England now includes these institutions in its Requests and has initiated the cash deposits scheme for other banks indicates that monetary control, to be effective, must take these institutions into account. There are no clear indications that Requests to these institutions will meet with the same success as Requests to the commercial banks. Developments could take place by more formal means of control, or the commercial banks might be encouraged to compete more actively with these institutions. Either of these developments pose difficult problems and raise far-reaching questions of monetary management, which will be developed in the next chapter.

6 Monetary expansion and contraction

We conclude that the proper spirit of approach to control of the money supply is a decent humility in the face of a highly complex task. Both old-orthodox and new-orthodox arguments are inadequate. The only policy for influencing the money supply on which practical reliance could be placed would be based on control, not of bank cash or of liquid assets, but of security sales to the non-bank public. If the authorities are to be criticized it is because of their timidity in experimenting with methods of controlling the gilt-edged market.

CRAMP, A. B. (June, 1966), 'Control of the Money Supply', *Economic Journal.*

The previous chapters have outlined briefly the financial sector of the British economy. A picture of the Bank of England and its relations with the government, the commercial banks, the discount market, other financial institutions and financial intermediaries has been built up. Also some of the interrelations of these institutions with each other have been indicated.

We now turn to the question: What determines the amount of money and liquidity in the economy? This will be tackled by looking first at what determines the amount of primary money and secondary money, and then considering broader issues which are introduced when acceptance houses, overseas banks and financial intermediaries are brought into the picture.

We should not make a common mistake and forget that money has a *demand* as well as a *supply* aspect. Thus the question, 'What is the potential power of the commercial banks to create money?' may not be the same as 'How much do they actually create?' The former question takes us over the whole field of government policy; the latter question brings in bankers' prudence and aspects which they take into account before granting loans and overdrafts. Again the monetary authorities can attempt to diminish the supply of money or they may be able to achieve the same ends by strengthening the demand for money or for government securities.

In looking at these questions, it will be found that the net flows of money to or from the Exchequer *vis-à-vis* the rest of the economy are the crucial factors, together with the ways in which the authorities and the commercial banks are able to deal with these flows. Much of this chapter is taken up in detailing these matters. One section is taken up with a discussion of how a government deficit in a particular year is financed. The next question goes into more detail of the factors affecting the size of a government deficit or surplus in a year. This is followed by a brief look at how the market is managed day to day. These factors are then drawn together to see how they influence the amount of money and liquidity in the economy.

Amount of primary and secondary money

Primary money has been defined to be coin, notes and bankers' deposits at the Bank of England.

Coin and notes need not detain us long. In Britain they are issued by the Bank subject to the formal consent of Parliament. They are kept at the level demanded by the public, so that issues reach a peak just before summer holidays start and before Christmas. For details of the mechanism of the note issued, the reader is referred to 'Note Circulation' (March, 1965).

The practical effect of an increase in the note issue is to lessen the Exchequer's need to borrow on other forms of debt. However, this is merely a by-product of the issue of a token currency. The government *does not* make an issue of notes to finance its expenditure: it does so because there is a demand for notes. Coin and bank-notes are, in a *Radcliffe* phrase, 'the small change of the monetary system'. We should expect to find in normal times that coin and notes bear a relatively stable relationship to national income, or to consumers' disposable income, after allowance has been made for seasonal factors referred to above.

So bankers' deposits at the Bank of England is the main item we should have in mind when we think of primary money. Transactions between the government and the rest of the economy will (except for sums that take place in coin and notes and in addition are not paid into the banking system) be reflected initially in a change in bankers' deposits. For example, to make a payment to the government, an individual will write a cheque on his account in favour of the Inland Revenue or appropriate department. The end-result is that, besides the individual's account being debited, bankers' deposits at the Bank will be debited and the government's account credited.

We know that commercial bankers maintain their cash reserves (bankers' deposits and till money) at 8% of deposits. Thus when implying that bankers' deposits are increased or decreased above this level, we are implying that commercial bankers alter their structure of assets and liabilities so as to maintain the desired ratio of 8% in a manner which has been outlined in Chapter 3.

Payments from the government that take place by way of cheques reverse the process: as well as an individual's account being credited, bankers' deposits at the Bank are increased, while the government's account is decreased.

What is relevant in this situation is the net flow of payments between the government and the rest of the economy and the way in which this flow is financed. To this we now turn.

The financing of a government deficit

Let us suppose that the Budget in a particular year, taking both above- and below-the-line items,[1] shows a deficit—that is, the government will be spending more than it receives, assuming no tax changes are made. The issue of notes and direct borrowing from the Bank of England have both been ruled out as a means of financing the deficit. *It will be met by the issue of securities: it makes a considerable difference whether these are long-term or short-term securities and to whom they are sold.*

We have two streams of payments to consider: on the one hand, payments from the government to the non-government sector in excess of payments the other way, so that individual and company accounts at commercial banks will be increased and, as we have seen, a consequence of this is that bankers' deposits will be increased. On the other hand, we have the consequences following on from the issue of securities. The first effect is a potential increase in purchasing power, while the second may be, but does not have to be, a potential decrease in purchasing power.

Let us first consider that the government attempts to finance the deficit by the issue of long- or medium-term securities (here a decision has to be made on what rate of interest they will be offered to the market, a point that will not be pursued at this stage). This issue may be taken up by:

(a) the public,
(b) the commercial banks.

[1] The distinction between above- and below-the-line items is historical. Items above the line were intended to cover expenditures met out of taxation and revenue derived from taxation; below the line items, expenditures and revenue derived from borrowing. The distinction has little economic merit. For a discussion of alternative ways to present Exchequer accounts see Peacock, A. T. (January, 1964).

(a) It is clear that if the public take up the whole of the issue they will draw cheques in favour of the government and bankers' deposits will be reduced. The increase in deposits brought about by the Budget deficit has been matched by a decrease because the public have been induced to exchange cash for bonds.

(b) Sales to the banks have similar effects to sales to the public. The increase in deposits brought about by the government deficit is matched by the banks' transfer of funds to the government in exchange for securities.[2]

Failure to sell long- or medium-term debt will result in the need to issue short-term securities—that is, Treasury bills. In the chapter on the discount market it was seen that the discount houses undertake to cover the tender. They can do this because they can always get accommodation at the Bank of England. In so far as the discount houses take up the securities, there is no offset to the government deficit. Sales to outside tenderers will reduce bankers' deposits by a like amount and reduce their liquid-asset ratio. However, Treasury bills present a potential spending power, since they are very liquid and their holders will, in any case, have money in three months.

We can summarize so far and say that notes and coin come into circulation because the public desire more or less notes. They are not of operational significance. Bankers' deposits and the amount of secondary money depend on the acquisition of debts by the commercial banks and the public, and is the result of the whole fiscal and budgetary process—that is, it depends on the stream of payments to and from the government and public and the method of financing any deficit.

Determinants of the government's annual surplus or deficit

The preceding section presented a static picture of how a deficit could be financed. We now examine more closely the factors that in any one year will determine the size of the government's surplus or deficit, and then go on to examine day-to-day management.

Table 1 presents a fuller picture of changes that occur in a year. The top part of the table presents the items that require financing in a year; the lower section shows how the finance was provided. The bottom is the inverse of the top. Thus net balance is either a deficit, and a figure will appear in the top half showing the amount that requires financing or a surplus, in which case a figure will appear in the bottom half showing the amount of finance provided.

[2] It is unrealistic to postulate the sale of long-term bonds to the commercial banks in current conditions as bonds with five years or less to maturity are preferred. See *Radcliffe Report*, para. 406.

Table 1

Exchequer Financing

(£ million)

Items requiring Finance	Year *1963-4*	*1964-5*	*1965-6*	*1966-7*	*1967-8*
1. Net balance or overall deficit	376	313	499	740	1,331
2. Increase in Exchange Equalization Account	—	—	128	—	—
3. Decrease in overseas holdings of British Debt	—	—	—	62	—
4. Reduction in the note issue and coin	—	—	—	—	—
5. Withdrawal of National Savings	—	—	118	197	5
6. Reduction in Tax Certificates	59	41	59	—	—
7. Reduction in Treasury bills	—	544	—	488	42
8. Reduction in government stocks	8	138	72	—	96
9. Reduction in net indebtedness to Bank of England	—	1	—	—	131
	443	1,037	876	1,487	1,605
Items providing Finance					
1. Net balance or overall surplus	—	—	—	—	—
2. Decrease in Exchange Equalization Account	55	118	—	112	234
3. Increase in overseas holdings of British Debt	13	611	85	—	1,228
4. Increase in the note issue and coin	205	123	212	123	123
5. Increase of National Savings	156	185	—	—	—
6. Increase in Tax Certificates	—	—	—	98	20
7. Increase in Treasury bills	—	—	396	—	—
8. Increase in government stocks	—	—	—	1,130	—
9. Increase in net indebtedness to Bank of England	14	—	183[3]	24	—
	443	1,037	876	1,487	1,605

Source: *Bank of England Quarterly Bulletins*, Table 1.

[3] Includes changes in the Banking Department's holding of government debt resulting from a special swap with the U.S. authorities and its repayment.

Item 1 thus shows the overall deficit in the year. This was the only item considered in the previous section.

Item 2. It may seem strange that an increase in the Exchange Equalization Account (E.E.A.) appears under the heading of items requiring finance and that a fall provides finance. The explanation is simple. When the E.E.A. increases its holdings of gold or foreign currencies (i.e. foreigners exchange their currencies for pounds) the E.E.A. draws on its reserves to provide these pounds. These reserves are mainly held in the form of tap Treasury bills, so that the Exchequer is obliged to replace these bills by borrowing from another source.

Likewise a fall in reserves (foreigners exchanging pounds for gold or other currencies) means that the E.E.A. has more of its assets in pounds. These as we have seen are held mainly in the form of Treasury bills.

Item 3. The change in overseas holdings refers to changes in amounts of government securities held by foreigners. Many of these changes will be accompanied by opposite changes in E.E.A. For example, when foreign currencies are converted into sterling with the E.E.A. (with the result we saw under item 2 of increasing the Exchequer requirements) and then invested in government debt, the Exchequer requirements will be unaffected; E.E.A. will hold less debt, foreigners more. In the same way, government borrowing from abroad usually results in opposite changes in E.E.A., so that it has no effect on the amount of Exchequer financing.

In addition to these movements, balances held in sterling may be put into, or taken out of, government securities with no attempts made to change into other currencies.[4] These movements will affect Exchequer requirements because of the need to replace the foreign holder by some other.

Items 4-6 are straightforward. A reduction in the public's holding of any of these items has to be financed in some other way. These items are 'passive' savings, in the sense that the government are

[4] These balances could, for example, be invested in local authority securities, in equities, or left on deposit with commercial banks. A full analysis would try to take into account the secondary effects of foreign funds being invested in one type of security rather than another. The most important of these would be the effects on the commercial banks, interest rates and on the lending, borrowing and spending of the private sector. For further details see 'Inflows and Outflows of Foreign Funds' (June, 1962). The tentative conclusion reached by this article was: '. . . It may be said that, in a period of restrictive credit policy, such as 1960 and 1961, a substantial part of an inflow or outflow is likely to occur in ways that directly cause no change in bank deposits and domestic spending. Nevertheless, some parts are likely to be in forms that do cause changes in the liquidity of banks and other credit-giving institutions' (p. 102).

always ready to issue Tax Reserve Certificates, Savings Certificates, Premium Bonds and the like on demand. The more of these that people are willing to take up the less need there is to sell other securities and vice versa.

From time to time these issues are made more attractive, but this is usually when the interest on them has fallen behind other rates.

Items 7 and 8. Again a reduction in the public's holding of these requires to be financed. The contrast between Treasury bills and stocks compared with National Savings is that the monetary authorities may actively be trying to alter the composition of the former. In particular, they may be trying to fund—that is sell long-term securities instead of Treasury bills.

Item 9. This item is not important in this context. It has already been explained that the indebtedness of the government to the Bank of England is minimal. The large sum appearing in 1965-6 is the result of a special swap with the United States authorities and its repayment.

From Table 1 and its depiction of actual changes that took place in the economy during the years in question, it is evident that the question of what determines the amount of money and liquidity in the system cannot be separated from consideration of the whole economic system. In particular, it is possible to imagine adverse circumstances for the authorities. Suppose the aim is to reduce the amount of money and liquidity in the economy. Adverse circumstances would be:

1. A budget deficit, i.e. a stream of expenditure being injected into the economy, and the need to increase debt as a result.
2. Inability to fund because of unwillingness of the public and the banks to buy bonds.
3. A large amount of government debt maturing which, because of 1 and 2, will mean short-term debt must be issued to replace it.
4. An inflow of gold or foreign exchange into the Exchange Equalization Account.

The embarrassment of an inflow of gold or foreign exchange may not seem a very realistic worry in present-day conditions. (This is not saying a gold inflow is bad; merely that this results in the Exchequer having to find alternative holders for the Treasury bills that the Exchange Equalization Account formerly possessed.) However, in the post-war period the adverse circumstances numbered 1, 2 and 3 have been present and have coloured a great deal of monetary policy. This being a period in general of overall deficits, of large amounts of debt-maturing, and of the cult of the equity share rather than fixed-interest stock.

The authorities had little choice but to increase short-term debt to provide the necessary finance. In these circumstances it is not surprising that the monetary authorities should feel that control of the banking system—of secondary money—by the traditional means of controlling primary money and liquid assets left something to be desired and sought to supplement control by other means.

Day-to-day management of money

So far we have seen that imbalance in the flow of payments out of, and receipts into, the Exchequer in a particular year results in a change in the amount of securities. Within the context of a deficit or surplus expected in a year, the flow of payments from day to day, which may be distinctly uneven, and from one time of the year to another, has to be evened out. The Bank, working closely with the Treasury, has the job of ensuring, if a deficit on the day is forecast, that finance is available; alternatively, if a surplus is forecast, that these surpluses are used to buy back Treasury bills from the market and so minimize the net cost of the National Debt.

From our point of view, the second connected task—that of managing the London money market—is more important. A new flow of payments to the government has the effect of reducing bankers' deposits. The banks are likely, as a result, to be drawing upon money lent at call to the discount market.

> . . . The discount houses find themselves short of funds in consequence, and unless the Bank take steps to relieve the shortage—usually by buying Treasury bills either from them (the so-called 'direct' method of giving help) or from the banks (the 'indirect' method)—they may be forced to borrow from the Bank at Bank Rate or over. The enforcement of such borrowing increases the average cost of the houses' total borrowings and is one of the main ways (short of a change in Bank Rate) in which the Bank of England exerts an influence on short-term interest rates and particularly on the rate at which the discount houses may be expected to bid for Treasury bills at the following Friday's tender. ('Management of Money Day by Day', March, 1963, pp. 15, 16. This article gives a detailed account of the management of money day by day.)

The monetary authorities are thus faced with a choice either of maintaining the existing structure of short-term rates, with the consequence that they relieve the shortage of money, or of maintaining the shortage and allowing short-term rates to rise. In practice the authorities normally try to create a shortage, to give themselves this option, by issuing Treasury bills slightly in excess of the Exchequer's estimated needs. At this point the issues become more controversial. See Cramp, A. B. (June, 1966) and references therein.

In considering how effective control by means of a money-shortage can be the controversy turns on whether or not the discount houses are able to escape from the penal rate imposed by borrowing at the Bank, either by reducing their share of Treasury bills or borrowing elsewhere. Either way of escape is unlikely to be effective in current conditions, because the discount houses undertake to 'cover the tender' and because the sources of outside finance are limited.

The reasoning of this section leads to the likely conclusion that the authorities would find it very difficult to control the commercial banks by controlling their cash base. Since the authorities are concerned with the level of short-term rates, they are prevented from provoking a severe and long-lasting shortage of money because of the effect this would have on short-term (and eventually long-term) interest rates. The authorities have to be concerned with the level of short-term rates for a number of reasons. A powerful one is the need to keep rates in line with foreign monetary centres so as to avoid undesirable flows of 'hot' money. Related to this is the effects of servicing the debt and the effects on the balance of payments if the debt is held abroad. Domestically they may also wish to keep interest rates from rising for a number of social and economic reasons.

The previous assertion that the amount of secondary money in the economy depends in a complex way on a number of factors, in particular on the fiscal and budgetary policy of the government, the public's attitude to government debt, and the reactions of the commercial banks, has now been justified and spelt out at some length.

Other financial institutions and financial intermediaries

The presence of a large financial sector, apart from the commercial banks, means that wider issues of credit and liquidity have to be considered. It has been argued that a number of factors have to be taken into account in considering the operations of the banks, and it is clear that these factors will also apply to these other financial institutions—for example, the public's choice between holding deposits with the commercial banks or holding them with the acceptance houses, overseas banks or building societies. The monetary authorities have also to take the amount and composition of government paper into account, not only because it affects the commercial banks, but because it is also important to these other institutions.

It was suggested at the end of the previous chapter that control by means of Requests of these other financial institutions may be less easy than control of the commercial banks. If this is so, one way of establishing more effective control would be to subject these other financial institutions to more formal arrangements as to their reserve ratios, of the kind already imposed on the commercial banks. The situation has altered a great deal since the Radcliffe Committee considered, and largely rejected, proposals on these lines. An alternative proposal (or it could be a supplement to control on the lines suggested above) is that commercial banks should compete more actively amongst themselves and with other financial institutions. Although this proposal is not novel, the first 'official' statement on these lines came, not from a monetary body, but the National Board for Prices and Incomes.[5] The major recommendation of the Board was that the convention by which the banks agree between themselves on the rate of interest to be paid or not to be paid on deposits with them should be abandoned:[6]

> We consider that this agreement has led to a loss in their power to attract deposits, to a loss therefore in their power to extend and diversify their lending activities, to an inability to secure to a larger extent the economies of scale which could follow on such an extension—in short, to a loss in their relative place in the entire financial system. A recovery of place for the banks requires in our view a greater degree of competition between the banks themselves for deposits and therefore between the banks as a whole and other financial institutions . . . (*Bank Charges* (1967), para. 182).

In earlier paragraphs the Board considered the implications for monetary policy. They rejected the idea that freeing rates would weaken monetary control and went on to suggest that it might strengthen the hands of the monetary authority. The present immediate link between changes in Bank Rate and clearing-bank rates while other rates lag behind would be likely to give way to a more evenly spread effect throughout the entire financial system. The Board indicated that this could be coupled with liquidity reserve requirements imposed upon non-bank financial institutions and perhaps also with the imposition of a reserve power over the maximum deposit

[5] *Bank Charges* (1967). This was so in spite of the fact that the reference of bank charges to the Board stated explicitly: 'It is not intended that the Board should concern itself with questions of monetary policy, such as Bank Rate and the general level of interest rates.' The Board interpreted this to mean: 'In so far, however, as we recommend changes in the system of bank charges, such changes are likely to have considerable implications for the techniques of monetary control. We have accordingly thought it consistent with our terms of reference to indicate what these implications might be and what possibilities by way of offsetting action might be open to the authorities' (para. 3).

[6] Other recommendations were abandonment of their agreement on rates to be charged for advances, complete disclosure of profits and reserves, the publication of a scale of charges for work done and the allowances made for credit balances, and more flexible opening hours.

rates offered for specific types of deposit.

The Board briefly considered the effect of freer rates on the level of interest rates and considered 'that our suggestions would have greater implications for the relative rates of different intermediaries than for the general level of lending rates'.

Summary

This chapter sets out to examine the forces that determine the amount of money (in the narrow sense of coin, notes and bank deposits) and the amount of liquidity in the economy, and whether the amount of money and liquidity is under the control of the monetary authorities. Not surprisingly, no simple answer emerges. Monetary control is never likely to be a precise instrument, since it depends on so many things—in particular, the whole fiscal and budgetary process and the attitudes of the public to saving and holding government debt. What emerges from this analysis is that while the monetary authorities can control the commercial banks, more or less, according to their wishes, control over other financial intermediaries is much looser.

Recent developments have included the extension of Requests to many of these intermediaries and the introduction of the cash deposits scheme for other banks. It has also been suggested that control would be more successful if the commercial banks competed more actively amongst themselves and with other financial institutions.

Part II
Public finance

7
Introduction to public finance

We cannot therefore settle on abstract grounds, but must handle on its merits in detail what Burke termed 'one of the finest problems in legislation, namely, to determine what the State ought to take upon itself to direct by the public wisdom, and what it ought to leave, with as little interference as possible, to individual exertion'.

KEYNES, J. M., *The End of Laissez-faire.*

The economic welfare of an individual is his command over goods and services. This command comes from a number of sources. It is derived from work, from accumulated wealth, from inheritance and gifts, and from government provision and legislation.

This book will not be concerned with the return from work as such. It is sufficient for our purpose to note that returns from different kinds of work are altered by society in various ways. For example, the beginning of this century saw the start of minimum-wage legislation. Today we see efforts to have a more extensive incomes policy. Of more practical importance has been the extension of the provision of education out of general taxation, so that entry to work requiring formal training is no longer confined to those able to afford the training. Within the existing framework of the returns from work, this section of the book examines how the individual and the corporation are influenced by taxation of income, wealth, inheritance and gifts and the effects of government provision and legislation.

Public finance is about the revenue, expenditure and debt operations of the government and the impact of these measures. The need for government spending (and therefore to raise revenue or debt) is argued on a number of grounds. A start can be made by considering the imperfections of the competitive pricing system.

Imperfections of competitive market prices

The model of a perfectly competitive pricing system has often been held up as an ideal: prices act as a guide-post to producers as to the things and quantities that they should produce and, assuming certain assumptions are met, output will be optimized. The usefulness of prices in this respect, in invisibly (but not costlessly) planning the immensely complex assortment of goods and services found in a modern developed economy, should not be underestimated. It is, however, the imperfections of the pricing system which give much of the interest to a study of public finance.

One drawback of a pricing system in allocating goods is that it only takes account of effective demand (that is, demand backed by money). If income and wealth is unevenly spread, deficiencies in allocation will occur. These deficiencies in allocation provide one reason for State intervention, either to redistribute income and/or wealth to some extent, or to ensure in other ways some standard for its citizens. This point will be developed later in this chapter.

Another important modification to the optimality of the competitive pricing system has long been recognized: it is usually discussed under the headings of 'collective goods', 'externalities' or 'neighbourhood effects'. These terms are used to draw attention to the fact that some goods confer large benefits, not only on the potential purchaser, but on other people. The opposite may also be true; disadvantages may be imposed on other people, e.g. noise, dirt and pollution. In the former case, where benefits are apparent this may result in the demand for this type of good being lower than the optimum level, as persons hope to benefit from the provision made by other people without providing any themselves. Minimum provision for sewerage disposal can be left to the individual in a sparsely populated area: concentration of population in towns makes it essential to ensure that sewage-disposal is adequate. It is no accident that serious plagues have been eliminated from developed countries. Services of this type usually result in 'natural' monopolies. The waste in having more than one company digging up the same street to lay sewage pipes is obvious. The principle applies to other services, such as gas, electricity, water-supply, telephones, and so on. This conclusion leaves open the question of whether in cases such as this the government should itself undertake the provision of the service and, if so, how the cost shall be met. Or whether the government should merely supervise, and, if it is needed, subsidize the private provision of the service. Where a good imposes a cost on the community (usually termed a 'social cost') there are likewise alternatives. The government may just forbid the nuisance—say, the disposal of waste in rivers—and thereby leave the cost of alternative means of disposal on those causing it (or on their customers), it may assist those concerned financially to make other arrangements, or the government itself may make the alternative arrangements and decide how the cost shall be met.

In extreme cases provision of a service at all means provision for everybody. These services are indivisible. Defence against external aggression and police protection are obvious examples. These are sometimes called 'pure public goods'. In cases such as this the pricing system cannot be operated. Provision of these services, if left in private hands, is likely to result in zero supply.[1] Finally the competitive sector may, if left unregulated, be subject to systematic periods of boom and slump.

The government sector

The above account of the inadequacies of the private pricing system helps to put a discussion of the public sector in perspective. Three questions are frequently posed:

1. How big should the government sector be?
2. How to determine how much to produce when the price system is inoperative, either by necessity or through deliberate choice to meet the cost out of general taxation.
3. How to ensure that expenditures are efficiently, and not wastefully, applied.

1. On the first question the writer believes that the economist, as economist, has no unique answer. The question indeed incorrectly implies that a level of activity can be specified which will be valid over time, valid under varying conditions, and which admits of a unique solution. 'Public goods' where externalities are large are not constant over time. The growth, and particularly the concentration, of population means that problems of health, such amenities as open spaces, clean air, water-supply, communications and so on have more externalities. Again, if size is measured by the amount of government expenditure, it is worth emphasizing that different decisions on the way to achieve a particular object will involve different levels of government expenditure. For example, a decision to maintain employment in the shipbuilding sector of the economy

[1] 'There is a still more fundamental bias in our economy in favour of products and services for which it is easy to collect payments. Goods that can be sold in packets to individual customers, or services that can be charged for at so much per head, provide a field for profitable enterprise. Investments in, say, the layout of cities, cannot be enjoyed except collectively and are not easy to make money out of; while negative goods, such as dirt and noise, can be dispensed without any compensation being required.

'When you come to think of it, what can easily be charged for and what cannot is just a technical accident' (Robinson, J., 1962, p. 124).

can be achieved by subsidies to shipbuilders, or by providing cheap loans to purchasers, which will raise expenditure, or by tariffs which will not. The conclusion to which this sector tends is that the level of government activity at any one time is, in a democracy, essentially decided by political means.

2. The question of how much to produce, say, of defence or public health, where the price system is inoperative is one that admits of no easy solution. The principle of achieving equal marginal benefits from various expenditures needs to be borne in mind. It may avoid crude waste of expenditure. For example, the argument is sometimes heard: 'If only one life is saved the expenditure [on say, a road modification or a particular safety device] is worthwhile.' If the objective is to save life, the question that should be considered is: 'In what way can this particular sum of money be spent so as to save the most lives?' However, as a practical guide to day-to-day decision-making—whether £1 million spent on hospitals would yield more benefit than £1 million spent on defence, or roads, it yields little practical help. This principle is likely to be more fruitful in allocating expenditure within a particular field, e.g. whether to spend £1 million on operating theatres in hospitals or on the provision of more hospital beds.

One possible way out of the difficulty of weighing up expenditure in disparate activities is to set up minimum standards of service that it is desired to obtain[2]—say a policeman for every 2,000 of the population, the elimination of serious epidemics, maximum size of school classes of twenty-five, maximum permitted levels of pollution, and so on. Provided these standards are based on the cost and benefits that flow from reaching these standards, these should aid decision-making. The standards will not be obtainable overnight, but the act of quantification of the costs and benefits and listing of the non-quantification advantages and disadvantages should enable more rational decision-making.

On the question of deciding how much of a particular good should be produced in the absence of price-guide-lines, no economist would claim that, with existing knowledge and techniques, he can do more than assist in decision-making. Intuition, judgment and flair have their part—perhaps the major part—to play.

3. The question of ensuring economy in public affairs in the sense that, after expenditure decisions have been made, the money is used efficiently and not wastefully is important. However, the process

[2] Suggested by Drees, W. Jr. (1967). This issue is devoted to the *Papers and Proceedings of the Twenty-second Session of the International Institute of Public Finance*. Many of the ideas touched on in this chapter are dealt with more fully in this volume.

whereby the government attempts to secure economy in this sense, the weaknesses of present methods and hopes for improvement by new statistical and other techniques must be considered outside the scope of this book.

It may be noted in passing that 'extravagance' may be an indication of too little rather than too much administrative expenditure, in the sense that the misallocation of resources might have been avoided wholly or in part if there had been more, or better trained, government officials. Aircraft development costs since the end of the Second World War seem an apt illustration.

The minimum level of government activity

The above outline enables us to discuss the minimum level of government activity—the level on which all reasonable people can agree.

Nearly all societies give some help to those who are incapable of helping themselves (mainly the young, the old, the sick and the disabled) and who have no one on whom they can depend.

Collective goods, such as the administration of justice and defence of the realm, will form part of the government activity for the reasons given. (There may be deep divisions of opinion about the nature and extent of defence, about whether it is necessary at all, but if the need is granted nobody seriously suggests that private armies be formed.)

Again, it is generally agreed that where an operation must, by its nature, be monopolistic in order to be efficient, e.g. sewerage and the supply of electricity, then the State should either control, or itself run, the service at the central or local government level.

General agreement obtains that where there are strong externalities government action is needed. Difficulties occur over those goods which have both a benefit to the individual and externalities: education is an example. Elementary education is recognized as having strong externalities; our present society would be impossible without a certain level of education of the population. Not everybody agrees that, as yet, higher education has sufficiently strong externalities to justify meeting the cost out of general taxation.

This is, then, the minimum scope of State activity: some form of aid for the unfortunate, justice, defence, the regulation of natural monopolies, and goods which have strong externalities. Public opinion in most societies would recognize this as the lowest common denominator of government action. Even at this level disagreements can creep in. If government action is admitted as necessary in a certain area—say, education—it leaves open the question of whether the government should itself undertake the provision of the service or merely supervise and, if it is needed, subsidize the private provision of the service.

Government activity, even at this minimum level, involves some redistribution of resources from the 'better off' to the 'worse off'. The questions raised by redistribution will now be tackled.

Redistribution of income and wealth

Redistribution in a community can take place by provision of services above the minimum levels just discussed, provided these are met out of taxes paid by the 'better off' or, alternatively, by direct money transfers from the 'better off' to the 'worse off'.

In talking about redistribution of income and/or wealth, three strands of thought are apparent. These will be discussed in turn. One is unavoidable if it is granted that help should be given to the unfortunate. The second strand of thought aims at deliberate redistribution above the level required to supplement the lowest incomes. The third strand is directed at changing the conditions which help create and foster the inequalities. In practice, these ideas may be interwoven, but conceptually much confusion can be avoided if they are kept separate.

If it is granted that a society should assist those who are incapable of helping themselves, then this implies that society has already made a decision that some redistribution of income and/or wealth is desirable. This conclusion is inescapable. The government cannot in these circumstances be neutral in its attitude to the redistribution of income and/or wealth, since a decision to help a needy section of the population entails redistribution from a 'better-off' to a 'worse-off' section.

Leaving to one side humanitarian arguments, the core of the case of those who advocate government provision or, alternatively, argue for some redistribution of income and/or wealth above the minimum level just discussed, is that, as we have seen, needs are not satisfied equally if income is unequally spread. That is, that economic welfare can be increased by government provision or redistribution. This case was well put by Dalton, H. (1959), 10:

> Income consists of the means of economic welfare, and great inequality in incomes in any community implies great inequality in the economic welfare attained by different individuals. But this is not all. For it implies also considerable waste of potential economic welfare. Put broadly, and in the language of common sense, the case against large inequalities of income is that the less urgent needs of the rich are satisfied, while the more urgent needs of the poor are left unsatisfied. The rich are more than amply fed, while the poor go hungry. This is merely an application of the economists' law of diminishing marginal utility, which states that, other

things being equal, as the quantity of any commodity or, more generally, of purchasing power increases, its total utility increases, but its marginal utility diminishes.

This quotation contains two ideas. One is that the economic welfare of different individuals can be compared. However reasonable such an idea may seem, particularly when we compare extreme positions, such as giving a loaf of bread to a man who already has plenty with giving a loaf to a man who is hungry, there are those who hold that we have no objective measure by which we can compare needs of different individuals. We need not enter into this controversy, because the second idea contained in this quotation is that the community should judge relative needs. Such judgment will not be to any absolute standard, but will change as ethical, political, social, economic and other conditions change in the community. Much of the study of public finance can be taken up with a consideration of how these changes in community standards have affected ideas about government spending and revenue. Chapters 8 and 9 look briefly at the changes in Britain since 1900.

The more fundamental problem is to change the conditions of society which create and foster the inequalities and this paradoxically seems to receive less practical attention. It is perhaps inherent in most of us to regard as 'normal and just' whatever framework of society exists at the time. Even Plato carried forward the conditions of slavery into his *Republic*. We shall examine two important examples of this tendency. One which will be examined at length in Chapter 11 on 'The Concept of Income' is concerned with the extremely narrow definition of income which has grown up for tax purposes. The second is concerned with the general tendency to regard the laws about inheritance and gifts as though they were ordained by the Almighty from the beginning of time. Far from this being the case, it is found that laws and customs about these matters show wide variation between countries, even when these countries have similar democratic institutions and roughly comparable economic development. Changes within the same country over time may be just as great, but come less to the notice of the observer. The substantial freedom of bequest in England is in large measure due to legislative changes in the nineteenth century, but this freedom is hedged about in important ways. When a person dies intestate, the State steps in to administer the estate according to law, and in the event of no surviving relatives the estate goes to the Exchequer. Where a will has been made, it is restricted in that the deceased cannot validly direct that his property should be destroyed, and there are restrictions imposed in the interests of morality and public policy generally. Property cannot be left in perpetuity and dependants have certain rights, even if they are not named in the will, over other beneficiaries. Far from the laws about inheritance being laid down from time immemorial, they are seen to be restricted both to place and time. Dalton, H. (1959), Part IV, Chapter VI, gives an interesting elaboration of these matters. However a great deal of the discussion that takes place is confined to rates at which taxes shall be applied within the current legislative mould. As we shall see in later chapters, questions about the nature of wealth and income are as important in discussing a tax system as the rates which happen to be applied at a particular moment of time.

Summary

By the economic welfare of an individual is meant his command over goods and services. This command comes to the individual from a number of sources. It is derived from work, from wealth, from inheritance and gifts, and from government provision and legislation.

Imperfections in the competitive marketing price system leave a vacuum for the community to fill. These are due to the uneven spread of income and wealth leading to deficiencies in allocation, the presence of goods which have strong externalities, and the natural bias of the private sector of the economy towards goods for which it is easy to collect payment.

It has been suggested that there is no unique solution to the question about what is the correct level of government activity. The level itself is likely to change with time, with changes in population, and in the complexity of society. Also changes in political ideals are likely to change ideas about goods which could be produced by the private sector, but which the State (for economic or other reasons) decides to control.

In deciding the quantities of goods to be produced, where no pricing system acts as a guide, the economist has a useful, if limited, role to play.

Government provision and legislation forms the backdrop of a public finance study. Government provision out of general taxation or transfer payments, such as pensions, are an obvious way of supplementing income deficiencies. Society judges the extent to which redistribution above this level is desirable. The economic justification for such provision is that command over goods and services is unevenly spread, and a democratic society, in no very exact fashion, judges the relative needs of its members and deems that some minimum needs must be met for all—that is, that some redistribution of command over goods and services shall take place.

8

The pattern of government expenditure since 1900

Crying wolf at the drop of an index.

MISHAN, E. J. (1967), *The Costs of Economic Growth.*

Conceptual difficulties

Government spending and taxation affects every individual. It is not therefore surprising to find that in public finance there are perhaps more attempts made by sectional interests to present biased information than in other economic fields. It is not uncommon to find people asserting opposite things, e.g. one will claim that public expenditure has gone up, another that it has gone down. Ignoring deliberate attempts to mislead by, for example, choosing a base period when prices were either particularly high or particularly low, or deliberately picking on the item which 'proves' the point in question and ignoring all the evidence to the contrary, there are still a number of difficulties to be overcome, which we shall look at briefly. After this the evolution of government spending during this century can be tackled.

First, figures of money expenditure, although useful in showing how expenditures on different sub-categories have changed relative to each other, tell us little about the share of government expenditure in relation to total resources. In order to measure the latter, it is necessary to make allowances in some way for changes in the value of money. This can be done by some form of price index which can be used to present the money figures in 'real' terms, i.e. in terms of command over goods and services, or by expressing government expenditure as a percentage of the gross national product. Unfortunately, all ways of allowing for price changes have limitations, which means, not that the results are useless, but that we must use them with care.

Secondly, items should be related to population. The longer the period under consideration the more misleading it can be to ignore this factor of government activity if population has changed significantly in composition or absolute numbers or both.[1]

Thirdly, we need to take account of the nature of government expenditure and draw a clear distinction between transfer payments on the one hand and direct government expenditure on goods and services on the other. Transfer payments are, as the name implies, payments made by the government, such as pensions, family allowances and interests payments on the National Debt.

Transfer payments do not involve the government in direct use of the nation's goods and services. Transfers may be classified in different ways—for example, transfers between persons, as between rich and poor; transfers over time, as the provision of pensions; and transfers to meet such contingencies as sickness or unemployment. Since the government does not work on the principle of earmarked funds the practical implications of transfer payments on these lines are not easy to sort out. The financing of National Insurance, outlined in the Appendix to Chapter 9, comes closest to the idea of a fund, since only 15% of the cost in 1967 came out of general taxation. However, the use of the word 'fund' can be misleading. It does not represent a transfer over time, in the sense that individuals pay now to build up a fund to pay for their future pensions and other benefits. Current payments are used to pay existing benefits. Pensions, for example, are largely a transfer from the working population, because they pay contributions, to the pensionable group. Existing workers in their turn, on the current method of financing, will have their pensions paid by the population working at the time they are retired. Over 73% of the cost of health is met out of general taxation: the transfer here depends much more on the impact of the tax system as a whole on the particular individual, as well as the benefit to the individual. Given this situation, it seems that the most meaningful concept of transfer between persons is obtained by looking at the whole system of taxation and benefits and taking their net impact on the individual. This will be done in Chapter 18.

Finally, a great deal of confusion is caused because different concepts of government are selected. Should government spending include spending by local authorities? Should it include spending by the nationalized industries? Fortunately, there is no need to seek a non-existing 'right' definition. Sometimes one definition, sometimes another is useful; what we must avoid is misleading conclusions from figures drawn up on different bases.

[1] Looked at from a different viewpoint. If the government undertakes exactly the same functions over a time period, it does not follow that expenditure, when allowance is made for price-changes and population-growth, will also be static. Age changes in the population will mean different amounts need to be spent on, for example, education and old age pensions.

Expenditure since 1900

Table 1 shows government expenditure for selected years since 1900. The definition of 'government' adopted will, throughout this book, include local government, but exclude the nationalized industries unless the contrary is stated. Nationalized industries have been excluded because they are not, as a rule, on the same footing as other government activities. Neither the nationalized industries' investment nor their charges form part of the Budget process in quite the same way as other government activities. This will be taken up in the beginning of the next chapter. Table 1 shows expenditures for central and local government separately and a 'Total' column with them combined. The figures are given in £ million, first at current prices—that is, at prices in the year in question—then in 1900 prices after allowance has been made for the growth of population. For the sake of completeness, a price index and population index are given. Attention to the footnote to this table will make it clear that the price index is intended only as a rough guide. In practice, expenditure in the period 1900-55 was broken down into various parts, e.g. capital-formation and goods and services, and appropriate price indexes were applied to each component part. The 'price' index shown gives a rough average of these price indexes. The index after 1955 is that for 'all goods and services sold on the home market' from the *National Income and Expenditure Tables* for 1968—adjusted to the base year, 1900.

The source of these figures, price index and population index up to 1955 is from Peacock, A. T. and Wiseman, J. (1961). No attempt has been made to match the sophistication of Peacock and Wiseman's price index. The adjustment for price and population changes after 1955 is only intended to serve as a rough approximation. For this reason a line has been drawn across the table and figures for the year 1955 appear from both sources.

Table 1 shows very clearly that government expenditure has increased markedly in this century. The rather meaningless comparison in money terms is an increase from £281 million in the year 1900 to £16,749 million in 1967, or a forty-seven-fold increase. However, prices increased nearly seven-fold in this period and population increased by 33%. When allowance is made for these changes, we get more than a six-and-a-half-fold increase in expenditure in real terms per head (either a staggering increase or a revelation of the fantastic underspending in earlier years, according to one's viewpoint!) The changes in expenditure have not occurred at a steady rate, a point which will be considered later. Central government expenditure has increased more rapidly than local government expenditure. As a proportion of the total, local government expenditure decreased from

Table 1

Expenditure of Central and Local Governments on Current and Capital Account at Current and at 1900 Prices per Head of Population. Selected years 1900-67

(£ million at Current Prices)

Year	Current Prices C.G.	L.G.	Total	%[2]	Gross National Product	Total Spending as % of G.N.P.
1900	182	99	281	35	1,944	15
1910	142	130	272	48	2,143	13
1920	1,275	317	1,592	20	6,070	26
1928	695	399	1,094	37	4,523	23
1933	676	390	1,066	37	4,141	26
1938	1,056	531	1,587	34	5,294	30
1950	3,479	1,060	4,539	23	11,636	39
1955	4,607	1,536	6,143	25	16,784	37
1955	4,848	1,622	6,470	25	16,974	38
1960	6,744	2,251	8,995	25	22,790	39
1961	7,305	2,578	9,883	26	24,392	41
1962	7,573	2,866	10,439	27	25,550	41
1963	7,882	3,142	11,024	29	27,163	41
1964	8,428	3,639	12,067	30	29,313	41
1965	9,310	4,112	13,422	31	31,310	43
1966	10,097	4,461	14,558	31	32,858	44
1967	11,684	5,065	16,749	30	34,292	49

1900 Prices deflated by Population Growth

Year	Price[3] Index	Pop. Index	C.G.	L.G.	Total
1900	100	100	182	99	281
1910	103	109	118	123	241
1920	282	106	432	101	533
1928	197	111	316	184	500
1933	173	113	344	201	545
1938	186	115	494	246	740
1950	380	122	765	215	980
1955	469	124	808	248	1,056
1955	469	124	833	279	1,112
1960	537	127	989	330	1,319
1961	553	128	1,032	364	1,396
1962	574	129	1,023	387	1,410
1963	585	130	1,036	413	1,449
1964	601	131	1,070	462	1,532
1965	632	132	1,116	493	1,609
1966	659	133	1,152	509	1,661
1967	675	133	1,301	564	1,865

35% or higher at the beginning of the century to around 25% after 1945, but in recent years it has shown a tendency to increase once more. The effect of two world wars on centralizing expenditure can be seen, expenditure in real terms by local government being lower after the wars than it was before. Part of the explanation of the change in local government expenditure is the transfer after the Second World War of gas and electricity services to national industries.

Table 1 also shows Gross National Product (G.N.P.) in current prices and total government spending in current prices as a percentage of G.N.P. The results, using deflated values for both sets of figures, do not differ very greatly from those using current prices, so the latter only have been shown in the table.

Government spending as a whole rose from 15% of G.N.P. in 1900 to 49% in 1967. In 1900 most of this expenditure was on goods and services and on capital account. By 1965 spending under this head accounted for 32%, spending on transfers and subsidies 17%, making up the indicated total of 49% of G.N.P.

These facts can be expressed rather differently. The money increase in G.N.P. of rather more than seventeen and half times between 1900 and 1967 has the effect, when allowance is made for price and population changes, of almost doubling real G.N.P. per head. Against this doubling of real product per head, in this period of sixty-seven years, government expenditure in real terms has increased six-and-a-half times; however, government spending on goods, services and capital account increased rather less than this at five and a half times, the difference being made up by the bigger increase in spending on transfers and subsidies.

Tables 2-4 use figures at current prices, but this does not matter,

---

[2] Total local government expenditure at current prices as percentage of total government expenditure (i.e. C.G. and L.G.).

[3] 1900 prices for the years 1900-55 were arrived at by breaking down government expenditure into various parts, e.g. capital formation and goods and services and appropriate price indexes were applied to each component part. The 'price' index shown gives a rough average of these price indexes. The index for the years 1955 onwards, shown beneath the line, is that for 'All final goods and services sold on the home market' from *National Income and Expenditure Tables*, 1966 and 1968, Table 16, adjusted to base year 1900.

Source: Source of figures, price index, population index and G.N.P. up to 1955, Peacock and Wiseman, *The Growth of Public Expenditure in the U.K.*, Table A.20, pp. 201-2, and Table A.2, pp. 153-4. 1955 and after: *National Income and Expenditure Tables*, 1966, Tables 1 and 48, and 1968, Tables 1 and 47.

Because of rounding, figures may not add up to the totals shown.

Table 2

Expenditure of Central and Local Governments at Current Prices on Current Account (Goods and Services and Transfers and Subsidies) and on Capital Account. Selected years 1900-67

(£ million at Current Prices)

Year	*Goods and Services* (1)	*Transfers and Subs.* (2)	*Current Account* (3)=(1)+(2)	*Capital Account* (4)	*Total Expenditure* (5)=(3)+(4)	*Capital Expenditure as % of Current Account*
1900	194·2	36·2	230·4	50·4	281	21·9
1910	171·8	55·1	226·9	45·1	272	19·9
1920	887·7	602·5	1,490·2	101·9	1,592	6·8
1928	451·9	534·1	986·0	108·7	1,094	11·0
1933	438·9	538·6	977·5	88·5	1,066	9·1
1938	822·7	545·6	1,368·3	218·7	1,587	16·0
1950	2,071	2,031	4,102	437	4,539	10·7
1955	3,192	2,333	5,525	618	6,143	11·2
1955	3,171	2,305	5,476	994	6,470	18·2
1960	4,163	3,260	7,423	1,572	8,995	21·2
1961	4,497	3,616	8,113	1,770	9,883	21·8
1962	4,822	3,822	8,644	1,795	10,439	20·8
1963	5,080	4,129	9,209	1,815	11,024	19·7
1964	5,395	4,307	9,702	2,365	12,067	24·4
1965	5,919	4,822	10,741	2,681	13,422	25·0
1966	6,436	5,182	11,618	2,940	14,558	25·3
1967	7,063	5,925	12,988	3,761	16,749	29·0

as we are here interested in how the proportions spent on various services have changed, and deflating by a price index is not likely to alter these in any significant way. Table 2 splits the total figures of Table 1 into expenditure on goods and services and expenditure on transfers and subsidies. The importance of this distinction has already been commented on in the beginning of this chapter. Together these expenditures equal the current account transactions. If to the current-account expenditures we add expenditure on capital account, we reach the figures of total expenditure, which agree with Table 1.

The bottom part of the table expresses these expenditures as a percentage. Taking the current-account transactions, we see that transfers and subsidies run at much higher levels in the later period. Sub-

Expenditure as a Percentage of the Total

Year	*Goods and Services*	*Transfers and Subs.*	*Capital Account*	*Total*
1900	69	13	18	100
1910	63	20	17	100
1920	56	38	6	100
1928	41	49	10	100
1933	41	51	8	100
1938	52	34	14	100
1950	45	45	10	100
1955	52	38	10	100
1955	49	36	15	100
1960	46	36	18	100
1961	45	37	18	100
1962	46	37	17	100
1963	46	37	17	100
1964	45	36	19	100
1965	44	36	20	100
1966	44	36	20	100
1967	42	35	23	100

Sources: 1900-55: Peacock and Wiseman, *The Growth of Public Expenditure in the U.K.*, Table 5, p. 71, and Table 6, p. 78. 1955 and after: *National Income and Expenditure Tables*, 1966, Table 48, and 1968, Table 47.

Because of rounding, figures may not add up to the totals shown.

sidies are mainly to agriculture; transfers either payment of interest on the National Debt or on social services. Variations in social-service payments will also cover very interesting variations, reflecting, for example, high amounts on unemployment pay during the slump of the 1930s, and more on education, health and housing in the later years. Interest payments exhibit interesting variations during this period. Greater detail is available in Tables 3 and 4.

Expenditure on capital account exhibits wide variation. This is not unexpected, since capital expenditures create durable assets. Neither the creation of the original assets nor their replacement is likely to be spread evenly over time. The mistake should not be made of equating capital expenditures with 'useful' expenditures and current expenditures with 'wasteful' expenditures. Both statements may be true, but both may be false. The tendency is all too apparent which regards expenditure on bricks and mortar as somehow 'better' than expenditure on training and pay of the staff to run the schools or hospitals or institutions once they have been built.

Table 3

Expenditure of Central and Local Governments on Current and Capital Account by function. Selected years 1900-67

(£ million at Current Prices)

Year	Administration and Other	National Debt	Law and Order	Overseas Services	Military Defence	Social Services	Economic and Environmental Services	Total
1900	17	20	10	1	135	51	48	281
1910	22	20	13	1	74	89	53	272
1920	72	325	33	3	520	412	228	1,592
1928	49	305	31	1	125	434	149	1,095
1933	44	228	31	2	112	497	151	1,066
1938	61	213	39	3	473	596	202	1,587
1950	175	507	79	179	836	2,094	669	4,539
1955[4]	182	707	115	80	1,606	2,739	714	6,143
1955	145	770	118	135	1,567	2,970	600	6,305
1960	194	1,025	174	213	1,612	4,122	1,145	8,485
1961	221	1,108	209	236	1,732	4,574	1,270	9,350
1962	250	1,118	224	230	1,853	4,892	1,367	9,934
1963	208	1,200	247	238	1,905	5,348	1,402	10,548
1964	206	1,263	272	281	2,006	5,871	1,580	11,479
1965	228	1,349	295	301	2,131	6,657	1,800	12,761
1966	253	1,475	339	315	2,246	7,108	2,042	13,774
1967	267	1,599	380	326	2,412	8,003	2,702	15,689

Current Prices expressed as % of Total Government Expenditure

1900	6	7	4	0·4	48	18	17	100
1910	8	7	5	0·4	27	33	19	100
1920	5	20	2	0·2	33	26	15	100
1928	5	28	3	0·1	11	40	14	100
1933	4	21	3	0·2	11	47	15	100
1938	4	13	2	0·2	30	38	13	100
1950	4	11	2	4·0	19	46	15	100
1955[4]	3	12	2	1·0	26	45	12	100
1955	2	12	2	2	25	47	10	100
1960	2	12	2	3	19	49	13	100
1961	2	12	2	3	19	49	13	100
1962	3	11	2	2	19	49	14	100
1963	2	12	2	2	18	51	13	100
1964	2	11	2	2	18	51	14	100
1965	2	11	2	2	17	52	14	100
1966	2	11	2	2	16	52	15	100
1967	2	10	2	2	16	51	17	100

[4] The totals after 1955 are less than those shown in Tables 1 and 2 because grants from the Central Government to local authorities, and other transactions in financial assets, are omitted to avoid double counting.

Sources: 1900-55: Peacock and Wiseman, *The Growth of Public Expenditure in the U.K.*, Table A-15, pp. 186-7, and Table A-16, pp. 188-9. 1955 and after: *National Income and Expenditure Tables*, 1966 and 1968, Tables 52 and 53.

Because of rounding, figures may not add up to the totals shown.

Table 4

Expenditure of Central and Local Governments on Current and Capital Account on Social Services at Current Prices and as a Percentage

(*£ million at Current Prices*)

Year	Education	Health	Social Insurance and Assistance	Housing	Food Subsidies	Total
1920	97	49	213	53	—	412
1928	105	66	202	61	—	434
1933	107	75	269	46	—	497
1938	139	99	278	80	—	596
1950	440	478	674	340	162	2,094
1955	675	582	1,015	420	47	2,739
1955	549	619	1,075	489	238	2,970
1960	916	919	1,574	468	245	4,122
1961	1,012	996	1,721	534	311	4,574
1962	1,172	1,046	1,843	503	328	4,892
1963	1,281	1,118	2,093	562	294	5,348
1964	1,417	1,224	2,214	772	244	5,871
1965	1,588	1,375	2,537	920	237	6,657
1966	1,768	1,515	2,719	898	208	7,108
1967	1,963	1,692	3,055	1,045	247	8,002

Expenditure as a Percentage of the Total

1920	24	12	51	13	—	100
1928	24	15	47	14	—	100
1933	22	15	54	9	—	100
1938	23	17	47	13	—	100
1950	21	23	32	16	8	100
1955	25	21	37	15	2	100
1955	19	21	36	16	8	100
1960	22	22	38	12	6	100
1961	22	22	37	12	7	100
1962	24	21	38	10	7	100
1963	24	21	39	11	5	100
1964	24	21	38	13	4	100
1965	24	21	38	14	3	100
1966	25	21	38	13	3	100
1967	25	22	38	13	3	100

Sources: 1900-55: Peacock and Wiseman, *The Growth of Public Expenditure in the U.K.*, Table 10, p. 92. 1955 and after: *National Income and Expenditure Tables*, 1966 and 1968, Table 53.

The period since the 1930s reflects the growth of Keynesian ideas that government spending can be used to take up the unemployment in the economy. In present-day conditions these ideas have been re-examined. The first crude idea of government expenditure acting as a regulator of the economy—expanding when the private sector contracts and vice versa—looks odd when the nature of much government expenditure is considered. Do we really wish to put off spending on roads, education or hospitals until such time as there is a danger of recession?

In the post-war period the authorities have been groping in a new direction. Fiscal and monetary policy is seen as a means whereby the private sector of the economy can be regulated. If the economy is slack, the private sector can be encouraged to undertake more capital investment by, for example, tax incentives, or attempts can be made to influence private expenditure on goods and services by reducing tax or other changes. This can be in addition to, or in place of, changes in government spending. In a like manner, in times of inflation the private sector can be discouraged from trying to undertake so much investment or consumption by tax increases; the full brunt of the adjustment need no longer be borne by the government sector.

There is probably wide agreement on the principle involved in trying to regulate the economy in the way outlined in the preceding paragraph. Disagreements occur on the ability of the government to undertake the regulation, and on the advantages and disadvantages of various monetary and fiscal weapons as the means to achieve the regulation. Value judgments enter when regulatory measures are at variance with equity aspects. These matters will be taken up in Part III.

Table 3 sets out information on government spending in the same two ways. The first part of the table gives figures in £ million. The second part expresses expenditure on each service as a percentage of the whole.

The following brief notes on the headings should make clear the nature of expenditure referred to and the main changes which have occurred:

ADMINISTRATION AND OTHER

A heterogeneous category covering the cost of tax-collection, government buildings and maintenance. While these have, of course, increased in money terms, they have not done so in percentage terms. Not surprisingly, they take a smaller proportion of the Budget.

NATIONAL DEBT

Simply interest paid to other than government sectors—that is, the so-called 'net' debt, which excludes inter-government transactions.

The National Debt interest payments show interesting variations. In the 1920s they amounted to well over a quarter of government expenditure, falling in the 1930s after the conversion operations in 1932 and 1934. The contrast in the proportion of the Budget going in debt payments after the two world wars is very striking, and reflects the very different ideas of paying for these wars held at the respective times. A great deal of the credit must go to the ideas of J. M. Keynes. In particular see Keynes, J. M. (1940). The difference between the two war periods reflects the greater use of taxation in the Second World War compared to the greater use of debt policy in the First World War. The Second World War also introduced a special war-time tax known as post-war credits. Sums paid in this form of taxation remain to the credit of the individual, returnable at the discretion of the government. At present these are paid back to a woman on reaching the age of fifty-five and to a man on reaching the age of sixty. Since 1959 interest at the rate of 2½% has been paid on sums still retained.

LAW AND ORDER: *Police, prisons, law courts, judges' salaries*

In view of the current emphasis on crime, it may seem surprising that a smaller proportion was spent on law and order in 1965 than in 1900. We can put this in another way: while government expenditure in real terms increased, as we saw from Table 1, about six and a half times, on law and order it increased about four times. This relative change in emphasis poses interesting questions which cannot be pursued here. It might be argued that we are spending too little on this service, that, for example, our prison system is largely a relic from the nineteenth century. On the other hand, it may be that increased expenditure on other services has redressed the balance and reduced the relative needs of this sector.

OVERSEAS SERVICES

Expenditure of the Foreign Office, colonial administration, the British Council and overseas broadcasting. From very small absolute and relative amounts prior to the Second World War, overseas services account for 2% of total government expenditure after 1955. Part of the difference is explained by loans to overseas governments and net lending abroad for private industry, etc., which were excluded from the figures above the line, but included in the figures from 1955.

MILITARY DEFENCE

This includes civil defence. Military defence has always occupied a significant slice of expenditure in this period. From around a third of expenditure pre-1914, a significant drop in the 1920s and 1930s to around a quarter of the Budget in the 1950s, the 1960-67 period shows the proportion slightly declining.

SOCIAL SERVICES

Education, child care, health, National Insurance (unemployment, sickness benefits, retirement pensions, etc.), national assistance, housing (subsidies and capital expenditure) and food subsidies. The importance of social service expenditure from the 1930s is evident from the tables, and now accounts for over 50% of expenditure. The figures hide important changes in the nature of the expenditure which will be looked at in Table 4.

ECONOMIC AND ENVIRONMENTAL SERVICES

Services to agriculture, forestry and fishing, and expenditure on industry and commerce (food subsidies appear under the social service heading). Provision of basic services: roads and public lighting, fire, water, sewage, refuse, land-drainage, coast-protection, town-planning, parks. These expenditures were a higher proportion of total expenditure in most of the pre-1939 period: they now account for 17% of the total.

Table 4 presents the main items of social service expenditure. Differences in classification at this more detailed level mean that the proportions shown for the period 1920-55 are not strictly comparable to those after 1955, but the broad trends are evident. While the proportion spent on education has accounted for nearly a quarter of expenditure during this period, expenditure on health has increased from around 12% to 22%. The most important category, social insurance and assistance, shows considerable variation, and the figures do not bring out the different nature of the expenditure in different periods. The high proportion shown for 1933 reflects the high level of unemployment and hence unemployment payments of this period, while the later figures reflect the growth of social insurance. The fluctuations in housing reflect to some extent the different emphasis put on municipal housing by the Conservative and Labour parties. Food subsidies reflect the relative decline in their importance from their Second World War levels.

Summary

Government expenditure has increased since 1900 in money and real terms per head of population. Of this expenditure the central government has increased its importance relative to local government.

Of the broad categories of government spending we selected, the increasing importance of the social services showed up clearly, and within the social services the largest increase in expenditure was on health. Military defence fluctuated, as we would expect, and it still accounts for a sizeable amount of government spending. Finally, the interest payments on the net National Debt showed interesting variations.

The rate of growth of the government's claim on the national product (as measured by expenditure on goods and services) is impressive if somewhat less than the rate of increase in government expenditure as a whole. Put the other way, expenditure on transfers and subsidies has increased faster than expenditure on goods and services.

9

The pattern of government revenue since 1900

It has been maintained—and the assertion is scarcely an exaggeration that the theorems of Euclid would be bitterly controverted if financial or political interests were involved.

FISHER, I., *The Purchasing Power of Money.*

Introduction

This chapter first of all takes a factual look at the pattern of government revenue since 1900. It then goes on to consider the aims of a tax system and principles of taxation.

In looking at the pattern of government expenditure in the previous chapter, it was possible to treat as a whole the expenditures of central and local government on both current and capital account. In presenting figures of revenue, a similar procedure will be adopted, whereby the items of tax revenue of central and local government will be presented. It is not the intention to present a complete balance sheet, and some revenue items, such as trading income and income from rents, interest and dividends, are not included.

The decision to exclude trading income is in line with the general treatment throughout this book. If, however, a government-run service is operated primarily as a tax device, this decision would clearly be incorrect. For example, some countries have a tobacco monoply, so that 'profits' from this service are no different from the large amounts raised in tax from tobacco in Great Britain. In a similar way, services run at a loss represent a subsidy to the users of the service met out of general taxation. In Great Britain lip-service at least is paid to nationalized concerns breaking even taking one year with another. Three industries do not fit very well into this formula. The postal services have for many years made a profit and contributed sums to the Exchequer but, on the other hand, the National Coal Board and railways have made much larger losses. There appears to be growing up, at least in respect of the railways, the idea that some parts of the service will always have to be run at a money loss, the social or neighbourhood effects of these loss services being held to justify the subsidy involved. In the absence of separation in the accounts of nationalized concerns of that part of the service run for social purposes as opposed to that part run on more commercial lines, taking account of the 'tax' or 'subsidy' involved, is bound to be an arbitrary process.[1] Therefore trading profits or losses are omitted. Our concern will be with the items of taxation which are regarded as variable in the Budget to suit the revenue needs of the government.

Revenue since 1900

Table 1 presents the information on revenue, first in current money prices and then in percentage form. Since our interest is in the amount of revenue drawn from various kinds of tax, we can work in current prices without worrying that price and population changes will seriously distort the picture: see the opening remarks in the previous chapter. A warning is needed that in looking at changes in the amounts yielded by different types of taxes the aggregate figures conceal changes in the rates of tax and of the income or goods which are subject to tax. The details of Customs and Excise taxes will be looked at in this chapter; details of the other taxes will be taken up in later chapters.

Income tax has accounted for a quarter or more of total revenue since the 1930s, and in much of the post-war period for around 31%. This tax is subject to almost annual changes, either as to the rates applied or to tax concessions granted. The impression that we have a steeply progressive tax system is frequently obtained because income tax and surtax are progressive taxes. However, together these only account for about a third of total revenue, and when all taxes are taken into account the picture is rather different.

The percentage yield from surtax shows a diminishing trend from a high of 6% before 1939 diminishing to 2% in the post-war period. It cannot be concluded from these figures that high incomes have diminished significantly in this period. Changes in rates and in the level of income subject to surtax, already mentioned, have to be taken into account and also the extent of legal avoidance. Faced with high tax on money incomes, employers and employees have taken advantage of the fact that many tax-free benefits can be given: free meals, generous expenses, top-hat pension schemes and so on. These benefit those concerned to the detriment of the revenue and of other taxpayers whose taxes are correspondingly higher. It may also

[1] The government paper *Railway Policy* (November, 1967), envisages that this —separation of social services from commercial activities—will be made in respect of the railway accounts. See also *Nationalized Industries: a Review of Economic and Financial Objectives* (November, 1967).

be possible to convert income into a capital gain which until recently was untaxed. For example, instead of a salary increase an executive may be offered share options or better pension prospects. Estate duties have also been eroded by avoidance to a much greater extent. Estate duty accounted for 12% of revenue in 1900, about 6% per cent in the 1930s and 3% post-war. Since death duties are now much higher than they were pre-war, amounting to 80% on estates over £1 million as opposed to 40%, it might be supposed that wealth is now more equally distributed. As we shall see, very little of the change in yield can be explained by redistribution effects. Rather, the explanation is to be sought in the fact that death duties are to a great extent a discretionary tax which can be legally avoided.[2]

Stamp duties cover miscellaneous items of revenue, of which the bulk is from *ad valorum* duties on the sale of houses, land and shares. Also included are the fixed duties payable on cheques and other deeds. A not insignificant source of revenue in the early years of the century, these items in the post-war period account for only about 1% of revenue.

Taxes on companies were introduced to gather some of the excess profits which some companies were able to make in wartime. The high percentage figure shown in 1920 for company tax is a reflection of the abnormal conditions still being felt as a result of the First World War. The corporate form of business has been growing in importance throughout this century, and in interpreting these figures this fact must be borne in mind. The yield has remained at about 4% in the post-war period. Whether companies should be taxed as companies, as opposed to taxing only the owners of the companies, together with the structure of tax and allowances, will be discussed in Chapter 13.

National insurance and health contributions show the biggest percentage increase of any tax in the table, and now account for 14% of total revenue. This increase thus mirrors the increase in expenditure on social services that was noted in the previous chapter. These contributions are in the nature of a poll tax, payable in part by the employer and part by the individual. They are therefore by nature regressive taxes, falling more heavily on small incomes. This has been modified

[2] Those who regard this statement as a wild exaggeration might ponder the advertisements in newspapers. For example, the *Financial Times* on December 16th, 1967, carried two advertisements on this theme. The largest, spaced over two columns, read:

'ESTATE DUTY IS ALMOST A VOLUNTARY TAX!'

'If you have an estate-duty problem and love someone more than the Exchequer, we can assist you.

'We have specialized in designing original schemes for Top People for over 20 years.'

Table 1

Sources of United Kingdom Tax Revenue

(£ million)

Year	Income Tax (Land and Property)[3]	Surtax	Estate Duties	Stamp Duties	Profits Tax[4]	National Insurance and Health[5]	Customs and Excise	Motor Vehicles[6]	Rates	Selective Employment Tax	Other	Total
1900	21	—	19	9	—	—	61	—	45	—	3	158
1909	37	—	18	8	—	—	63	—	68	—	4	197
1920	320	42	41	23	290	29	283	—	119	—	297[8]	1,443
1928	251	61	77	27	2	80	251	25	188	—	86	1,048
1933	252	61	77	19	2	88	288	28	165	—	30	1,010
1939	336	63	77	21	22	104[7]	341	36	214	—	23	1,236
1939	346	65	77	19	28	104[7]	382	34	214	—	23	1,292
1950	1,404	114	190	53	277	440	1,583	59	338	—	16	4,474
1955	1,964	132	184	75	223	594	1,990	85	475	—	17	5,739
1960	2,285	178	236	94	262	913	2,366	123	771	—	28	7,256
1961	2,565	196	259	97	317	1,072	2,540	141	831	—	32	8,050
1962	2,846	230	266	95	379	1,197	2,687	164	916	—	33	8,813
1963	2,823	174	308	92	388	1,303	2,721	182	1,013	—	38	9,042
1964	2,942	179	308	83	408	1,444	3,034	194	1,092	—	46	9,730
1965	3,373	184	290	76	466	1,685	3,425	192	1,228	—	71	10,990
1966	4,120	210	315	78	120	1,806	3,617	174	1,358	298	65	12,161
1967	3,666	279	339	92	1,146	1,908	3,729	196	1,475	429	78	13,337

Year	Income Tax (Land and Property)[3]	Surtax	Estate Duties	Stamp Duties	Profits Tax[4]	National Insurance and Health[5]	Customs and Excise	Motor Vehicles[6]	Rates	Selective Employment Tax	Other	Total
1900	13	—	12	6	—	—	39	—	28	—	2	100
1909	19	—	9	4	—	—	32	—	34	—	2	100
1920	22	3	3	2	20	2	20	—	8	—	20	100
1928	24	6	7	3	—	8	24	2	18	—	8	100
1933	25	6	7	2	—	9	28	3	16	—	4	100
1939	27	5	6	2	2	8	28	3	17	—	2	100
1939	27	5	6	1	2	8	29	3	17	—	2	100
1950	31	3	4	1	6	10	36	1	8	—	—	100
1955	34	2	3	1	4	11	35	2	8	—	—	100
1960	31	2	3	1	4	13	33	2	11	—	—	100
1961	32	2	3	1	4	14	32	2	10	—	—	100
1962	32	3	3	1	4	14	31	2	10	—	—	100
1963	31	2	4	1	4	15	30	2	11	—	—	100
1964	31	2	3	1	4	15	31	2	11	—	—	100
1965	31	2	3	1	4	15	31	2	11	—	—	100
1966	34	2	3	1	1	15	30	1	11	3	—	100
1967	28	2	3	1	9	14	28	1	11	3	—	100

[3] Land and assessed taxes were about £2·5 million until 1924 and thereafter declined in amount. Refer to note 3 to explain revenue changes in 1966 and 1967. Net receipts from capital gains tax is estimated to be £1·5 million in 1963-4, £2 million in 1964-5, £2·5 million in 1965-6 and £15·5 million in 1966-7. These sums are included under income tax.

[4] Profits tax, called at various times excess profits tax, corporation profits tax, national defence contributions (profits), etc. Now known as corporation tax; the switch to this tax is the reason for the unevenness of revenue in 1966 and 1967.

[5] From 1965 Redundancy Fund contributions are included.

[6] Prior to 1921 motor licences were included under Excise. From 1965 export rebates were introduced; these have been excluded from the figures.

[7] Refers to year 1937.

[8] Mainly receipts from the sale of war property.

Sources: 1900-39 Financial Accounts of the U.K. and Statistical Abstracts of the U.K. 1939 and after: *National Income and Expenditure Tables*, 1966 and 1968, Tables 41, 42 and 45.

only slightly by the recently introduced graduated contributions for pension and supplements in respect of sickness and unemployment and industrial injuries. The social services at the present time represent a not very happy mixture of services which are intended to be self-financed, some which are intended to be partly met by way of contributions and partly met out of general taxation, and some met solely out of general taxation. In current conditions the idea of earmarked taxes is a polite fiction that bears little relation to government accounting, a fact which has long been recognized in the case of the Road Fund. The adoption of the total accretion principle which will be discussed in Chapter 11 would abolish this fiction entirely. An appendix to this chapter gives more details on the financing of the national insurance and health services.

The broad category of taxes labelled 'Customs and Excise' has always represented a sizeable portion of revenue. Gladstone called them the 'two fair sisters'! They have accounted since the 1930s for roughly the same proportion of revenue as income tax. Table 2 gives the breakdown of Customs and Excise duty in 1967.

Table 2

Customs and Excise Duty in 1967

		(£ million)	%
Alcohol		725	19
Tobacco		1,038	28
Hydrocarbon oils		949	26
Purchase tax		748	20
Rest: protective duties and temporary import charge	189		
Betting	69		
Other	11	269	7
		3,729	100

Source: *National Income and Expenditure*, 1968, Table 41.

From Table 2 it can be seen that the three standbys of the Exchequer are alcohol, tobacco and hydrocarbon oils, which accounted respectively for 19%, 28% and 26% of Customs and Excise revenue in 1967. Purchase tax is spread over a large number of products: the tendency in recent years has been to simplify the structure by reducing the number of rates and increasing the number of products subject to the tax. Further details are given below. The remainder of Customs and Excise revenue comes chiefly from protective duties, with betting contributing a small amount.

PURCHASE TAX

Purchase tax was first imposed in 1940, and is levied on certain goods, whether home-produced or imported. No services are charged in this way. The tax has been as high as 125% of the wholesale value of certain items. In recent years a simplification in the number of rates charged has taken place. Today goods are charged at one of four rates, 13¾%, 22%, 36⅔% or 55% of the wholesale value.[9]

The tax is charged on registered persons: these are normally manufacturers and wholesalers whose sales of goods exceed £500 a year. The effect is to create a tax-free 'ring'. Goods may pass tax-free between registered traders, but tax is charged when the goods pass outside this ring, i.e. normally to a retailer or final buyer. As a rule, the goods are invoiced with the full value of the tax added on.

In general, the lower rate is applied to garments, footwear, gloves and to goods used in the home, such as floor coverings, wallpaper, fabrics, furniture, hardware, table-ware and kitchen-ware. The second rate is levied on confectionery, beverages, ice-cream, and since 1969 prepared pet foods. The third rate of 36⅔% applies to motor-cars and most durable consumer goods and luxury goods, except for those taxed at the top rate. The top rate applies to furs, jewellery, watches and clocks, gramophone records, smokers' requisites and photographic goods, pictorial reproductions, diaries, calendars and greeting cards, fancy and ornamental articles, perfumery and toilet preparations. Foodstuffs, raw materials used in industry and exports are the main goods exempted from the tax.

The revenue shown under motor vehicles covers the annual licence duty, which for private motor-cars was raised to £25 per annum in 1968. Commercial vehicles are charged at a higher rate, and goods vehicles are subject to a rising scale of charges, based on the unladen weight of the vehicle. Cars are also subject to purchase tax and fuel

[9] In 1963 the number of rates had been reduced to three: 10%, 15% or 25%. An increase of 10% was imposed under the Regulator power given to the Chancellor. The Regulator also applies to duties imposed on tobacco, alcohol and hydrocarbon oils. This was consolidated with these old rates in the Budget of 1967. The Chancellor then estimated the yield from this surcharge as in excess of £150 million a year. The Budget of 1968 increased the rates to 12½%, 20% and 33⅓% and introduced a top rate of 50%. The yield from these changes was estimated to be £163 million a year. In November, 1968, an increase of 10% was again imposed, under the Regulator power and consolidated in April, 1969, giving the rates shown in the text. The yield was estimated to be £250 million a year.

is taxed; the receipts for these appear under the heading 'Customs and Excise'.

In view of the annual outcry that is made against rates, it is perhaps surprising to find that rates as a percentage of revenue show a sharp decline from nearly a third of revenue in 1900 to 11% in 1965. Rates are a local authority's only major source of revenue that is independent of the central government. They are levied by local authorities at so much in the pound on the value of premises. One reason for the unpopularity of rates could be laid on the local authorities themselves. Rates are levied in two annual instalments, so that the householder or ratepayer is faced with two payments to make of quite large magnitude, whereas most income tax is deducted by the employer under 'Pay as You Earn' and indirect taxes in the price of the article subject to the tax. Local authorities are now required to allow payment of rates by instalments. One reason for the decline in the share of revenue from rates is due to derating: this is the exemption, whole or in part, from rates for certain kinds of property. These first occurred in the Depression of the 1930s and have continued with modifications ever since. At the present time buildings of charities are 50% derated and agricultural land and buildings are wholly exempt. Manufacturing premises were 50% derated, but were brought back into the rating system in 1963. Legislation in 1966 takes the amount due for rates into account in assessing the needs of applicants for pensions or other assistance.

Comment

The two main sources of revenue, income tax and Customs and Excise, show only a small percentage change in the twenty-eight-year period from 1939 to 1967 in spite of a world war. The changes in this period have been the decrease in the percentages obtained from surtax, death duties and rates and the increase in sums raised by way of national insurance and health contributions.

The tabulation of the existing sources of revenue that has been carried out in this chapter hides a curious feature. This could be brought out more clearly by having many more headings showing nil returns. The majority of taxes shown in the table fall on current income: wealth as such is virtually untouched, apart from the small amounts raised by death duties and a portion of stamp duty that can be attributed to wealth movements. An outsider looking at this tax system might well conclude that our society despised and generally tried to discourage earned income while it looked up to and tried to encourage inherited wealth. A deeper probe of the system to be found in Chapter 11 on the concept of income will reveal that it is only income very narrowly defined which is heavily taxed. Spending power that comes in the form of gambling winnings, capital gains or gifts was virtually untaxed in the period covered by the table.

The table does not bring out important changes that have been made in recent years, as these have as yet made little impact on the revenue received. A capital gains tax of a very restricted kind was introduced in 1962; a more thoroughgoing tax was introduced in 1965. Chapter 12 on 'Personal Income Taxation' gives details. From the point of view of equity between persons, this change is a major breakthrough, but from the revenue side it will be many years before the capital gains tax brings in very much revenue, as it is only gains made since the passing of the Acts (with offset for capital losses) which have been made relevant for tax purposes. Details of recent changes in taxes on betting and gambling and the selective employment tax will be looked at in the next chapter.

Aims and principles of taxation

A fiscal system serves various purposes besides the obvious one of providing revenue. Following Musgrave, R. A. (1959), 5, these will be collected under three headings:

1. *Allocation of resources.* This aspect of taxation is concerned with the allocation of resources between, for example, private and public goods and between investment and consumption goods. It is also concerned with correcting deficiencies in the pricing mechanism due, for example, to monopoly elements, the existence of external economies or diseconomies, and cases where social costs diverge sharply from private costs.
2. *Distribution of resources.* Chapter 7 has already indicated that the distribution of income and wealth depends on a number of factors, including work, educational opportunities, inheritance, gifts, and from government fiscal policy and legislation. The distribution heading is concerned with the adjustments that society decides to make in order to correct for deficiencies in the distribution of income and wealth.
3. *Stabilization of the economy in terms of current objectives.* Current objectives usually include equity, obtaining and maintaining a satisfactory level of growth, maintaining full employment, ensuring stability in the value of money and maintaining a satisfactory balance of payments.

It should be noted that, until recently, only 1, the allocation of resources, has been considered as a part of public finance. After about 1900 the distribution of resources began to be considered.

Stabilization of the economy is due to the ideas of Keynes in the 1930s.

Within the aims selected by society as relevant, persons have been looking for centuries for a general principle that could be used as a guide to apportion taxes in an equitable manner. Two principles have long been canvassed:

The benefit principle and ability to pay

These principles have mainly been discussed in relation to the allocation of resources. When the aims of public finance are drawn more widely to take in the distribution and stabilization aims, neither will be found without fault, but both can contribute to our understanding of the problems involved. A detailed discussion of these principles will be found in Musgrave, R. A. (1959), Chapters 4 and 5.

The benefit approach dictates that taxes are apportioned to individuals according to the benefits they derive from government activity and spending. Taxes are treated as a payment for the goods and services provided by the government. The provision of government goods and services will, like the provision of private goods and services, be dictated by market demand. In a society where the aims of government are conceived in minimum terms of defence against external aggression and the administration of justice, as in eighteenth-century England, this approach is understandable. The existing structure of wealth and income was taken as given, and the economy was conceived as self-regulating. These ideas have given ground on all fronts. It is generally conceded that private provision will seriously underestimate the need for various social services where there are strong neighbourhood effects. Some redistribution of income and wealth is granted as necessary in all developed countries, and stabilization of the economy since the 1930s is now taken for granted. With these wider aims the benefit rule is clearly ruled out as a principle of general application. The more the government did to help the needy, the more the needy would have to pay. The whole transfer process which has been seen taking place, particularly in this century, would be frustrated. Again the allocation of some benefits—for example, defence—would be an arbitrary process. And the aims of stabilization would not necessarily be carried out by following the benefit principle of taxation. The benefit principle, nevertheless, may have application in limited areas where a close relationship between outlay and benefit can be established. Thus where a government undertakes the provision of a service, which could equally well be undertaken privately and there are no strong externalities present, the danger of not charging according to the benefit principle is that demand for that service is likely to be stimulated at the expense of services where costs are allocated to users. This may represent an uneconomic use of the nation's resources. For some services, e.g. health and education, this extension of demand is deliberately aimed for: neighbourhood effects apply. In others, e.g. government provision of some forms of transport or some forms of fuel, failure to charge users with the costs of the service or commodity is likely to have the effect of distorting the use of the nation's resources in an undesirable way. No general solution emerges: it is necessary in each case to weigh the social benefits and costs involved in charging users for the full costs of the service and in meeting these costs out of general taxation, or of some compromise between these two methods.

The ability-to-pay approach is concerned with the equitable distribution of taxes according to the stated taxable capacity, or ability to pay, of an individual or group. It leaves the correct contribution that government provision should make to be decided on political grounds. This rule, in terms of the objectives stated at the beginning of this section, enables the distribution and stabilization objectives to be carried out in an equitable manner. Its disadvantage, that the allocation objective has to be decided by other means, has just been stressed. With the ability-to-pay principle, the criterion on which ability is to be judged must be identified: whether it is to be income, wealth, income and wealth, or spending power. This will form the main concern of Chapter 11. In their usual formulation these criteria do not take into account benefits from government expenditure that accrue to the individual. However, it is possible to define the criteria to include these benefits. This partial synthesis of the two approaches will be developed further in Chapter 18.

Summary

Income tax and Custom and Excise duties each account for about 30% of government revenue, proportions that have changed relatively little since pre-war. In 1967 73% of Customs and Excise duties came from tobacco, hydrocarbon oils and alcohol; purchase tax, charged at one of four rates on a wide range of commodities, accounts for a further 20%. National insurance and health contributions show the largest increase and now account for 14% of total revenue. The proportions raised from surtax, estate duties and rates show a sharp decline. It is not correct to conclude that high incomes, or the distribution of wealth, have diminished significantly in these years.

Recent years have seen the introduction of a number of important taxes: on capital gains, on betting and gambling and a selective employment tax. Wealth continues to be taxed lightly, in spite of nominally high rates of duty, compared to earned income, because of the ease of avoiding the full impact of estate duties.

A fiscal system is aimed at providing revenue and also serves other purposes. These were collected under three headings: allocation of resources, distribution of resources, and stabilization of the economy. Within the aims selected by society as relevant two principles of tax have been put forward: the benefit principle and ability to pay. Neither of these principles, in present-day conditions, is without fault, but an understanding of them is useful in trying to formulate a satisfactory fiscal system.

Appendix
Financing of National Insurance and National Health Services

A list of the major public social services is given below. Finance comes from diverse sources. These vary from contributions from local authority sources, contributions from employed persons and from employers, part-payment from the users of some of the services and contributions from the State out of general taxation.

SOCIAL SECURITY

National insurance: pensions
unemployment and sickness benefit
maternity benefits
industrial injuries

Family allowances

Social security supplementary benefits (old title 'National Assistance') to meet exceptional need.

PUBLIC HEALTH

National Health Service: hospital and general practioner services.

Environmental Health Services: sewerage, home-refuse, water-supply, etc.

EDUCATION

HOUSING

OTHER SERVICES, as: employment exchanges, retraining, town and country planning, highways, administration of justice, child care, parks and the arts.

With the exception of national insurance, these services are financed in the main out of general taxation of the central government with the lesser part being financed from local authority sources. Attention will be confined to discussing the financing of national insurance and the National Health Service. The use of the term 'contribution', in talking of employees' payments to national insurance followed in this appendix, is conventional. Since payment is compulsory the term tax could equally well be used.

The financing of the services covered by these two schemes has differed from the start. The National Health Service is not an insurance scheme; benefits do not depend on the payment of contributions: it is basically a service available to all. The flat-rate contributions paid by employed persons and their employers for National Health covered only 11% of the cost of the service in the year ending March 31st, 1967.

In looking at the National Insurance Scheme, the position is less clear-cut. Whether the term 'insurance' is the correct one to use has been debated since its inception. There are two basic principles of private insurance; the less important one is basing the premium to be paid on an assessment of the risks involved. Thus a thatched house pays a higher premium against fire risk than a similar house with a tiled roof; motor-insurance premiums may vary with the age of the insured, his accident record and occupation, type of car, etc. A person in chronic poor health or over a certain age is unlikely to be accepted at all in a private medical care scheme. In contrast, State insurance was instituted on the principle of collective risk and flat-rate contributions and benefits. Recent departures from this principle will be noted.

The more important principle of private insurance is the actuarial aim that premiums should more than cover the claims paid out. There has been disagreement from the start whether State insurance should operate on similar lines. The idea that the State should build up a fund to meet future contingencies was not contemplated: the issue is between those who wish to see a 'pay as you go' system and those who wish to see the whole, or part, of the expenditures met out of general taxation. Lord Beveridge, whose Report formed the basis of the extension of the National Insurance Scheme after the war envisaged the scheme as being financed on a tripartite basis: from employers, employees and the State (*Social Insurance and Allied Services*, 1942, and Beveridge, W. H., 1944). It was envisaged that employers' and employees' flat-rate contributions would provide the bulk of the necessary revenue. It was foreseen that the State would need to contribute a large amount for many years towards the provision of pensions, since people nearing retiring age at the start of the scheme would not be able to contribute much towards the scheme.

The meaning of a State 'pay as you go' scheme, largely financed by flat-rate contributions, is assessing the rate of contribution at the minimum age of entry to the scheme which, say, a male would have to pay over his working lifetime to ensure the benefits on an actuarial basis. This rate, or some lesser sum if the State is to bear part of the cost of the services, is the flat-rate contribution for all males. In any one year such a scheme will leave the State with a larger, or smaller, contribution to make, depending on many factors, such as the age-structure of the population, the degree of sickness and unemployment.

Many commentators have pointed out the weakness of this idea. Financing the bulk of the service by flat-rate contributions sets a limit to the amount that can be collected without imposing undue hardship on the poorest paid in the community. The amount so raised may bear little relation to the needs of the community. This fact and the general inflation of money which has occurred since the war has eroded to some extent the concept of self-financing outlined. These ideas of self-financing, on the one hand, and of meeting expenditures out of general taxation, on the other, continue to be debated (e.g. Titmus, 1963).

There follow three tables, one giving the weekly contributions paid by employed persons and their employers and two setting out costs and sources of finance.

At present persons are categorized for payment of flat-rate contributions according to whether they are male or female and whether they are over or under eighteen years of age. Different rates are paid by employed persons and self-employed persons, and other categories are separated, e.g. part-time workers and students.

Table 3

Class I employed persons' weekly contributions from May 6th, 1968[10]

	Paid by Employee				*Paid by Employer*				
	N.I.	N.H.S.	I.I.	Total	N.I.	N.H.S.	I.I.	R.F.	Total
	s. d.	*s. d.*	*d.*	*s. d.*	*s. d.*	*d.*	*d.*	*d.*	*s. d.*
Man	12 8	3 2	10	16 8	14 1	8	11	10	16 6
Woman	11 0	2 6	7	14 1	12 3	8	8	5	14 0
Boy	8 8	1 7	5	10 8	9 6	8	5	—	10 7
Girl	7 1	1 7	3	8 11	7 10	8	4	—	8 10

N.I.=National Insurance.
N.H.S.=National Health Service.
I.I.=Industrial Injuries.
R.F.=Redundancy Fund.

[10] These flat-rate contributions are to be increased for employers and employees by 1*s.* a week for men and 11*d.* for women from November, 1969.

Table 3 lists the contributions paid by Class 1 employed persons who have not contracted out of the pension scheme. It covers the most numerous category.

These sums are paid by the employer fixing a stamp of the appropriate value to the employee's card; the employer deducts the employee's contribution from his wage. The stamp must also cover the employer's contribution to the selective employment tax in respect of each worker, but since this tax is not part of the social insurance scheme, this has been omitted from the tabulation.

It will be seen that a man pays 12*s*. 8*d*. a week for National Insurance, or £33 a year, and 3*s*. 2*d*. a week for the National Health Service, or £8 4*s*. 8*d*. a year. The employer pays £36 16*s*. 8*d*. and £1 14*s*. 8*d*. respectively per year for each man employed. Since 1961 an element of graduation was introduced into the pension part of the insurance contribution. This has not been taken into account in the table of weekly contributions above. Employed persons over eighteen who have not contracted out and whose remuneration exceeds £9 a week, together with their employers, each pay an additional contribution of 4¼% of earnings between £9 and £18 a week. These contributions entitle those who pay to an additional graduated benefit in addition to the flat-rate pension. Persons can only contract out of this graduated scheme if the employer has a private scheme at least as good as the provisions provided by the State. The position is therefore that every person covered is entitled to a flat-rate pension. Those whose wage is above the minimum will, in addition, receive an additional benefit from their firm or from their additional graduated contributions, or both. Those with a wage of £18 a week or more will pay at the highest graduated rate, unless contracted out, and will receive the highest graduated pension.

As from October 5th, 1966, a contribution at the rate of ½% of earnings between £9 and £30 is paid by both employer and employee (whether or not contracted out) to meet the cost of earnings-related benefit supplements under the National Insurance Act, 1966. These supplements are in respect of sickness, unemployment and industrial injuries. From November, 1969 these rates are increased to 2¾% for those who earn between £18 and £30 a week, so that a man earning £30 or more a week will pay 7*s*. 7*d*. and women 7*s*. 6*d*. a week. Employers' contributions are increased by the same amount.

Table 4 shows that for the year ending March 31st, 1967, the Exchequer financed directly 73% of expenditure on health. The Exchequer also, through the rate-support grant finances a proportion of local authority health expenditure. National Health Service flat-rate contributions financed 11% and charges on users 4%. Over half of this expenditure was on the hospital service.

Table 4

Health finance for Year ending March 31st, 1967, to nearest £ million

Cost		£m.	%	*Sources of Finance*	£m.	%
Hospitals: current	685			Exchequer	987	73
Capital	80			N.H.S. contributions	147	11
	——	765	56	Payments by users	55	4
General medical		97	7	Rates and Exchequer grants to L.As.	166	12
Pharmaceutical		142	11	Rest	3	0
General dental		70	5			
Local health authorities		126	9			
Administration		16	1			
Other		142	11			
		1,358	100		1,358	100

Source: *Annual Report of the Ministry of Health, 1967.*

Table 5

National Insurance Funds for Year ending March 31st, 1967, to nearest £ million

Cost	£m.	%	*Sources of Finance*	£m.	%
Retirement pensions	1,272	68	Flat-rate contributions (from employers and insured persons)	1,165	63
Sickness	262	14	Graduated contributions (from employers and insured persons)	346	19
Widow's	141	8	Exchequer contributions	287	15
Unemployment	78	4	Other	65	3
Maternity	37	2			
Administration	62	3			
Other	24	1			
	1,876	100		1,863	100
Excess of payments over receipts	13				

Source: *Annual Report of Ministry of Social Security, 1967.*

Table 5 shows that in the same period flat-rate contributions from employers and insured persons accounted for 63% of finance to the National Insurance Funds. Graduated contributions accounted for 19% and the Exchequer contributed 15%. On the expenditure side, the major part is accounted for by flat-rate benefits, of which retirement pensions constitute the bulk. Graduated retirement pensions, as yet, hardly figure on the expenditure side. In 1966, the last year for which figures were given, they amounted to less than £2 million.

Proposals after 1972

In January, 1969 a White Paper—'National Superannuation and Social Insurance'—was issued which proposed substantial changes in pensions and social insurance.

The basic change envisaged is earnings related payments coupled with earnings related benefits paid in respect of pensions, sickness and unemployment.

The most important part of these proposals concern pensions and the most controversial part the suggestion that these new earnings related pensions be paid only to those who have paid earnings related contributions, so it will be twenty years after the start of the scheme before pensions at the full new scheme rates are paid. Contributors who reach pension age during the twenty-year build-up period will earn pensions at intermediate rates.

Citizens in otherwise equal circumstances will therefore be differentiated according to the number of years contributions they have made. Based on the illustrative figures given in the White Paper, for a single man assumed to earn the national average of £22 a week we find:

						Existing pension
a man aged	70	in 1972	would be aged	90	in 1992.	£4. 10. 0.[11]
						Proposed pension
,,	60	,,	,,	80	,,	£5. 14. 0.
,,	55	,,	,,	75	,,	£6. 19. 0.
,,	45	,,	,,	65	,,	£9. 7. 0.

[11] Plus a supplement of a few shillings under the existing graduated scheme. The basic pension for a single person will be increased to £5 in November, 1969.

These proposals which differentiate, not according to need but according to the time a person has contributed to the new scheme, can be contrasted with the proposals introduced after the Second World War. Then, as now, it was envisaged that pensions should be on the basis of 'pay as you go' but then it was accepted that to bring those near retiring age into the scheme would entail a contribution out of general taxation for a period of years. The scheme was largely set up on this basis.

The figures used in the illustration above will not, of course, be the actual rates payable in 1992. The White Paper proposes:

'The government will be required by law to undertake a review every two years of the main rates of benefits in payment, both under the present scheme and under the new. The increases made will, as a minimum, compensate for any rise in prices during the two year period. The amounts of increases beyond this will be decided by the government of the day, in the light of the general situation on each occasion' (para. 6).

The proposals to make the review of pension bi-annual can be unreservedly welcomed as an improvement on the present system whereby pensions receive most attention at times of Parliamentary election. However the issue taken up here is not about the level of benefits, but about the degree of differentiation. If the spread of pensions is maintained as shown in the table, £4. 10*s.* 0*d.*—£9. 7*s.* 0*d.*, it is not difficult to forecast that for those near retirement age at the present the closer he or she will be to poverty as they get older. The White Paper, paragraph 9, tells us that nearly one-third of the 7,000,000 pensioners in 1965 were eligible for some form of additional assistance, or in other words had inadequate pensions. If levels of national assistance had been £2 a week higher about three-quarters of all pensioners would have been eligible for assistance.

Proposed rates

The new scheme proposes to charge employees up to a level of earnings of about £33 a week, 4¾% of total earnings for superannuation and 2% for social insurance benefits, so that a deduction of 6¾% from earnings is proposed. Employers will be charged 6¾% on their total payroll with no earnings ceiling. Collection of both employers and employees contributions will in most cases be administered through the 'Pay as You Earn' system of tax collection.

Contributions from employees are therefore not progressive but proportional. However, some redistribution of income is provided because the fully mature pension rates will be based for a single person on 60% of earnings up to half the national average earnings, and 25% of the remainder up to the ceiling of £33 a week. From the table below it can be seen that this results in a man earning £33 a week or more paying 3 times as much as a man earning £11 a week whereas his pension is 1·8 times as much. The table on p. 110 lists the proposed new total contributions for pensions and social insurance.

Level of weekly earnings	*Proposed employees total contribution per week*	*Change on present contribution*	*Fully matured new pension rates*[12]
	s. d.	s. d.	£. s. d.
£11 (½ national average)	14 10	− 3 0	6 12 0
£16 10s. (¾ national average)	22 3	− 9	8 0 0
£22 (national average)	29 8	+ 5 0	9 7 0
£27 10s. (1¼ national average)	37 1	+11 10	10 15 0
£33 or above (1½ national average)	44 7	+19 2	12 2 0

Women pay the same rates as men under the new scheme.

[12] That is pensions payable after 20 years of earnings-related contributions, assuming April, 1968 earnings levels.

10
Government expenditure and revenue (concluded)

They [politicians and experts] have to say whether it is better to try for a surplus or to acquiesce in a deficit. They both have to consider economic and political consequences. But, so far as taxpayers are concerned, all such questions are subsidiary to the critical issue of distribution. . . . It is usually assumed that other problems may be best resolved by shifting the burdens elsewhere. And there is no lack of ingenuity in providing the necessary rationalizations for the desired results.

EISENSTEIN, L. (1961), *The Ideologies of Taxation.*

To explain adequately the changes in expenditure and revenue would require a full-scale social and economic history of the period. Similar trends to the ones observed in this country can be seen in most developed countries over the same period. In this chapter the main pressures that have helped to mould the system are outlined.

Pressures on government spending

As long ago as the 1880s Adolph Wagner was predicting that public expenditure would increase (at least for a time) at a faster rate than national output. We get a law of 'growing public expenditure'. He based his observations on the results of a study of developed Western countries and on the grounds that State activity would need to increase as a result of social progress. To date Wagner's prediction has proved to be accurate. The extent to which it will continue to hold good in the future is more problematical. The fact of adult male suffrage in 1887 and the start of female suffrage in 1918 is likely to have played a very important (though largely unquantifiable) part. With adult suffrage, Parliament is likely in its spending and revenue to reflect the needs of the community as a whole more closely than before, because Members of Parliament depend on the goodwill of the majority of the community for their seats.

Not always stressed as much as it deserves to be is the pressure on public spending caused by the *growth* of population and the *concentration* of population. Services which can be safely left to the individual in a sparsely populated country have to be undertaken by the community in a more populated country, sewage and water-supply being obvious examples. The process is still at work today. Government spending or regulation on smoke-abatement in large urban areas is beginning to take on the nature of a social necessity, and we can expect expenditures on this head to increase in the future. The motor-car is creating its obvious pressures on the public purse, and so on.

It is sometimes possible to distinguish two trends under this general heading. One which has been referred to under 'externalities' refers to the benefit which the whole community derives from the service. Leaving the provision of such a service to the goodwill of the individual, who is likely to take only his private benefit into account, would result in serious deficiencies, to the general detriment of all. The basic services referred to in the previous paragraph come into this category.

Secondly, we can distinguish cases where technical considerations apply, where, in order to obtain a better use of resources, collective provision is needed. Thus the generation of electricity could be left to the individual, but each building with its own generator is a very inefficient way, at the present time, of obtaining electricity. The State usually steps in at the local or central level to run the service, or to supervise the provision of the service if monopoly powers are granted to a private concern. New processes and inventions change these technical considerations in no very predictable manner. We have already reached the stage where it is technically an extremely inefficient use of resources for each building to supply its own needs for heat and hot water. Centralized provision of hot water to houses and other buildings could yield large economies in the use of fuel, as well as yielding benefits in terms of cleaner air and better living conditions.

In contrast to the neighbourhood and technical effects stressed above, social reasons for public spending—that is, the wish to spread benefits to the community at large—have played an important (but once again hard to determine) part. This is particularly noticeable in the extension of education, health and the social services generally. The desire to spread income and wealth more evenly has also helped to shape the expenditure and the revenue side of public finance. Finally, since the depression of the 1930s most governments accept that they have a positive role to play in keeping the economy in balance, avoiding both the extremes of slump and of severe inflation. This compensatory aspect will lead to a larger rather than a smaller government sector.

Pressures on government revenue

To pick out some of the pressures that have shaped public expenditure is analogous to explaining price by looking at demand and ignoring supply. If we look at public expenditure and revenue over time we find that they are uneven. In particular, we can single out wars as causing large jumps in government expenditure. By itself this is not a surprising feature: what is interesting is that government expenditure does not go back after the war to its former level. This observation is apparent even when allowance is made for price-changes and when war-related expenditures are excluded.

Peacock, A. T. and Wiseman, J. (1961) use the term 'displacement effect' to cover this phenomenon. Once again we find that many strands knit together to cause this effect. Peacock and Wiseman develop the idea that in normal times there is a dichotomy between the desire for public goods and services and the level of taxation which is considered tolerable. A large-scale disturbance, such as a war, may create an upward displacement of the level of taxation considered tolerable, so that new levels of public spending can afterwards be maintained.

In wartime new methods of raising revenue may be accepted; there is some release from the 'bonds of the revenue'. 'Pay as You Earn' is an example introduced in the last war. War also focuses attention on social ills. 'It has taken the catastrophe of war to bring home to those in power that economic progress does not automatically disseminate the benefits of education and health' (Peacock, A. T. and Wiseman, J. (1961), 93). Such a period may also see an acceleration in reorganization of government accounts, statistical information and in Civil Service procedures. Periods of crisis, such as war and the severe slump in the earlier 1930s, thus seem to act as a catalyst. We do not know what would have happened in the absence of these disasters, but in the light of hindsight they appear to break the 'cake of custom'.

Recasting the system of revenue?

The period 1960-7 is a remarkable one in that, without a marked crisis of the kind previously referred to, major changes have been made on the revenue side. These changes have, apart from the selective employment tax, made little impact to receipts of revenue but their potential is great.

The inequalities of income taxation have been tackled indirectly by subjecting some of the spending power which escaped income taxation to other forms of tax. The most notable change has been the capital gains tax. Wealth has received less practical attention. These matters will be taken up in later chapters. In the rest of this chapter an outline is given of two taxes which have been recently introduced, the selective employment tax and the taxes on betting and gambling.

The selective employment tax

The selective employment tax (abbreviated to S.E.T.) was introduced in September, 1966. It is a tax on labour imposed on all civil employers in the private and public sectors. It varies for men, women, boys and girls, and is differentiated according to which industry employs them. At first the tax was 25*s.* a week for every man, 12*s.* 6*d.* for women and boys and 8*s.* for girls. Boys and girls are those under eighteen years of age. Establishments fell into three categories: those who got back after a six months' delay more than the tax, those who just have the tax refunded, and those who get no refund. Amendments were announced in the Budget of 1967 in respect of part-time workers and staff absent overseas: and considerable changes were made in September and November, 1967 and the budgets of 1968 and 1969. These will be outlined shortly.

General establishments classed as manufacturing came into the first category, and received back, in addition to the tax paid, an extra 7*s.* 6*d.* in respect of each male employee, 3*s.* 9*d.* in respect of women and boys, and 2*s.* 6*d.* for girls. Broadly speaking, transport, agriculture, horticulture, shipping, nationalized industries, local government and universities come into Category 2 and receive back the amount of tax paid. Service, distribution and construction come into Category 3 and get no refund.

Two justifications were given in the White Paper, *Selective Employment Tax* (1966), for this tax. The first, and generally agreed, aim was that service and distributive trades should bear a portion of the tax bill. This has the important advantage of allowing the government to restrict consumer-demand without affecting those industries that are already subject to purchase tax and Customs and Excise duties. The second, more controversial, aim was that it would in the longer term encourage the redeployment of labour from the service, distributive and construction trades to industry. The tax also had the effect of acting as a mild stimulus to exports, since wage costs in manufacturing industries were lowered. However rebates are now confined to manufacturing industries in development areas and are due to end there in April, 1970, and S.E.T. unlike a value-added tax cannot be rebated on exports.

If a system of indirect taxes is in operation, the only economic arguments for taxing a small range of goods and services is ease of collection. On social grounds it may be desired to tax goods consumed mainly by the rich, but such goods are not easy to discover. On economic grounds the case for taxing all goods and services, rather than taxing more heavily fewer items, is that consumer prices will reflect more closely their relative costs. In turn this is likely to lead to a more efficient allocation of resources. In the past, relative prices of services and manufactured goods have been distorted because the former were untaxed while the latter were subject to various rates of tax. Under any system of tax, some items, such as alcohol and tobacco, will probably be taxed more heavily for social reasons: but here the deliberate intention, as well as to raise revenue, is to choke off some of the demand for these products.

If it is decided to tax a wide range of goods, the problem then arises as to the best method of collecting the tax. On this point disagreement is sharp. The reason given for this rather clumsy method of taxing all industries and then giving rebates to some, in order to tax the service sector, was that the only machinery readily available was the Ministry of Pensions and National Insurance organization for receiving the national insurance and health contributions. The insurance contributions do not draw any distinction between employees in different industries, and therefore this method was adopted.

The second aim of encouraging redistribution of labour by giving what is in effect a subsidy to manufacturing establishments is more open to criticism. Manufacturing as well as other concerns may be guilty of hoarding labour, and the S.E.T. does nothing to encourage the manufacturing sector to use its labour wisely—rather the reverse.[1]

The tax also came under attack because it discriminates against part-time and disabled workers, who are subject to the same rates of tax. This may have the paradoxical effect of causing a reversal, or a slowing down, in the distributive trades of the trend towards the employment of more part-time workers—in particular, the employment of married women. The 1967 Budget modified the tax, with effect from September, 1967, in respect of part-time workers, but not disabled workers. In establishments not entitled to a refund—that is, in general the service, distribution and construction industries —one-half of the tax payable in respect of adult employees who normally work less than twenty-one hours a week will be refunded. In effect, these industries are charged 12*s.* 6*d.* for every part-time male employee, 25*s.* for full-time male employees and 6*s.* 3*d.* for part-time female employees. Employers with staff who are absent overseas for over three months had a concession whereby their S.E.T.

[1] The element of subsidy to manufaucturing firms is effectively reduced to the extent that the services bought by the manufacturer will be increased in cost.

would be refunded. This was intended to help the construction industry with long-term contracts abroad.

Further changes were later announced in *Development Areas Regional Employment Premium* (1967). These charges came into operation from September, 1967. The tax was now envisaged as a major way of increasing employment in the development areas. Since January, 1966, development areas are defined to include, except for small areas deemed to be sufficiently developed, Scotland, northern England (i.e. the four northernmost counties of England, plus the North Riding of Yorkshire), Wales, Merseyside and the south-western area, which takes in much of Devon and Cornwall. Premiums to manufacturing industries in these areas are to paid out for not less than seven years and then phased out over another two or so years. The premiums are in addition to the refunds already received, and amount to 30*s.* for men, 15*s.* for women and boys, 7*s.* 6*d.* for girls, with part-time employees getting half of the premium in each case. The premiums will be worth about £100 million a year to the development areas.

The aim of these premiums is to reduce the disparity in unemployment levels between the development areas and the rest of Britain; if successful this would have the effect of helping Britain's growth without, it is thought, adding to inflationary pressure or leading to any worsening in the balance of payments, and without the need to increase taxation. These desirable effects will be brought about, it is believed, because any increase in demand for imports will be offset by increased exports, and the competitive loss by maufacturing industry in the rest of the country will offset the extra demand deriving from the higher levels of income and output in development areas. Therefore higher levels of tax will not be required to release resources for the subsidy. The White Paper discounted the idea that the premiums would only result in increases in wages, and that firms would use them to increase profits and not reduce prices. It remains to be seen whether the assumptions which have just been outlined are correct.

In November, 1967 at the time of Britain's devaluation of the £1, it was announced that the rebates (7*s.* 6*d.* in the case of full-time male employees) would be withdrawn from manufacturing industries outside the development areas, but retained within them. This measure goes a little further in favouring the development areas. However it is proposed to stop this premium in April, 1970.

The Budget of 1968 announced that rates of S.E.T. for full-time employees would be increased by 50% from September 1968, and some minor modifications were made. Part-time employees were not subject to the increase. Also workers over sixty-five (about 190,000 in 1968) on whom employers at present pay the full rates will be charged only at the same rate as part-time employees. A minor concession was also announced whereby hotels, inns, boarding-houses, and other small establishments with a minimum of four bedrooms in certain rural parts of development areas would be entitled to a refund of payments.

In July, 1969 the rates of S.E.T. were increased by a further 28% so that the rate is 48*s*. a week for an adult male employee, 24*s*. for women and boys, and 16*s*. for girls.

What emerges from this is that a powerful new fiscal tool has been made. The net yield, that is after allowing for refunds and premiums to manufacturing industry in development areas, is about £600 million a year. The tax as shown by the changes that have already been made, is extremely flexible. It is now used to discriminate between different regions of the country, different sectors of the economy, and by age, sex and time worked. More controversially, it could be developed to discriminate between efficient and inefficient firms.

The real question-mark that hangs over the S.E.T. is whether it should be replaced by a value added tax. This will be considered in Chapter 14.

Betting and gambling

To the future historian the most surprising thing about betting and gambling may well be the length of time that elapsed before they were taxed. This was so in spite of the example, from a number of other countries, that large sums could be raised from this source. The reasons for this immunity have been partly objections on moral grounds and partly difficulties of collection. Winston Churchill's betting levy between 1926 and 1929 was a failure, and may have acted as a deterrent.

A pool betting tax was introduced in 1947. This was a tax virtually confined to football pools, which were taxed at 33⅓% on weekly turnover. At 10% totalisator tax on dog-races was also imposed at the same time.[2] The pools tax was reduced to 25% on weekly turnover when football fixed-odds betting was introduced at 25% in 1964. The totalisator tax on dog races was reduced to 5% at the same time.

It was not until the Finance Act of 1966 that an attempt was made to tax gambling and betting more comprehensively. This Act intro-

[2] In 1963 bookmakers at dog-tracks were required to have an excise licence varying from £6 to £48, according to the number of enclosures. In 1964 the licence fees were halved. The duty was abolished with the Finance Act, 1966.

duced a 2½% tax on the amount staked with a bookmaker or on a totalisator, so that the tax on dog-races was again reduced. The tax on football pools remained at 25%. In addition, gaming was taxed by requiring premises where gaming was carried on to have an annual gaming licence.

The Budget of 1968 increased the betting tax from 2½% to 5%, and raised the pool betting duty to 33⅓%. Fees for gaming licences were also raised.

COLLECTION OF THE BETTING TAX

The betting tax on the amount staked on any bet with a bookmaker on or after October 24th, 1966, is now standardized at the rate of 5%, regardless of the type of event or contingency which is the subject of the bet.

The bookmaker or operator of a totalisator is responsible for payment of the duty, which is due when the bet is made and *not* when the account is settled. The collection of the tax is administratively straightforward. The operator of the totalisator normally pays the tax weekly. The most usual method for a bookmaker is to purchase betting-duty sheets in advance of the duty becoming due, on which summarized details of the bets have to be recorded. The sheets are available in various denominations, from £1 to £500.[3] The alternative method of paying the tax applies only to off-course bookmakers, who may apply to make monthly returns. Approval is subject to the bookmaker's satisfying minimum security arrangements in order to safeguard the revenue. Since 1969 an annual licence for premises used for off-course betting has to be taken out. The cost is three times the rateable value of the premises, or £150 in the case of premises with no rateable value.

INCIDENCE OF THE TAX

Bookmakers have not yet, it appears, settled standardized procedures for passing on the betting tax. Initially some appeared to be bearing the tax themselves while others changed the odds so as to recoup

[3] In respect of betting premises, the value of the sheets purchased must be at least equal to the duty liability incurred in the last week but one during which the bookmaker carried on bookmaking on the premises concerned, less any duty credit or plus any duty debit brought forward from that week. In respect of on-course bookmakers, the value of the sheets are related to the price of admission to the track for horse-racing and to the number of enclosures for dog-races.

themselves. An increasing number either deduct the tax from winnings or charge the tax on the money staked.[4]

GAMING

Gaming was first brought into the tax net in 1966 by requiring premises where gaming was carried on to have an annual gaming licence. The cost of this licence varies with the rateable value of the premises and according to whether bingo only is played or other gambling games. In 1969 the system was changed in respect of places where bingo only is played. These are now subject to a duty of 2½% of the stakes plus one thirty-ninth of any amount by which the value of the prizes exceeds the duty. Premises where other gambling games are played are still subject to duty by an annual licence whose cost varies with the rateable value of the premises as follows:

Rateable value of premises	Duty per annum
Not exceeding £1,000	£750
Between £1,000 and £1,500	£7,500
Between £1,500 and £2,250	£20,000
Between £2,250 and £3,000	£40,000
Exceeding £3,000	£100,000

Also an annual licence is required for a gaming machine (one-armed bandit) in a club. If operated by a coin of 3*d*. or less this now costs £50 for a single machine and £150 for each subsequent machine. If operated by a 6*d*. the cost is £100 for the first machine and £300 for subsequent machines. Machines for gambling with prizes in amusement arcades have since 1969 been taxed at £25 for the first and £150 for subsequent machines if operated by a 6*d*. and at half these rates if operated by a coin of 3*d*. or less.

CONCLUSIONS

So soon after the passing of the Betting and Gambling Act only tentative conclusions can be drawn. The overall impression seems to be that the tax is working well, and revenue has been greater than was estimated.

[4] The procedure is sometimes adopted of deducting 6*d*. on winnings (or stake money as the case may be), up to 10*s*., 1*s*. between 10*s*. and a £1, and pro rata. So that a bookmaker with four 5*s*. bets collects 2*s*. This is almost certainly in excess of his expenses incurred in collecting the tax and his liability to pay 1*s*. in the £1 on the amounts staked, an example, with many previous precedents of a sum greater than the tax being passed on to the consumer.

The idea of taxing some forms of betting at 33⅓% and others at 5% is hard to justify. The rate of 5% looks ridiculous when it is compared with the high marginal rates of income tax and surtax and many indirect taxes. The argument is sometimes put forward that betting and gambling reflects a circular flow of income, with most of the stake-money being returned to the winners and being restaked and so on, and that to tax at higher rates would kill the industry. Since all economic activity can be represented as a circular flow, this argument hardly provides a case for lower taxes on betting and gambling.

The device of taxing gambling by grouping rateable values of the premises in five sizes is obviously an extremely crude procedure. This is not the place to examine alternatives, but examples from a number of foreign countries show that there are feasible and better alternatives.

Summary

Britain, in common with other developed countries, shows a marked increase this century in government expenditure, and hence in tax. Political pressures, growth and concentration of population, the wish of the community to spread income and wealth more evenly can be selected as major forces that have helped to shape expenditure and revenue. From the side of revenue, two world wars, as well as focusing attention on social ills has enabled fiscal innovation to take place and given governments larger tax resources after the war to continue a higher rate of expenditure.

Two recently introduced taxes were examined. Selective employment tax, introduced in 1966, is a powerful new fiscal weapon that is extremely flexible. As well as raising considerable amounts of revenue, it is used to discriminate between different regions of the country, different sections of the economy, and by age, sex, and time worked. The harsh comments on this tax, from many quarters, may be a tribute to the success it is having in achieving some of these objectives, but it is too soon to make any objective judgment. The adoption of a value-added tax (necessary if Britain joins the Common Market) would almost certainly replace S.E.T., and it is difficult to see any future Chancellor of the Exchequer being able to give up such a flexible and lucrative tax as S.E.T. for anything less than a tax on value-added lines.

The Finance Act of 1966 introduced a much more comprehensive tax on betting and introduced a tax on gambling. This area of taxation still exhibits many illogicalities, with different forms of betting taxed at different rates and gambling taxed by the crude method of taxing the rateable value of premises where the activity takes place. It is still the case that a person who has spending power from earning will be likely to pay a great deal more in tax than a person who has the same sum as a result of a bet or by gambling.

11
The criterion of ability to pay

There is still much of sham even in our big redistributional reforms. Our taxation is advertised to be, and is commonly believed to be, steeply progressive, but by various devices the tax laws are permitting the rich to become richer while they live well, in spite of their paying most of their 'incomes' in taxes. In Britain and some other countries, where generous means are provided for avoiding inheritance tax by giving away the wealth in advance of one's death, the situation is almost scandalous, though it is largely concealed from workers and salaried people who are really pressed by taxation and social insurance payments. In Sweden and the United States the tax system is more rigorous, but even there the real incidence of taxation is very different from what it seems to be.

GUNNAR MYRDAL (1960), *Beyond the Welfare State*.

From the discussion in Chapter 9 of the benefit and ability to pay approaches it was clear that, given the current objectives of society, the benefit principle by itself cannot serve as an adequate guide to taxation policy. Some form of criterion based on ability to pay is needed and this is now examined.

Horizontal and vertical equity

The ability-to-pay criterion has to be seen in a broad setting. One of the few principles in public finance that commands wide acceptance is the so-called principle of *horizontal equity*—'that people in equal positions shall be treated equally'. On *vertical equity*—that is, the treatment of people in unequal positions—there is no such agreement. Regressive, proportional and progressive taxes have all been advocated at different times. There is probably widespread agreement today that taxes that fall on the 'better-off' rather than the 'worse-off', and are progressive rather than proportional, are to be preferred. Widely differing views are held on the degree of progressiveness that is desired. The author's opinion is that the economist, as economist, has no special competence to decide this question, which is essentially an ethical one. In democratic societies the decision is decided by political means. The economist can help in pointing out the likely economic consequences of this or that degree of progression, but society as a whole has to decide how much these factors shall count.

In the search for a correct criterion to judge ability to pay, in order to achieve horizontal equity, claims are put forward for income, wealth and expenditure.

By 'wealth' is meant the accumulated assets of a person or institution as opposed to 'income', which are receipts that accrue per period of time. Taxing wealth by itself is unlikely to provide sufficient revenue, and the issue is between those who would like to see wealth taxed separately and those who would like to see the definition of income broadened so as to take in changes in wealth. The latter solution is developed in this book, although reference is made to the alternative of taxing wealth separately.

As an alternative, expenditure has been put forward as the better criterion (see Kaldor, N. (1955)). Any distinction between income and wealth becomes irrelevant with an expenditure tax: both are taxed, not as they accrue, but when they are spent. However, the difference in principle between these concepts is not as wide as it might appear at first glance. The issue is not, it should be stressed, one of progressiveness. It is possible to build into a tax system on either base whatever degree of progressiveness is required. An expenditure-based tax does not have to entail the detailed recording of expenditures. These can be computed as the difference between certain money incomings and outgoings. Forms to compute expenditures in this way would be somewhat more complicated than the current income tax form, but not unduly so. The real difference between taxes on these different bases lies in the exemption from tax of savings under an expenditure tax. In a general way, using consumption (i.e. expenditure) as a base is taxing according to what a person takes out of the common pool; income with what he puts into the common pool.

There are a number of reasons for not developing the idea of an expenditure-based tax here, besides the necessity to keep this book within limits. One is that an expenditure tax has been brilliantly elaborated by Kaldor in his book cited above. Another that has just been noted is that in practice the only major difference between an expenditure tax and the tax on total accretion lines that is developed here lies in the different treatment of savings. Most of the problems that have to be dealt with are common to both. The pros and cons of the argument of whether it is desirable (since savings increase with wealth and income) to exempt savings from tax are discussed by Kaldor. It should be noted that because he is arguing for a progressive tax on expenditures, this mitigates to some extent for not taxing savings. Finally, there is the practical consideration that most countries do not use an expenditure-based system. It is income which is used, and the concept has been elaborated over many years. To this problem we now turn.

Definition of income

One concept of income has gained wide acceptance, and is termed *total accretion*. Income is defined to equal consumption during a given period, plus increase in net worth valued at market prices for the beginning and the end of the period. Income is thus defined to include consumption, savings and changes in wealth. The principle is uncompromising: all accretions to wealth are included, in whatever form they are received or from whatever source they accrue. In practice the principle may have to be modified, but if it is accepted as a principle it gives a basis from which to judge our present tax system and proposed changes. The principle accepts that a change in net worth may be negative—in other words, gains and losses should be allowed for.

The Memorandum of Dissent to the *Royal Commission on the Taxation of Profits and Income Final Report* (June, 1955), sets out very clearly the rationale behind this definition (para. 5):

> In our view the taxable capacity of an individual consists in his power to satisfy his own material needs, i.e. to attain a particular living standard. We know of no alternative definition that is capable of satisfying society's prevailing sense of fairness and equity. Thus the ruling test to be applied in deciding whether any particular receipt should or should not be reckoned as taxable income is whether it contributes or not, or how far it contributes, to an individual's 'spending power' during a period. When set beside this standard, most of the principles that have been applied at one time or another, to determine whether particular types of receipt constitute income (whether the receipts are regularly recurrent or casual, or whether they proceed from a separate and identifiable source, or whether they are payments for services rendered, or whether they constitute profit 'on sound accountancy principles', or whether, in words of the Majority, they fall 'within the limited class of receipts that are identified as income by their own nature') appear to us to be irrelevent. In fact, no concept on income can be really equitable that stops short of the comprehensive definition which embraces all receipts which increase an individual's commands over the use of society's scarce resources—in other words, his 'net accretion of economic power between two points of time'.

It cannot be emphasized too strongly that the consequence of adopting this definition of income would be that current rates of income tax could be reduced without a loss in revenue, or indirect taxes could be reduced, or some downward reduction made in both. In other words, at present income, in the narrow sense, bears a disproportionate share of tax precisely because spending power other than income is taxed less or not at all. For example, capital gains are taxed differently according to whether they are made within twelve months or longer: if realized within twelve months they are taxed at income rates, otherwise if, after offset for losses, they exceed £50 they are taxed at what for a standard-rate-payer will be a lesser rate. Betting and gambling is taxed at flat rates, Earned income is taxed less than unearned income. Inherited wealth is not taxed according to the position of the recipient, but according to the wealth of the donor. Gifts were not taxed at all unless the donor died within five years of making the gift. This was changed to seven years in 1968, so that a gift *inter vivos* remains fully dutiable for four years. In the fifth, sixth and seventh years relief is given of 15%, 30% and 60% respectively. Enough has been said to make it clear that the present system is the result of the haphazard growth of the tax and benefit system over the years.

Is the principle workable?

It is one thing to talk about a principle. Is it workable in practice? As a preliminary we shall deal briefly with the drawbacks of the present system, and then go on to deal with the difficulties of implementing the accretion principle. These difficulties are present in our existing system; some would be emphasized in the system of accretion.

Possibly the main drawback of the present system has already been mentioned. It is curious that it has not received more attention. That is, by the present very narrow definition of income, any receipt unfortunate enough to fall into this category is liable to a steeply progressive tax. Widening the base would give the authorities room to manœuvre: a greater range of small incomes could be exempt from tax, or rates throughout the range could be reduced, or some compromise made between these two.

From this advantage it would follow that there would be no gain in reshuffling assets (from, say, income to capital gains), because both would be income and subject to the same tax. The so-called 'blight' of modern times, the amount of time, money and effort which goes into tax-avoidance, would be lessened. (Avoidance is used here to mean legal means to reduce tax.) Tax-avoidance has always, and probably always will be, a profitable occupation, but the great reductions in taxation that can be achieved under the present system has virtually made it into an industry. It is not the purpose of this book to specify the means of avoidance at length, but the subject is important enough to merit mention. Estate-duty-avoidance is looked at in Chapter 15.

Numerous devices have been thought up to reduce tax on income. Some of the practices mentioned have now been stopped, or modified to limit abuse, but efforts to find new loopholes may be expected to continue unabated, given the present very diverse rates of tax on different receipts. Employers, instead of a salary increase to their top executives, may offer generous non-contributory pensions, a wide range of 'fringe benefits' and lavish entertainment expenses. An old favourite is to turn income into capital gains, which formerly went untaxed and now, if long-term gains, are taxed at a maximum rate of 30% if in excess of £50. Share options to employees and various forms of 'dividend stripping' were the best-known among these devices. It will be pointed out in the chapter on 'Personal Income Tax' (Chapter 12) that advantages may accrue to the person who is able to arrange his affairs under the mantle of company status.

Titmus, R. M. (1962), 72, has pointed out that

> The British system of taxation is almost unique in the world in recognizing a payment voluntarily undertaken by the taxpayer as a charge on his income, provided that payment (*a*) is made under a promise backed by a deed of covenant extending to a period of more than six years; (*b*) is not made in favour of an unmarried infant of the convenantor; (*c*) is not in exchange for value received from (or goods or services rendered by) the recipient.

In a footnote to this section he adds:

> Covenants by men in favour of their mistresses can only be regarded as ineligible for tax relief if the Inland Revenue can establish that they are given 'for services rendered' (see Monroe, J. G., 'Annual and Other Periodical Payments', *British Tax Review*, December, 1956, 289).

Implementation of the total-accretion principle

The total-accretion principle is defined as accretion to wealth, which is equal to consumption plus increase in net worth valued at market price for the beginning and the end of the period. The chief problems are presented by (1) valuation, (2) inflation or deflation, (3) fluctuating income, (4) the tax-paying unit.

VALUATION

As anybody who has had something to do with valuation for purposes of estate duties will know, valuation can cause a great deal of work and involve a great deal of arbitrariness. There is little problem with items which are standardized and traded regularly, such as quoted company shares. Unquoted shares, unique items, such as original paintings, plots of land and so on, are much more difficult to value, short of actual sale in the market-place. On the grounds of practicality, it seems that annual or periodic valuation is ruled out. The item would be brought into the tax-net on sale, or on death of the owner, when valuation has to take place in any case. It is argued against this that such a process discriminates in favour of people who enjoy unrealized accretion. This is true, but it seems to have little weight against the bigger distortions that have been mentioned, caused by not taxing some items at all. Similar considerations apply to the argument that treating as income on sale will interfere with the market process of buying and selling. Once again it is necessary to weigh any loss likely to be caused in this way with the undoubted losses and distortions caused by the present system.

INFLATION OR DEFLATION

Should the valuation of assets and liabilities allow for changes in the value of money—that is, for inflation or deflation? It is argued that a gain of, say, £100 on selling shares is a gain in money terms only, that what should be relevant is the gain in real terms—that is, the gain in command over goods and services. In inflationary conditions this gain will clearly be less than £100 and vice versa.

Most commentators agree that in principle changes due to changes in the value of money should be allowed for all receipts, whether income, capital gains or anything else. That is, in principle, it should be in real terms. However, most also agree that in practical terms money values will have to be used. The difficulties of finding a correct index, or indexes, with which to obtain real values are a serious deterrent to working with deflated values, and allowing for inflation would be administratively complex. Because of these difficulties, it is by no means clear that a system which attempts to take account of inflation and deflation would be more equitable than one that doesn't.

To argue for compensation for changes in the value of money for all receipts is not, however, a good argument for compensation for some of these receipts.

At the moment a money-wage increase which restores the real purchasing power of wages to the level of the previous year nevertheless results in more tax being paid if tax rates are unaltered. The claim that one particular slice of income should be protected from changes in the value of money thus begins to look like special pleading on behalf of interested parties.

If the principle is good for one, it is good for all, but of course, adjustment for all loses much of its point. The government starts out with clear ideas of the amount of revenue it wants from the economy; if adjustments were made on the income side for price changes adjustments would have to be made on the revenue side to tax rates to secure that the tax revenue target was reached. The only change from the present system is that the government obtains more revenue[1] from inflation at the moment if it keeps tax rates the same. If adjustments were made automatically to income, then the present hidden increase in tax revenue would not occur. In other words, if the government wanted more revenue it would have to increase rates rather than rely on the automatic increase brought about by inflation.

A similar argument is used when it is asserted that, since capital gains can accrue over a long period of time, it is unjust to tax them at income rates. The valid point in this argument is that the realization of capital gains will, under a progressive tax structure, raise the tax liability in the year in which the gains are realized, over the liability which would have been incurred if the gain had been realized evenly over time. The remedy for this is some form of averaging of income for tax purposes, a measure which is desirable under any form of progressive tax. This will be touched on in the next section. The assertion that capital gains are different from other income cannot be sustained under the total-accretion concept. This concept seeks the 'taxable capacity' of a person: it is irrelevant whether one person has a higher taxable capacity than another, due to higher earnings, receipt of a legacy, receipt of a capital gain or in some other way. A person who invests money in shares which show a gain in money terms is better off than a person whose shares show no gain or a loss: the degree of inflation or deflation cannot alter this conclusion.

It is also argued that a capital gain is illusory if the proceeds are to be reinvested in a similar asset. Thus in the case of a house purchased for £1,000 and sold for £3,000, it is probable that the whole of the proceeds will be needed to reinvest in a similar type of property. This is easily seen as a case of special pleading: that house-owners should be protected against inflation as opposed to other groups. The person who invests £1,000 in a house in the above example gains over the person who invests the £1,000 in securities and makes the same gain. The latter person will pay tax on his gain and be at a disadvantage in entering the housing market in competition with

[1] Whether the government gets more revenue in real terms with inflation depends on the degree to which its expenditures are affected by the inflation, the people who obtain an increase in income and the degree of progression of tax to which these people are subject.

the former householder. The fact that owner-occupied houses are exempt from capital gains for social and political reasons should not be allowed to obscure the fact that once an owner obtains a house (on the assumption that his property moves in line with the general market trend in house prices) he is largely indifferent to the subsequent trend in house prices. A wedge is driven between those who have houses, who are largely protected from subsequent inflation in house prices, and those who subsequently enter the market.[2]

Although housing was selected as an example, the principles involved apply to any asset; exemption from tax confers benefit on existing owners of the asset *vis-à-vis* the rest of the population. It is not suggested that no case can be made for the exemption of certain assets, but that the nature of the privilege being conferred needs careful examination. No presumptive economic argument can be set up that particular assets merit exemption.

PRO OR CON?

In the mass of words on the subject of inflation and capital gains the assumptions of the protagonists are seldom made explicit.

Those who argue that capital gains should take inflation into account presumably have in mind some concept akin to 'keeping capital intact'. If this is the correct premise, it is clear that taxing a paper gain is unjust.

Those who argue against this view take as their starting-point that what is relevant for taxation and equity purposes 'is the relative income positions of taxpayers'. If this is the correct premise, a person who has a capital gain in money terms is better off than a person who has no such gain or a loss, and should be taxed. On this assumption, not to tax a paper gain is unjust *or*, alternatively, everything should be adjusted for price changes.

This argument seems particularly protracted because the principle of 'keeping capital intact' is both a sound accounting principle and an unsound principle of public finance. The point has been investigated by successive Royal Commissions in relation to depreciation allowances for companies and whether these allowances should be based on historic or replacement cost. Allowances based on the latter would, of course, allow for price changes. Such a change has been decisively rejected. These questions will be discussed in some detail in Chapter 13 on 'Company Taxation'. The viewpoint adopted here is that, however desirable it may be for the individual to maintain

[2] This aspect of protection must also increase the demand for houses, and so be responsible in some degree for the rise in house prices.

his wealth position, it is no part of the fiscal system to do this for him. This aim of the fiscal system is not to maintain the status of those who happen to have wealth or to make gains. On the contrary, at any one time society aims for a certain degree of progression and a certain redistribution of income and wealth. The argument adopted here for the rejection of compensation for inflation is clear: inflationary and deflationary conditions affect all sectors of the community in different degrees; compensation for one sector results in less equity, not more. See Hockley, G. C. (January-February, 1968) and Wheatcroft, G. S. A. (January-February, 1968).

FLUCTUATING INCOME

The difficulty posed by any progressive tax is the inequity between those persons whose income fluctuates from year to year and those who receive their incomes in regular equal amounts. Authors, artists, sportsmen, farmers, fishermen and a number of people in professional occupations who rely on fees are likely to be in the former category.

As an illustration of inequity, an unmarried actor on rates of tax applicable in 1966-7, who receives £10,000 for a film and nothing for the next nine years, will pay about £4,284 in tax and surtax. On the other hand, a single man who receives a salary of £1,000 a year for ten years will pay approximately £186 in tax a year, or £1,860 in tax over ten years.[3]

The only provisions for spreading or averaging income at the moment apply to authors, to patent royalties and, since 1969, to painters and sculptors. The author of a literary, dramatic, musical or artistic work who sells the copyright or an interest in it for a lump-sum payment, or is in receipt of royalties from such a work, can sometimes spread his tax payments. This applies if he was engaged on the making of the work for more than twelve months. He can spread the payment over two years if the period of production does not exceed twenty-four months, and over three years if the period was longer. A person who is chargeable for tax in respect of a capital sum received on the sale of patent rights is entitled to spread the sum in equal amounts over the year of receipt and the five succeeding years. There is a further provision for spreading royalties received as consideration for more than two years' use of a patent. In this case the payment is spread back in equal annual instalments,

[3] The matter is not quite so simple as this example suggests. The actor will pay tax in arrears under Schedule D, while the salary-earner will pay as he earns under Schedule E. Claims for expenses are usually treated more leniently under Schedule D. This point will be taken up in Chapter 12 on 'Personal Income Tax'.

subject to a limiting number of six. The Budget in 1969 enabled painters and sculptors to spread the receipt for a work over the period during which it was made.

It needs to be stressed that the problem of fluctuating incomes occurs under the present tax system. The Royal Commission on the Taxation of Profits and Income in 1955 were of the opinion that 'it was quite impossible to regard as satisfactory the present position of fluctuating incomes' (para. 197). The problem becomes more acute under the accretion principle of income because more income will be volatile. Legacies and gifts are examples of receipts which cannot be expected regularly.

The seemingly straightforward solution of aggregating income over, say, a five-year period or a lifetime falls to the ground because if a person has a drop in income in any year, his tax bill in that year will be based on his average income over the relevant period which may be higher than his current income. The fact that a rising income gives a correspondingly lower tax bill does not compensate for the hardship which is likely to be involved in meeting high tax payments during periods of reduced income.

The usual assumption of averaging is that the total sum of taxes paid over the averaging period should be the same as if the income had been received in equal amounts in each year of the averaging period. With a five-year plan, tax could be computed by finding the average income over this period (that is, total income for the five years divided by five) and reworking the tax liability for each of the past years on the basis of this average. Not surprisingly, the Royal Commission on Tax (1955), para. 189, rejected proposals on these lines 'since the administrative burden of operating it cannot be contemplated'. However the assumption of the Commission that to achieve averaging, tax for past years must be reworked, is not a feature of all schemes of averaging. The Royal Commission on Taxation in Canada (1966) suggested the use of special averaging schedules which would mean that only one computation of tax would be necessary instead of a new computation for each year averaged. An alternative, using the current year's cumulative average income and subtracting from this the amount of taxes already paid for earlier years of the averaging period, is outlined by Vickray, W. (1947), 172-95 and 417-27. The deliberations and recommendations of the Royal Commission (1955) follow.

THE ROYAL COMMISSION ON THE TAXATION OF PROFITS AND INCOME, 1955

The Royal Commission considered a scheme of averaging income over five years. This was rejected on the grounds of an 'enormous volume of additional work that is inherent in averaging' (para. 198), and they came up with more limited proposals.

The 'enormous volume of additional work' came, it seems, from the necessity to ascertain income in virtually every case where there was any income at all. At the period the Commission were considering (1953-4), of the 20 million individuals in the U.K. with incomes above the exemption limit of taxation, 4¼ million were relieved of tax by the operation of allowances, and it was merely necessary to ascertain that such persons are free of liability. It was also stated that 'there would be a formidable task of recomputing the tax payable in each past year of the permitted period' (para. 199). Finally it was noted that this would add to the work of employees, in that their present dispensation from keeping P.A.Y.E. records of certain employees earning under £3 5*s*. a week could hardly be maintained.

On the first point the Report is not clear where the enormous volume of work comes from, since under the present system of tax it is necessary to establish whether a person has enough income to subject him to tax. Averaging does not necessary imply a change in tax allowances, and the number of persons assessed to tax need not be very different in the two cases. The necessity to recalculate past income is a characteristic of a particular scheme of averaging, but is not necessarily a feature of all averaging schemes. On the final point the number of employees below the exemption limits must be small.

At present a great deal of administrative effort goes into providing a large number of benefits. Chapter 18 suggests a possible simplification of these. A scheme of tax on the lines of the accretion principle of income with averaging and simplification of benefits might, after the change had been put through, result in a saving of manpower when both the Inland Revenue and other services are taken into account. Developments since 1955 in the field of computers may also have simplified the administrative task. The more limited proposals for averaging, on which the majority and minority reports of the Royal Commission agreed, was:

> Any taxpayer who can show that his total income for any year was not more than 50% of his total income for the previous year shall be entitled to have his total income for each of those two years assessed as if the aggregate income of the two years had accrued evenly throughout the period (para. 203).

If income again fell below 50% of the preceding year, averaging would occur over three years, and so on. It was recognized that special provisions would be needed when a taxpayer retired from active employment. This scheme was, it was said, 'nothing better than a rough-and-ready means of giving some alleviation to extreme cases of fluctuating income'.

Conclusion. Failure to adopt some form of averaging is unfair to those who have fluctuations in income. Any form of averaging will result in some complication of the tax system compared to a similar system without averaging: but not necessarily compared to a modified tax and benefit system. The amount of difficulty that would result from the introduction of averaging was greatly overstressed by the Royal Commission in 1955, because they worked on the assumption that tax in past years of the averaging period would have to be recalculated.

Even if it was found that an averaging scheme would take some years to work into the system, a simpler compromise could be used in the meantime. One possibility is to implement the suggestion of the Royal Commission. That in cases where a drop in income of 50% over the previous year's income occurs, the taxpayer should have his tax recalculated over the preceding year, and to supplement this with forward spreading of income in cases where income increases by 50% or more over the previous year. These situations would be mutually exclusive. The former situation, where income can be spread over the current and previous year being designed to cover the case where a taxpayer suffers a sharp reduction in earned income. The latter situation, where income can be spread in equal amounts over the year of receipt, and, say, the next two or three years (on the lines of current provisions for spreading a capital sum received on the sale of patent rights) being designed to cover exceptional receipts, such as the receipt of a large gift or legacy or exceptional income earned in one year.

These proposals are still 'rough-and-ready', but they do go some way to achieving equity. The scheme of the Royal Commission involves the greater administrative effort, but was considered feasible at the time. Forward averaging of exceptional receipts is not a great administrative burden. Provision could be made for a taxpayer, if he wished, to pay a provisional sum in tax in the year in which his large income occurred. This would be based on his estimated income in the years over which averaging was to take place. Adjustment would be made in future years if actual income differed from estimated income. The sum payable immediately could be discounted by a suitable rate of interest (since a deferred tax liability enables the capital to be invested and earn interest). The taxpayers concerned could then, if they wished, safeguard themselves against not having funds to meet their future liabilities.

THE TAX-PAYING UNIT

The problem of the tax-paying unit has been described as the most neglected problem in public taxation. If the structure of society is such that the composition of all tax-paying units is the same—say, a husband, wife and two children—we have little difficulty. But taxpayers differ greatly from those who are single with no dependants to look after, to married persons with large families and many dependants.

The Royal Commission on Taxation (1954), reported as follows:

> We have come to the conclusion that the taxation of the combined incomes of husband and wife as one unit is to be preferred to their separate taxation as separate units because the aggregate income provides a unit of taxation that is fairer to those concerned. That is why we do not recommend a departure from the present system. The combined incomes of married persons are sometimes described as a joint purse. We do not think that so wide a generalization can safely be made on such a question of social habit: but it does appear to us, on the one hand, that marriage creates a social unit which is not truly analogous with other associations involving some measure of joint living expenses and that to tax the incomes of two married people living together as if each were equivalent to the income of a single individual would give a less satisfactory distribution than that which results from the present rule. Such a method of taxation would mean that one married couple bore a greater or less burden of tax than another according to what must surely be an irrelevant distinction for this purpose—namely, the proportion in which the combined income was divided between the partners . . . (para. 119).

The Commission were sensitive to the abuses that can arise with separate assessment for husband and wife by the transfer of income from the spouse with the highest income (and therefore under a progressive tax to higher tax) to the partner with the lowest income. This abuse is most likely in the case of unearned income, as it is much more difficult to transfer earned income to another before tax is paid. The exception to this is provided by some private companies where the husband or wife can be paid a director's remuneration although they have little or nothing to do with the running of the business.

On the other hand, aggregation is hard on those married couples who both have high incomes. This point makes itself felt in particular where both spouses can earn high incomes. The extreme is found where the spouses earn equal amounts. For example, as single persons, people can earn up to £5,000 without paying surtax. As a married couple their joint income of £10,000 will attract £894 15*s.* in surtax. In addition, a joint salary of this magnitude will attract

£138 more in income tax, because the earned income allowance by which two-ninths is allowed to be deducted from earned income before tax is payable is diminished to one-ninth on incomes above £4,005, and disappears entirely on incomes above £9,945.

We have reached one of the many conflicts in public finance. To make the unit of taxation the individual may seem unjust to single persons who are not in a position to spread their incomes to a wife. To make the unit of taxation the married couple may seem unjust to the married couple when both can earn high incomes. The argument can be extended to children. Should their income be included in the income of their parents? In other words, why should we draw the line of the tax unit at husband and wife, rather than the family or the household? If the family or the household, how should these be defined?

This problem is one that is inherent with any system of progressive taxation. The moral, if one is to be drawn, is that our current system is likely to be far from perfect, that changes in tax modify the impact on the individual and on the family and, in the absence of any clear criteria for finding an equitable tax unit, would seem to call for periodic examination of the current tax position. Such an examination will be deferred until Chapter 18, where it is broadened out to account not only for taxes paid but also for benefits received by single persons and married persons with and without children.

THE TAXATION MIX

It should be clear from what has already been said that the total-accretion principle is an attempt to achieve horizontal equity. The assumption is made that the source of income is a matter of indifference. Whatever the source, it represents purchasing power, and should therefore be included in income. It should also be clear on reflection that other types of tax do more or less violence to the principle of horizontal equity. Taxes on consumption goods will fall unequally on persons in equal positions if they have different consumption patterns. Most noticeable, if tobacco and alcohol are to retain their present very high rates of tax for social reasons, then two individuals in equal positions, except that one smokes and drinks and the other does not, will pay very different amounts of tax.

In Chapter 9 the benefit principle of tax and the social cost argument were examined. It is clear that the application of either is likely to violate the ability to pay approach of the accretion principle.

The impossibility of laying down a universal principle of tax which will be valid under all conditions is that the extent of government activity varies widely. In a mixed economy the government may be providing services which would not be provided at all, or provided on an insufficient scale, if left in private hands. In such cases as this, the benefit principle is not applicable, and defining ability to pay is essential if equity is to be achieved. At the other extreme the government may be providing goods and services which could equally well be provided by private enterprise (albeit under some form of monopoly regulation). Steel, telephones, railways and power are cases in point. Here failure to charge on the benefit principle is likely to cause a misuse of the nation's resources.

A division on these lines is, in a rough-and-ready manner, apparent in our society. The nationalized industries are expected to pay their way—although at any one time this instruction may fail to be realized. It has already been argued that if these industries are to be expected to pay their way, and this is desirable on allocation grounds, then it is essential that social functions which these services are expected to serve should be clearly separated from their strictly commercial activities. Then the commercial side can be expected to pay its way, and the activities that are continued for social reasons, because the social benefits outweigh the money cost involved, should be subsidized out of general taxation based on ability to pay.

Thus the following conclusions are drawn: many government services either cannot be charged to individuals, such as defence and justice, or should not be charged because of neighbourhood and social effects, e.g. transfer payments, education and health. For these services, taxation according to ability to pay is necessary: the accretion principle has been set out as a method of judging ability to pay. Commercial activities should be charged on the benefit principle.

These conclusions do not still controversy. General agreement is, however, likely over a wide range of services which can be classified unambiguously in one category or the other. Some areas remain controversial, e.g. some people argue that higher education should be financed by loans on a benefit basis rather than grants. Here it is necessary to weigh the advantages and disadvantages that flow from the alternative ways of financing. Charging the beneficiary is likely to deter the use of the good or service, and this needs to be weighed against the social loss involved.

Company taxation is rather more controversial. It can be argued that companies belong to individuals and that company income (both distributed profits and undistributed profits) should be allocated to individuals as part of their income. Imputing undistributed profits to shareholders is not difficult administratively, but is impractical for incentive reasons. A case can be made for taxing companies as well as individuals. This will be further considered in Chapter 13 on 'Company Taxation'.

Whether estate duties should continue is once again a wider issue that a democratic country has to decide through the polls. The accretion principle would, we have seen, include bequests and gifts, along with other additions, as income. The issue is whether estate duties should be imposed as well. On the grounds of the very marked inequality of wealth in Great Britain, a case can be made for additional estate duties in some form.

It is estimated (by Revell, J. R. S., quoted by Meade, J. E. (1964)) that in 1960 the wealthiest 1% of the population owned 42% of personal wealth and the wealthiest 5% owned 75%. In this example the population is taken as individuals over twenty-five years of age in England and Wales. The difficulty in interpreting these figures is to know what degree of concentration of wealth is to be expected. If wealth was accumulated only out of savings, the natural progression would be for a person to have low or negative wealth under, say, thirty-five years of age as family commitments are taken on. Ages fifty on to retirement would see wealth at a peak, with gradually diminished wealth after retirement. Even more important is whether wealth is primarily held by husbands, by wives, or jointly. It is likely that those with very much wealth will adopt some form of sharing in order to minimize the impact of death duties.

Table 1 sets out the home population of England and Wales as given by the 1961 Census of Population, divided into males and females and those below thirty-five years of age and those thirty-five and over.

Table 1

(Thousands)

Age	Total Population	Males	Females
All	46,105	22,304	23,801
Below thirty-five	22,492	11,427	11,065
Thirty-five or over	23,613	10,877	12,736

Source: *Annual Abstract of Statistics, 1967*, Table 8.

On the assumption that wealth is owned by both males and females over thirty-five years of age, this would mean that wealth would be owned by 23,613,000 persons, or 51% of the population. On the extreme assumption that wealth is owned only by males over thirty-five, this would be 10,877,000, or 24% of the population, as potential wealth-owners.[4] The figures above give 5% of the population, or 2,305,250 persons, as owning 75% of the wealth. This represents a marked degree of inequality on any reasonable assumption about the sector of the population that can be expected to hold wealth.

In concluding this brief section on the coexistence of different types of tax, we again come up with the problem that not all the considerations involved are economic ones. In trying to establish horizontal equity between taxpayers, we find that other taxes usually breech this principle. However, principles of taxation are set up as a guide to policy not as inflexible rules. There may well be social and other reasons for deliberately departing from a principle in particular cases. This does not make the principle invalid. On the contrary, it illustrates the use of the concept very well: instead of taxing in the present haphazard way, it enables taxes to be justified; it makes it that much harder for particular groups to indulge in special pleading.

Summary

Horizontal equity—that people in equal positions shall be treated equally—presents few problems of principle. The correct treatment of people in unequal positions, or vertical equity, is more difficult. Even when, as in all developed economies, progressive tax is generally agreed on, the precise degree of progression is an open one that has to be decided by political consensus.

Even in setting aside questions of progression as a political decision, the important point remains as to the criterion on which equal and unequal positions shall be judged—that is, what shall be the taxation base? Two claims have been put forward and generally acknowledged. One is that taxation should be based on expenditure. On this criterion, the source of spending power, whether it comes from income or wealth or exceptional receipts, is irrelevant: taxation accrues as spending takes place, not as accumulation proceeds. The other base broadens the definition of income so as to take in changes in wealth and other receipts. These concepts, at first sight so very different from each other, turn out to have only one major difference in principle: that expenditure as a base exempts savings from taxation while the other does not. The problems posed by valuation, inflation and deflation, fluctuating incomes (or fluctuating expenditures) and the tax-paying unit which are detailed in this chapter are common to both and indeed to any system of taxation.

[4] This assumption is clearly unrealistic for older persons. On average, women live longer than men, and it is known that in the upper age-groups, wealth is concentrated into the ownership of women, particularly widows.

12
Personal income taxation

Albert Einstein once admitted that working out his income tax was beyond him: he had to go to a tax consultant. 'This is too difficult for a mathematician,' said Einstein. 'It takes a philosopher.' *Time*.

In this chapter an outline will be given of the main taxes on personal income. However, as will be shown, it is impossible to treat personal tax entirely separately from tax on businesses. It is necessary to distinguish between the individual, the incorporated business, usually termed a company, which has a separate legal entity, and what will be termed unincorporated businesses. The most common form of unincorporated business is the partnership. Income of the unincorporated business is treated as the income of the persons concerned, but, as we shall see, treatment for tax differs in important respects from the tax treatment of the individual. Incorporated company tax will be treated in the next chapter.

This chapter deals first with income tax. Income tax was introduced by Pitt in 1797 as a temporary tax to help finance the Napoleonic Wars. It ended in 1816. It was reintroduced by Gladstone in 1842 again as a 'temporary measure', and has continued ever since. In the course of looking at income tax, the position of unincorporated businesses will be taken up. Surtax is then considered and an evaluation of income tax and surtax is made. Consideration is then given to the tax on capital gains.

The structure of income tax

Income tax is imposed by a Finance Act introduced every year, which determines the rates of tax and other details which are to apply to the next year beginning April 6th. The tax is chargeable under a number of schedules:

Schedule B applies to woodlands managed on a commercial basis.
Schedule C covers interest on public loans.

Schedule D covers income of a professional and business nature, namely:

Trades, including farms,
Professions and vocations,

and in addition income from a variety of sources, e.g.

Interest not taxed at source, e.g. bank interest.
Foreign securities.
Foreign possessions.
Miscellaneous profits, e.g. from letting.
Furnished accommodation.
Short-term capital gains.
Rents and other receipts from lands and buildings.

Schedule E covers income from employment—that is, wages, salaries, pensions and the like. The tax is collected by the employer under the system known as 'Pay as You Earn', so that the employee receives his remuneration net of tax.

Schedule F covers assessments on companies in respect of tax deducted by them from interest and dividends.

The missing Schedule A used to cover the imputed income from owning land and property before it was abolished in 1964-5. The important schedules for the majority of individuals are Schedules D and E.

The individual is allowed to make certain deductions from his income before tax is charged. The main deductions are:

(1) In the case of earned incomes, including pensions, a deduction of two-ninths is made on the first £4,005; on income between £4,005 and £9,945 one-ninth is deducted. Thus (ignoring other allowances for the moment) a person who has an income of £9,945 or more from investment income will be assessed for tax on the whole amount. Whereas, if the income is wholly earned, the maximum reduction is £1,550, leaving £8,395 to be taxed from an earned income of £9,945. Thus although it is common to regard the marginal rate of tax as the standard rate of tax in force (at present 8*s.* 3*d.* in the £1) this is incorrect for the majority of earned incomes. Relief of two-ninths brings the marginal rate down to 6*s.* 5*d.* in the £1. The marginal rate of tax refers to the amount of tax paid on the last £1 of income.

(2) Since 1969 from the sum arrived at under (1) a married man deducts £375, single persons, including widows and widowers, £255. If a wife is working, she is also, in effect, allowed an allowance equal to that of a single person if her salary or wage is great enough; otherwise she gets a proportion of the allowance.

(3) Further deductions are made in respect of children: £115 for each child under eleven, £140 for each child over eleven but not over sixteen, £165 for each child over sixteen. The latter allowance is subject to the child's receiving full-time educational instruction. Moreover, if a child has income in its own right exceeding £115 the allowance is reduced by the amount of its income in excess of £115.[1]

(4) Deductions are allowed to cover a variety of circumstances: for a widow or widower who has to employ a housekeeper; for dependent relatives; in respect of age and blindness; in respect of life assurance and interest payments on house mortgages. Since the 1969 Budget, interest on bank overdrafts is no longer generally allowed as a deduction.

(5) The Budget in 1967 allowed single women, widows and separated wives who are the sole supports of a dependent relative an increase in allowance from £75 to £110. Also the additional personal allowance of £40 for single people with single-handed responsibility for bringing up children was increased to £75 and increased again to £100 in 1969.

(6) Certain expenses occurred in obtaining the income are deductible before tax is charged.

The allowances outlined in (1) to (5) above apply to all individuals. As we shall see, the treatment of expenses, (6) above, differs according to whether tax is paid under Schedule D or Schedule E. After the appropriate allowances have been deducted, the first £260 of the remaining income is taxed at 6*s*. in the £1, the balance at 8*s*. 3*d*. in the £1. However, the computation of the income which is subject to tax differs for Schedule D and for Schedule E taxpayers.

Schedule D and Schedule E

The most important category falling under Schedule D are shopkeepers, professional persons working on their own account and

[1] These child tax allowances should not be confused with children's allowances, which are paid irrespective of income. These were introduced in 1946 at the rate of 5*s*. a week per child for all children except the first. This was raised to 8*s*. in 1952 and again by 2*s*. per week for third and subsequent children in 1956. From April, 1968, these were increased to 15*s*. for the second and 17*s*. for each younger child, and in October, 1968, these rates were increased by a further 3*s*. Although child allowances are paid irrespective of income, the increased benefit above 8*s*. is confined to small-income families, as tax allowances are changed so as to recoup the increase from income-tax-payers. This supplementation was well below the estimate of Beveridge of the average cost of subsistence of children, and still remains so, with the result that many low-income families have to seek Supplementary Benefit (see Hemming, M. F. W. (August, 1965)).

other unincorporated businesses; wages, salaries and pensions are covered by Schedule E.

In the case of wages, salaries and pensions, the matter is straightforward. Income as defined by current law (not to be confused with the definition of income under the total-accretion principle) is, using standard-tax terminology, called 'gross income'. From this gross income the appropriate personal allowances are deducted in order to arrive at 'taxable income', which is charged under Schedule E through the system known as 'Pay as You Earn'.

In the case of income from trades, farms and professions, it is necessary to ascertain the total statutory income; from this sum adjustments are made to cover the using up of capital involved in the business in order to arrive at the figure of taxable income. If more than one person is involved, the taxable income is allocated to the partners in whatever proportions the partnership has agreed on. This portion of the profits is then the 'gross income' of the person concerned, and after the personal allowances have been deducted we arrive at the taxable income of the individual as before.

First- and second-class citizens?

The growth of unincorporated and incorporated businesses in this century, and the increase in tax rates, brings up some of the most contentious problems in taxation. Incorporated businesses are taxed separately from individuals; the method of tax will be treated in Chapter 11, on 'Company Taxation'. A problem in equity arises if the incorporated company is in effect a 'one-man business' or partnership rather than a company owned by a large number of shareholders. Profits retained in the business do not count as income of the owner and are not therefore subject to progressive rates of personal income. This problem has long been recognized, and provision is made for a closely-controlled company which makes inadequate distributions to be charged income and surtax on the shortfall, except to the extent that it can show that retention of profits is necessary or advisable for the maintenance and development of its business. In the past this provision appears to have been used only rarely, and some income must have been subject to lower tax as a result.

A not dissimilar problem is in achieving equity between taxpayers who receive their income by way of wages and salaries and are therefore subject under Schedule E and those who receive income from unincorporated businesses and pay under Schedule D. The latter are able to deduct for the using up of capital before arriving at a figure of taxable profit,[2] and expenses are dealt with more leniently under Schedule D. Both the majority and minority reports of the Royal Commission on the Taxation of Profits and Income (1955) had much to say on this aspect of tax. The following quotations are from the Minority Report; the paragraph references therein refer to the majority report:

The other main aspect in which the present legal definition of taxable income causes inequality of treatment between classes of taxpayers concerns not receipts, but outlays. As the majority point out one particular source of these differences consists in the allowances given for the wastage of capital. The original theory which ignored the wastage of capital altogether 'has been profoundly modified in the course of time, but not to the same extent or in the same way in respect of all the different sources of income' (para. 38). While incomes derived from trades, vocations or professions 'now received a full allowance out of taxable income to make good money expended in acquiring assets that are used up in the production of the income' (para. 39), no allowances are given with respect to the capital expenditure incurred in vocational and educational training or for the expenditure which a man incurs 'in developing and improving his expert knowledge' (para. 41). . . . Another and, in our view, even more important cause of such inequality arises out of the difference in the legal definition of deductible expenses in respect of income from a trade, profession or vocation assessed under Schedule D, and in respect of income from an office, employment or pension assessed under Schedule E (paras. 19 and 21).

Both the Majority and Minority Reports of the Commission were agreed that it would be impracticable to extend the scheme of capital allowances to expenditure incurred on investment by the individual in the human person. The Minority Report adds: 'we believe therefore that short of withdrawing capital allowances altogether—a course that, on grounds of expediency, we should not favour—the difference in treatment cannot in this respect be avoided and ought therefore to be recognized and compensated for' (p. 361). Compensation could be achieved by taxing individuals at a lower rate or by imposing an annual charge, perhaps graduated to the size of the business, for the privilege of company status, whether of unincorporated or incorporated form.

On the 'even more important' point of deductible expenses no obviously best solution emerges.

[2] The taxable sum may be more or less than the profits shown in the books of the company. For example, if capital items have been charged to revenue this will be disallowed, as will purely personal expenditure of the proprietor. That is, these sums will be added back to arrive at a figure of taxable profit. Certain types of capital investment attract allowances, but the details of these will be left to Chapter 13.

> Advertising and entertaining are typical examples of expenses incurred for building up the goodwill of a business, which though fully chargeable against the current year's receipts, are frequently linked with receipts, if at all, only through the enhancement of future rather than current earnings.
>
> Nothing similar to this would be a deductible expense under Schedule E. The wage- or salary-earner cannot charge as expenses the cost of entertaining his present or his potential future employers even though the expense might be 'wholly and exclusively' incurred with a view to securing for himself a better job. Nor could he charge the cost of training or education (whether in the form of a capital allowance or as current expenses) or the annual wear and tear to his physical earning powers. For all these reasons 'income' under Schedule E is not analogous to the net profit under Schedule D; it is more analogous to some conception of a 'gross profit' of trade, before the deduction either of depreciation or of all those other expenses which are not directly associated with the current receipts from trading activity (paras. 113 and 114).

The minority report goes on to point out the economic distortion that can result from these expense provisions. It refers to the 'very considerable subsidy from the Exchequer on outlays of doubtful value, which it might not have been worth the trader's while to incur at all in the absence of taxation'. The argument against extending these expense provisions to taxpayers under Schedule E is that these 'outlays of doubtful value' would be extended rather than curtailed. The argument against stopping these provisions is the difficulty of separating legitimate business expenses from other outlays, and the handicap which exporters would face if their overseas competitors continue to receive tax advantages.

Since the Report of the Royal Commission, action has been taken on two fronts. Deductible expenses under Schedule D have been tightened up and a slight relaxation of allowable expenses has occurred under Schedule E. The position, perhaps inevitably, still leaves many loopholes, and further changes are likely in the future.

If a value-added tax is adopted this would provide an opportunity to look afresh at the whole concept of capital allowances and deductible expenses. The agreed system of taxes towards which the Common Market countries are working would mean, if adopted in Britain, that her exporters would not be under a competitive disadvantage *vis-à-vis* European competitors.

Schedule D: other items

The other item under Schedule D which calls for comment is short-term capital gains. These are gains realized within twelve months of purchase. The types of gain which attract this tax will be dealt with in the section on the capital gains tax.

Surtax

Surtax was first introduced in 1909. It is an additional tax payable on incomes exceeding a certain amount. The practical effect of the tax is that since 1961 it is payable on earned income of a single person exceeding £5,000 and earned income of a married couple exceeding £5,120. For unearned incomes the figures are respectively £2,000 and £2,120.[3]

The actual computation of surtax need not concern us, because reliefs are allowed for children, dependent relatives and a housekeeper; the figures given above are the minimum figures at which surtax is payable. Because of these allowances, the figure at which an individual actually pays the tax will vary.

Income above the surtax limit is liable at the following rates:

	s.	*d.*	
On the first £500	2	0	in the £1
„ next £500	2	6	„ „
„ „ £1,000	3	6	„ „
„ „ £1,000	4	6	„ „
„ „ £1,000	5	6	„ „
„ „ £2,000	6	6	„ „
„ „ £2,000	7	6	„ „
„ „ £2,000	8	6	„ „
„ „ £3,000	9	6	„ „
On all beyond £15,000	10	0	„ „

The tax-paying unit

Chapter 11 looked at the problem of the tax-paying unit. In Great Britain the general rule is that income of husbands and wives is aggregated for tax purposes. The position of children's income depends on the source of the income. If the child has earned income in its own right, this is not aggregated with the income of the parent. However, for income, earned or unearned, in excess of £115 (the tax-allowance figure for a child) the parents lose a £1 of allowance for every £1 the child's income exceeds £115. For unearned income the general rule is that if parents settle property on their child the income is nevertheless counted as part of the income of the parents. This rule is an obvious one to reduce tax-avoidance. At the present time

[3] It is by virtue of a rebate on earned income and an additional earnings allowance of £2,000 that the starting-point of surtax for a single person is raised from £2,000 on unearned income to £5,000 on earned income. The corresponding figures for a married couple are £2,120 and £5,120 respectively.

there is a loophole: if the income is accumulated for the benefit of the child until he, or she, reaches twenty-one years of age surtax is not payable. The Chancellor announced in his Budget speech in 1968 that he was intending to alter this provision in 1969.

At the present time, where a grandparent or other person not being the parent makes a settlement of capital on a child (provided the donor receives no material benefit from the gift), the income thus produced can be applied for the child's benefit, e.g. for school fees, and this income is not aggregated with that of the parent. However, as from the tax year of 1969-70 this income will be aggregated with that of the parents. This change is on the lines suggested by the *Report of the Royal Commission on Tax* (1954), 77ff. The Budget in 1969 following the recommendation to reduce the age of majority from 21 years to 18 years also reduced the age for the aggregation of children's unearned income with parents' income to 18 years.

Evaluation of current income tax and surtax

A number of criticisms have been made in previous chapters. The prime one is not about the nature of income and surtax in itself, but the definition of income which is subject to these taxes. In this chapter attention has been drawn to some of the advantages which many individuals can obtain by forming themselves into unincorporated or incorporated companies.

Another criticism can be made: that reliefs given by way of tax concessions do not help the most needy. The present tax system, as we have seen, makes fairly elaborate provision for differences in taxpayers' circumstances. To recapitulate: earned income relief, single person's allowance of £255, married person's allowance of £375, allowances for dependent children, dependent relatives, in respect of age, for blind persons, and for certain interest payments, e.g. house mortgage payments, and life assurance premiums. In addition, the first £260 of taxable income is liable at 6*s*. in the £1, and the balance at 8*s*. 3*d*. in the £1.

Thus, because of earned income relief and a single person's allowance of £220, using the figures that applied up to April, 1969, a single man does not start paying tax until his income is just under £300; the corresponding figure for a married man is nearly £475. Thus the additional reliefs that a person might be entitled to are of no value to a single man whose income is below £300 and a married man whose income is below £475. To take an example, a married man with income below £475 obtains no benefit from the children's allowances even though he has children.

In a similar way, if we take children's allowances into account, a couple with one child do not start paying tax until their income is nearly £600, with two children over £700, with three nearly £900. Because of reduced rates of tax on the first £300 of taxable income, then, these figures become £900, £1,000 and £1,200 respectively before full tax relief is obtainable on further concessions, as, for example, interest or mortgage payments.

The tax system thus has built into it a system which helps those who are relatively well off without assisting the really poor. The surtax-payer gains most from the system of reliefs, the poorest members nothing. This paradox of the tax system is inseparable from the system of giving reliefs via income tax.[4]

It has been suggested that tax concessions should be extended to all citizens. Those citizens, for example, who have children and an income below £475 should receive a supplement equal in value to the allowance for a standard-rate taxpayer. Thus for a child under eleven the allowance against assessable income is £115, which at standard-rate tax of 8*s*. 3*d*. in the £1 is worth £47 8*s*. 9*d*. The present housing mortgage scheme was designed to overcome the drawback discussed above: a person can opt from 1968 either to pay the market rate of interest and claim a deduction from his assessable income or to take a loan at a reduced rate of interest. The basis of the social services and social provision is currently undergoing a reappraisal, and it can be questioned whether the housing scheme does more than partly patch up a system which needs more drastic remodelling. It can be argued, for example, that the need to extend the current tax concessions on life insurance is as great as in the case of mortgage interest. These matters will be extended in Chapter 18.

A look at the tax rates in force and working out a few examples will soon convince the reader that both the average rates of tax (income divided by tax) and the marginal rates of tax (tax paid on the last increment of income) do not impinge on higher and higher income levels in a smooth progression. Income tax is nearly a flat-rate tax, over £5,000 of earned-income surtax leads to progression.

The high rates of tax on very high incomes have frequently been said to act as a disincentive to effort, or to drive high-rate taxpayers

[4] Abel-Smith, B., and Townsend, P. (1965). This survey indicated that in 1960 there were 7·5 million persons, or 14% of the population, who were not living at a higher standard than 140% of the basic National Assistance scales. Poverty, as thus defined, *showed an increase* over a previous survey for the years 1953-4. The immediate causes of poverty were mainly old age and large families. The number of children in these households was estimated at 2¼ millions. They conclude (page 66): 'On the whole the data we have presented contradicts the commonly held view that a trend towards greater equality has accompanied the trend towards greater affluence.' See also Cole, D. and Utting, J. (1962) and *Circumstances of Families* (1967).

to take up residence abroad, although empirical evidence on this matter is largely lacking. Taking the latter point first, it has already been shown that these high rates are to some extent a sham because of the way income is at present defined. If the definition of income is reworked on the lines of the total-accretion principle then it may well be that the degree of progression in the system and the levels reached by the highest rates will have to be looked at anew. The present levels may well be tolerated because people reason that rough justice is being done: high rates on some parts of income being offset by low or no tax on other parts of income. The waste that this causes by the reshuffling of income and assets has already been noted. If income is redrawn on total-accretion lines and comes to form the main source of revenue, then also the problem of jumps in the degree of progression take on a more serious aspect.

A glance at the table on sources of revenue that appears in Chapter 9, on 'Revenue', will reveal a common error. There seems to be an almost universal tendency to take a particular tax in isolation from the rest of the tax system and to make judgments about the regressiveness or unfairness in one way or another of that particular tax. A particularly blatant form of this error is to assume that, because income and surtax, taken together, are highly progressive, we therefore have a highly progressive tax system as a whole. However, as the revenue table shows, income and surtax together account for roughly 33% of government revenue. Some of the other sources of revenue are regressive in their impact—for example, many of the Customs and Excise taxes and National Health contributions.

Capital gains tax

Sufficient has already been said to make it clear that the position before a capital gains tax was introduced was far from satisfactory.

The Finance Act, 1962 (passed by a Conservative government), was the first attempt at taxing capital gains. The importance lies not so much in the Act itself as in introducing the principle of taxing capital gains. The debate that preceded and followed the Act did much to blow fresh air into this corner of taxation, and made the passage of the more throughgoing Act of 1965 much easier. In 1965 the debate was hardly about the principle of taxing capital gains, which was now no longer a matter of party politics. Brief details of these two Acts follow before we attempt an evaluation of how far they succeeded in clearing up the previously unsatisfactory situation.

THE FINANCE ACT, 1962

This Act introduced the taxation of short-term gains. The short-term was defined as six months, except for land and buildings, where the period was three years or less. The tax applied to new transactions only: disposal of an asset acquired before April 10th, 1962, was not subject to the tax.

Assets chargeable to the tax included all forms of property other than those specifically excluded, whether situated inside or outside the United Kingdom. Thus stocks, shares, securities and land were included. The main assets excluded were an individual's main residence, tangible movable property and buildings (factories, shops, etc.) and ancillary land occupied and used solely for the purposes of a trade, profession or vocation, in the case of an acquisition and disposal by a person who occupies and uses them for such purposes.

Capital gains on chargeable assets, after allowance had been made for any capital losses, were treated as unearned income and taxed accordingly. The tax did not apply to gains on property passing at death.

It will be seen that this tax was a discretionary one in the sense that keeping assets other than land for six months and one day, and land for three years and one day gave complete immunity from the tax. Its importance, it has already been suggested, was in introducing the idea of taxing capital gains.

THE FINANCE ACT, 1965

This Act introduced a two-stage tax on capital gains realized by persons on the disposal of assets which occurred after April 6th, 1965 (companies' capital gains are charged to corporation tax). The first stage is a tax on short-term gains realized from the disposal within twelve months of acquisition of assets acquired after April 6th, 1965. These, as we have already seen, will be charged as income. They can thus be taxed at zero rate, or at surtax, or some intermediary rate according to the tax status of the recipient of the gain. The second stage is a long-term capital gains tax, i.e. on gains disposed of twelve months or more from the date of acquisition. These will be taxed at a flat rate of 30% unless it is to the individual's benefits to have the gains taxed on an alternative basis.

The alternative basis is that an individual may elect to settle his liability for tax (on the whole capital gain) by having part of the gain taxed at his marginal rate of income or surtax, as the case may be. The fraction of the gain to be counted as income is: (*a*) one half where the net gains are less than £5,000, (*b*) where the net gain is more than £5,000, the sum of £2,500 is deducted from the total net gain. This alternative is a substantial concession. Rule (*a*) can be stated as: one-half of the marginal rate of tax is payable on the whole net capital gains where gains are below £5,000. With the standard rate of income tax at 8*s.* 3*d.* in the £, this is equivalent to a tax of 20·6% instead of 30%.

From the tax year 1967-8, long-term capital gains of individuals will be exempt from tax if, after deducting allowable losses, they do not exceed £50 for the year.

THE SHORT-TERM TAX

This tax followed the previous Act in charging short-term gains to income tax, but widened the range of assets and extended the time-period from six to twelve months. The range of assets is the same as that for long-term gains and will be dealt with under that heading. The 1962 time-limit of three years for land was abolished, land being treated in the same way as other assets chargeable under the short-term tax if realized within twelve months, or the long-term tax if over twelve months. However, since the Land Commission Act, 1967, land is now treated separately if it is sold for a new use. Details of this Act are given in Chapter 16. A gain made on the change of ownership of land where no change in the land's existing use occurs is still taxed as a capital gain.

The short-term tax does not, however, apply to capital gains deemed to be realized at death. These gains, even though the assets have been owned for less than twelve months, are chargeable to the long-term tax, i.e. at what in most cases will be a lower rate.

Losses can be offset against short-term capital gains and, if necessary, carried forward; offset is not allowed against long-term capital gains or other income.

THE LONG-TERM TAX

The long-term tax applies to assets sold after April 6th, 1965, which have been held for one year or more. The time of acquisition of the asset is immaterial: it could have been acquired before or after 1965, but the tax is not retrospective. For assets owned on April 6th, 1965, only the proportion of the gain attributable to the period after April 6th, will be taxable. The gain can be ascertained in one of two ways. One is the difference between the amount actually received on sale and its market value on April 6th, 1965. In the case of securities quoted on the Stock Exchange, there is no difficulty in ascertaining market value at this date; in some other cases this may be difficult if a valuation of the asset has not been undertaken. The second method of ascertaining the taxable gain is a straight time-apportionment formula. Thus an asset acquired for £100 one year prior to April 6th, 1965, and sold one year after for £200 would attract tax on half of the gain, i.e. £50. If the asset had been kept for two years after April 6th, 1965, and if it was still sold for a gain of £100, then two-thirds of this sum would attract tax, i.e. £66⅔.

ASSETS CHARGEABLE

The general presumption is that all assets are chargeable to either the short- or long-term tax unless they are exempt. The main exemptions are a principal private residence to the extent that it is occupied as such, Savings Certificates, Premium Bonds, Defence Bonds, and National Development Bonds, normal life-assurance policies on surrender or maturity, tangible movable property (i.e. chattels) disposed of for £1,000 or less and, since March, 1958, tangible movable assets which are wasting assets; important works of art and other objects of national, scientific, historic or artistic interest, provided that they remain in this country and are not sold otherwise than to a national institution, university or local authority, the first £5,000 of net gains (i.e. gains less losses) deemed to be realized at death, gifts of chargeable assets, provided that their value does not in total exceed £100 for each individual donor each year, and private motor vehicles. Since April 1969 government securities, or securities issued by a public corporation and guaranteed by the government, are not chargeable to long-term capital gains tax or, in the case of long-term gains of companies, corporation tax. This budget also excluded from the long-term capital gains tax, gains that do not exceed £50 in any year.

OFFSET FOR CAPITAL LOSSES

Losses can be offset against capital gains in any year, and if gains are not sufficient, net losses can be carried forward without time limit and set against gains of future years. Losses, however, can be offset only against long-term gains, and cannot be offset against short-term gains or other income.

GAINS ON BEQUEATHED PROPERTY

Assets are deemed to be realized on the death of their owner and capital gains are taxed at the long-term rate (even if the assets were acquired within twelve months); however, the first £5,000 of net gains are exempt from the tax.

EXEMPTION FROM THE TAX AND SPECIAL CASES

A number of bodies which are normally treated in special ways for tax purposes are exempt from the tax. These are chiefly charities, approved superannuation funds, friendly societies, registered trade unions and local authorities.

Trustees are in general liable to pay capital gains on assets in the trust, with some provisions to ease the number of times the assets are deemed to be realized. An important clause makes discretionary and other trusts which have no limited interests in possession liable to tax on their accrued gains every ten years.

Evaluation of the capital gains tax

How does the capital gains tax stand up to the standard of the 'total accretion of income'?

The first thing to note is that the revenue from this tax is likely to be quite modest for many years to come. An asset acquired twenty years ago may have appreciated several hundred times in value, but the change in value from April 6th, 1965, is on the valuation basis all that matters for the purpose of the tax. If the asset in question depreciates in value from this date then a loss is available, which can be offset against other gains, in spite of the fact that the asset may have appreciated many times in value over its purchase price. This criticism does not apply if the time-apportionment formula is used. There is a general presumption against retrospective legislation, and in particular retrospective tax legislation. There may be very good grounds for circumscribing a government's power in this direction, but at the same time it must be pointed out that it gives an excellent weapon to vested interests to resist changes that are not in their interest, but could conceivably be in the nation's interest. In view of the sharp rise that has taken place in many capital values since the war, and in view of the general agreement that the old system was inequitable, a case can be made that the tax should have been back-dated for a number of years, or at least that where the value of the assets was known at April 6th, 1965, the overall gain should be taken into account before allowing loss offset.

Although the revenue gain is likely to take many years to build up, the tax represents in principle a major breakthrough—one of the few major changes in the fiscal system that has come about in peace-time conditions. Some of the criticisms that can be made of the tax comes from the inevitable conflict that results from putting principles into practice. Of this kind is the exemption from tax of gifts of chargeable assets, provided that their value does not in total exceed £100 for each individual donor each year, and exclusion of chattels disposed of for £1,000 or less. Because of the ease of evasion and the cost of trying to collect tax on small sums, it is almost inevitable that such exemption should be given, and is the reason for the exclusion of the first £50 of gains from the long-term tax since 1967-8. The same reasons of ease of evasion and cost of collection are given for the exclusion of gambling winnings (presumably without offset for gambling losses). It may well be that separate taxation of these winnings is preferable.

It is much more difficult to justify the taxation of long-term gains at a maximum flat rate of 30%. The principle of progressive taxation of 'income' (narrowly defined) has long been accepted, and it seems illogical to charge a flat-rate tax on part of income when this is more widely drawn. It seems little justification to argue, as some commentators have done, that current income tax rates are too high. Income tax rates are to some extent as high as they are because income is so badly defined, and one of the benefits to be expected from widening the scope of income is that tax rates and the progression of the tax can be looked at anew. The conclusion seems inescapable that if it is right to charge short-term gains, arbitrarily drawn at one year, to income tax, it is right to charge long-term in the same way. The fact that short-term gains may result from speculation is, under the total-accretion principle, irrelevant.

The only valid case that it seems possible to make, on total-accretion lines, for the more lenient treatment of capital gains is the present inability to spread fluctuating income over a number of years. In Chapter 11 on 'The Criterion of Ability to Pay', it was argued that some form of averaging was desirable under any form of progressive tax. The argument against taxing that part of the gain which is due to inflation was dismissed on the grounds that there is no case for protecting one section of income from inflation.

Since capital gains on a significant scale are likely to accrue to a very small section of the population, the case for a flat rate appears even more inequitable. A single man with an earned income of £10,000 will pay just over £4,280 in tax and surtax. A capital gain of £10,000 will be liable to a maximum tax of £3,000, regardless of how much or how little income and wealth the owner already possesses. The peculiar ethic that it is only income, narrowly defined, which should be taxed at highly progressive rates has still to be excised from the system.[5]

[5] It may be argued that the man may have less 'real capital' after realizing his gain of £10,000 than when he made the original investment, and that he is paying £3,000 of tax on a non-existent real gain. The pros and cons of this argument were dealt with in the previous chapter at some length. It was there concluded that public finance should be concerned with a person's relative tax position, changes in the value of money affect all sectors of the community in different degrees, compensation for one sector results in less equity, not more.

In view of the very unequal distribution of wealth in this country, which has already been commented on, the exclusion of the first £5,000 of net gains at death seems indefensible in a country where all political parties pay lip-service to the need for some redistribution of wealth. Redistribution at death is the least painful way of achieving this end, and the one likely to cause least economic disturbance.

It was argued in Chapter 11 on the 'The Criterion of Ability to Pay' that the total exclusion of owner-occupied houses from the capital-gains tax confers a benefit on house-owners as compared with those who rent property, and is, in addition, likely to inflate the demand for houses. In America, where capital gains have been taxed for many years,

> Gain on the sale of a residence is taxable as a capital gain but a loss is not deductible. Since 1954, for the federal tax, the capital basis of a residence sold may be transferred to a new one acquired within 18 months if the cost of the new is the same or higher than the sale price of the old, and pro rata if the cost is less, so that capital gains is in effect postponed for such 'paired' transactions. In 1964, Congress allowed additional exemption for gains on homes sold by persons over age 65.
>
> Shultz, W. J. and Harriss, C. L. (1965), 249.

Amendment on these lines would appear to be desirable. Owner-occupied houses would then be liable for capital gains, either when the proceeds were used for other purposes or at death.[6]

[6] The complete exclusion from tax of capital gains in the case of owner-occupied houses serves to further entangle what has been for many years an illogical, absurd and unjust situation. The only people who do not receive a subsidy from public funds are the occupants of privately rented houses. About half of these private tenants are 'subsidized' by their landlords because their premises are subject to rent-control. All tenants, both private and council, pay rents out of taxed income, but most council tenants receive subsidies. A much larger element of subsidy usually accrues to the owner-occupier while he is buying his house, because of tax relief allowed on interest payments. Since the abolition of Schedule A tax, no income is imputed to the owner for the value of the services of his property, so that this tax relief results in a direct reduction in tax.

Always an unpopular tax, we are unlikely for political reasons to see the reintroduction of Schedule A, however desirable this would be on grounds of equity. An alternative way is to allow a private tenant to offset the part of his rent that goes towards interest payment on the capital sum invested in his house against tax, in the same way that an owner can offset his mortgage payments. This proposal, while it would go some way to achieving equity between persons, suffers from administrative complexities and the drawback noted previously that the poorest section of the community derive no benefit from income-tax concessions. More drastic remodelling of the system is required if we are to break out of the present near-tragic situation. For a discussion on this and other aspects of housing, see Hemming, M. F. W. and Duffy, H. (August, 1964), 39-59.

Finally, some word should be added on the cost of administering this tax. The exclusion from the long-term capital gains tax of individuals where, after deducting allowable losses, the gains do not exceed £50 for the year will simplify the administrative task, at a sacrifice of some degree of equity. It should be noted that, in so far as it is now less profitable to switch assets around for a pure tax advantage, in time it could lead to a more productive use of manpower, even though the Inland Revenue staff may have to be increased. The costs of tax-collection do not form a large percentage of the amount of revenue collected, but there is no doubt that the capital gains tax will increase costs for some time to come. In the author's opinion, the serious distortions present in the old system justify this increase in cost. The 'cake of custom' has been broken. It can be hoped that a fruitful period of public discussion can now take place on the kind of modifications still needed.

Summary

Past attempts to allow for differences in individual and family circumstances has resulted in a complex code of personal income taxation which nevertheless fails to help the most needy in the community.

In recent years differences between citizens who obtain their incomes from an employer and those who obtain their income from a business have been accentuated, and has led many who are able to do so to arrange their affairs in this form. The latter are able to deduct for the using up of capital before arriving at a figure for tax, profit retained in the business is not, generally speaking, subject to the progressive rates of tax of personal income, and, finally, they are able to claim more generous expenses. Suggestions have been put forward that individuals should be taxed at a lower rate to compensate for these advantages or that an annual charge should be imposed on businesses for these privileges. Both suggestions are not without their difficulties. If a value-added tax is adopted this would provide an opportunity to look afresh at the whole concept of capital allowances and deductible expenses.

The capital gains tax, in spite of the small amount of revenue received at present, represents a major shift in principle. The distinction between short-term gains, already changed from six to twelve months and taxed as income, and long-term gains taxed at a maximum rate of 30% does not appear to be based on any valid grounds except the present inability to spread fluctuating income over a number of years. If a scheme of income-averaging is adopted, the case for counting all gains as income would be very much strengthened.

13
Company taxation

This indirect benefit of incorporation [retained profits on which surtax is not payable] cannot fairly be ignored in framing the tax system applicable to corporation profits. It is a fiscal matter and bears upon the proper distribution of the burden of tax upon different kinds of income. The difficulty remains, however, that the saving achieved is achieved on behalf of the shareholders as a whole; the money is in most cases outside the control of any one individual shareholder and is certainly not directly at his disposal as free personal income.

Royal Commission on the Taxation of Profits and Income (1955), para. 54.

Company taxation is a complex matter in which the public-finance, accounting and legal aspects twist and interweave. This chapter attempts to give a broad description of company tax, concentrating on important issues. It starts with a factual description of changes in company tax. This leads to a discussion of the principles of company tax and to a discussion of the value or otherwise of tax discrimination against distributed profits. With this necessary background, the tax system before the Finance Act, 1965, can be understood and the important changes introduced by the Act with the introduction of corporation tax. One aspect of this, the taxation of companies trading overseas, is treated at some length. The next section then treats important, and even more controversial, matters relating to the concept of profit which is subject to tax. Finally, it looks at the important system of investment allowances and grants which has grown up since the war.

Company tax in this context is used to cover the ordinary meaning of taxes levied directly on company profits. It will be clear from previous chapters that a number of other taxes affect companies, and may be paid in whole or in part by them. Purchase tax has been previously considered and treated as a tax on consumers. As a general rule this is probably correct, but changes in purchase tax may have sharp repercussions on industry in altering demand for the products concerned. This will be taken up in Part III of this book. Capital gains tax, the selective employment tax and employers' National Health and pension contributions were looked at in previous chapters and will not be developed further.

Changes in company taxation

During the years immediately following the First World War a special tax was levied on the profits of companies to absorb some of the excess profits companies were able to make as a result of the war. In 1937 a national defence contribution was imposed. This continued until 1947, when a profits tax (paid on profits above a certain amount) was levied. This differentiated according to whether the profits were retained in the business or distributed to shareholders. The tabulation below lists the changes made in this tax. This was adapted from Rubner, A. (June, 1964), 347-59. For a comment on this article see Harcourt, G. C., and Whittington, G. (1965), 373-8. An opposing view is given by Feldstein, M. S. (December, 1967), 947-53.

Table 1

Year	*Income Tax*	*Net Profits Tax* On Undistributed Profits	On Distributed Profits
	%	%	%
1947	45·0	5·4	13·8
1949	45·0	5·4	16·5
1951	47·5	5·2	26·3
1952	47·5	2·5	22·5
1953	45·0	2·5	22·5
April, 1955	42·5	2·5	22·5
November, 1955	42·5	2·5	27·5
1956	42·5	3·0	30·0
1958	42·5	10·0	10·0
1959	38·8	10·0	10·0
1960	38·8	12·5	12·5
1961-6	38·8	15·0	15·0

The column under 'Income Tax' merely reflects the changes in the standard rate of income tax to which taxable profits of the preceding accounting year were subject. The next two columns show the additional profits tax which were levied on profits of the current year if these were above £12,000 with reduced rates for profits between £2,000 and £12,000. Except for the period from 1958 to 1966, a heavier—sometimes a much heavier tax—was levied on that part of profit which was distributed to shareholders than on that part which was retained in the business. The discrimination, which seems to be based on no clear logical principle, was at its highest in 1956, when profits tax was 3% on undistributed profits and 30% on distributed profits.

The principles of company tax

The erratic gyrations of the net profits tax lead to the question of whether or not it is possible to find any principles on which company taxation should be based. On reference back to the section on total accretion of income, it will be found that if we are adhering strictly to this principle and if we are trying to treat people in equal positions equally, then it is the shareholders, as owners of companies, that should be taxed rather than the companies themselves. It is only in the case of profits retained in the business that a problem of reallocation arises.

It is sometimes suggested that company tax should be reduced or abolished and that the whole of company profits should be allocated to the owners. In the case of public companies, shareholders would receive with their dividend warrants a statement of their portion of the profits which the company had decided to retain in the business. The shareholder would be liable for tax on both sums.

This solution has weighty objections. It is usually rejected on the grounds that a person should not be liable for more tax than the sum he receives. This could occur under this scheme, e.g. where a top-rate surtax-payer is a shareholder in a company that retains most of the profit in the business. Even if this argument is accepted in principle, it is one which is likely to carry less weight under the total-accretion principle, since the adoption of this would enable a revision of tax rates to be made. The argument that this would stop the flow of funds to companies, from high-tax-payers, even allowing for the adjustments of tax rates under the accretion principle, is more serious. However just on grounds of equity, it seems unlikely, for this reason, to be a practical proposition.

The adoption of the accretion principle of income would greatly reduce the problem of inequity. Distributed profits would be part of the income of the recipient, as at present. Retained profits, to the extent that they enhance the value of the business, would also be taxed as income when the gains are realized. This solution favours the investor, both because he has a deferred liability for tax and because he has a tax cushion if retained profits do not enhance the value of the business. This degree of inequity may be thought tolerable because of the incentive it is likely to give to investment.

The solution outlined above leaves open the question of whether companies should be taxed as entities in their own right, apart from taxing shareholders. On the one hand are those who hold that the only problem is to achieve a system that will tax shareholders as closely as possible to the position that would be reached if all profits were distributed; on the other hand are those who argue that, in effect, companies can be considered as entities or personalities in their own right and should be taxed accordingly. Before definite answers can be given, it is necessary to know the incidence of company taxation—whether, that is, this ultimately falls on the shareholder, the workers or the consumer. The importance of this question also tends to merge with that of tax incentives to business investment, which is taken up at the end of this chapter.

Does tax discrimination against distributed profits help investment?

Post-war British governments have been concerned with increasing capital investment; the changes in tax on distributed profits, as opposed to undistributed profits, reflects to some extent a conflict on ways of achieving this. The rationale behind sharp discrimination against distributed profits is that this should encourage capital investment by the ploughing back of profits.[1] A number of factors have to be weighed in order to evaluate this. Firstly, it can be said that discrimination against paying dividends, by itself, causes no incentive to material investment, since firms may merely acquire liquid assets. The number of take-over bids that took place after dividend discrimination had been in force for some years is often quoted as evidence that this is so, since in a number of these take-overs the excessive liquid position of the company being taken over was an attraction. As many factors enter into the decision to take over another company, this evidence is hard to quantify.

More serious is the question of how important different sources of finance are to companies. Relying on ploughing back profits limits a company to a growth rate that is compatible with its profits. A company wanting to expand faster than this must seek funds from

[1] It is sometimes suggested that discrimination against distributed profits is in effect discrimination against consumption by shareholders. In view of the facilities for consumption given by capital appreciation in the post-war period, this argument is not very sound.

outside. Borrowing on fixed interest by way of debentures or preference shares has its limitations. Too high a 'gearing'—that is, the level of its fixed-interest payments compared to its ordinary or equity shares—leaves a company very vulnerable if profits should fall. In a bad year equity dividends can be reduced or passed over altogether, but fixed-interest payments must be met or, as a rule, the debenture or preference holders have a right to supersede the management by appointing a receiver or other person to look after their interests. An equity issue means that the market for the shares needs to be a good one, and one of the most important means of ensuring this is to have a liberal dividend policy. We thus come to a direct conflict. If dividends are deliberately discriminated against in order to encourage investment, the effect may be to hamper those companies which want very fast growth and need to go to the equity market in order to do so.

What value should be placed on this argument? There is some evidence that equity finance has been important for many fast-growing companies (see Tew, B., and Henderson, R. F. (1959)), but before we conclude that dividend-discrimination has been bad in this respect, it is necessary to establish that the discrimination has been sufficiently severe to draw funds away from the company sector to some other sector of the economy—that is, that there has been a general shortage of funds for company finance. The evidence does not point in this direction; certain sectors—for example, small companies and new companies—may have had difficulty in getting funds, but this has always been so and has little to do with dividend-restraint. Company dividend policy, in spite of high tax at times on dividends, has nevertheless resulted in an attractive market. If company dividend policy is, for one reason or another, inflexible—and there is some evidence for this (Rubner, A. (June, 1964))—we reach the position that it is possible that Britain, by taxing retained profits less than distributed profits, has nevertheless taxed the shareholder more on balance than those countries who discriminate, on grounds of equity, more heavily against retained profits. This argument depends on the assumption that companies have an inflexible dividend policy, that whatever the level of tax on distributed profits they will try to pay out a fixed proportion of profit. The argument should not be pushed too far!

A further point sometimes made against the discrimination of distributed profits is that such a policy favours the *status quo*. Companies making large profits have the ability to grow, but these may not be dynamic companies. Distributing the profits to shareholders leaves them free to invest in any company. The extent to which dividends are used directly or indirectly to finance new investment is once again a field where little empirical evidence is available.[2]

What emerges from this mass of contradictory opinion? It would appear that many factors influence the real investment of companies. These factors are not likely to be stable over time for one company, nor for companies as a whole to lead at one particular time to a predominant influence of any particular factor. This negative conclusion has policy implications. Simple-minded theories that investment will be increased or decreased by this or that amount of dividend discrimination seem incorrect: such discrimination is unlikely to make any substantial difference one way or the other to investment.

The system of tax before the Finance Act, 1965

A company's taxable profits of the preceding year were liable to tax at the standard rate of income tax, and in addition the taxable profits of the current year, if large enough, were subject to profits tax. From 1961 profits tax was an additional 15% if profits exceeded £12,000 per year. The rate was scaled down for profits between £2,000 and £12,000: below £2,000, profits were only taxed to standard rate of income tax. Under this system it was thus a matter of indifference (from a tax viewpoint) to a company whether it paid out profits in the form of dividends or whether it retained these in the business. The system before 1961 was, as we have seen, one where distributed profits were taxed more heavily than retained profits. (The recipient of the dividend was credited with the standard rate of tax paid by the company, so that he had no more to pay if he was himself a standard-rate income-tax-payer. If he paid at lower or higher rates, he was entitled respectively to a rebate of tax or indebted to the Inland Revenue for the difference.)

One reason why it is very difficult to link changes in tax on companies with changes in their investment behaviour is that both their current-year profits and preceding-year profits were liable to tax because the liability to income tax was lagged by one year. Since companies are under no obligation to keep standard accounting dates for making up their accounts, the time over which tax changes affecting companies was spread amounted to two or more years.

The Finance Act, 1965

The Finance Act of 1965 introduced a corporation tax in place of

[2] This argument is important on 'welfare' grounds. If it is good that capital should be mobile and the rate of return should tend to equality in different use, it would seem desirable to distribute profits and let the recipients reinvest (or consume) them as they think fit.

the two-tier system just described. The corporation tax separates the taxation of companies from that of individuals. Companies are liable to this tax on their taxable profit, including capital gains, but will not be liable to income tax. Payment of interest (e.g. on debenture stock) is treated as a charge against profits, and will not therefore be subject to corporation tax. The initial rate of the tax was 40%, increased to 42½% from April, 1968 and to 45% from April, 1969. However, shareholders will be liable to income tax and, surtax, where appropriate, on dividends and other distributions, and, as a matter of machinery, companies will be required to deduct income tax, at the standard rate, from payments to shareholders and hand the sums over to the Inland Revenue. In essence, companies pay a flat rate of tax of 45% and split dividend payments into two, one part of which they send to the shareholders, the balance to the Inland Revenue.

This is back to the position of effective discrimination against dividends that operated before 1958. It is also back to the questions that were raised in the previous discussion to which no satisfactory answers could be given. If dividend policy is very inflexible, this is saying in effect that it is a matter of indifference to company directors how much they have to split off from their dividend payments to send to the Inland Revenue, so long as the flow of funds to the company sector is not adversely affected. On the other hand, it can be argued that directors will reason that every £1 of profit retained in the business is worth 11*s.* after paying corporation tax at 45%, whereas to the average taxpayer it is worth very much less, because the shareholder will in addition be liable for income tax on this 11*s.* If the result is not to affect dividend policy, then the shareholder is in effect taxed more heavily compared to other taxed income on that part of profits which is distributed to him and less heavily on that part which is retained in the business.

In these circumstances, whether the shareholder gains or loses from the tax compared to the position he would be in if he was credited with the whole of profits and liable to income tax depends on the shareholder's tax position. If, however, the result is to cause companies to retain more profit in the business, as well as the problem of deciding the equity position, we have the more serious problem, in this context, of deciding whether it is to the benefit of the economy as a whole to encourage firms to retain profits.

The corporation tax made other changes with far-reaching results, which will now be considered.

Basis of assessment

The old system of tax was concerned, as has been shown, with two years' profits. The new tax fixes the rate of corporation tax each financial year, and that rate will be applicable to the profits of that financial year. Normally, the tax will be payable nine months after the end of the company's accounting year or, for the majority of existing companies, on January 1st. The financial year referred to above starts on April 1st and ends the following March 31st.

If a company's accounting year coincides with the dates of the financial year, no problem arises as to the rate of tax that is applicable to those profits. If, however, the two do not coincide, then a time-apportionment basis will be used. Thus a company whose accounting year ends on December 31st, 1968, will have one-quarter of its taxable profits charged at the rate fixed for the financial year ending March 31st, 1968, and the remaining three-quarters at the rate for the financial year ending March 31st, 1969. (Obviously, if the tax rate remains unchanged, no problem of time apportionment arises.)

General opinion seems to be that this method of assessment, once the complications of the changeover have been assimilated, is a welcome simplification of the tax structure, companies being subject to an assessment on one year's profits rather than two.

Taxation of company profits earned overseas

The corporation tax has been heavily criticized because of its treatment of companies who earn profits overseas. In order to decide whether this criticism is just or whether the corporation tax merely ended a favoured tax position, it is necessary to go back and establish the procedure in force before the change.

The essence of the problem

The essence of the problem can be quite simply stated: should companies who earn profits overseas and who pay taxes to overseas governments be given any allowance against taxes that they are liable for in their home country?

Over the years a general principle has been established that income so earned should be subject to home taxation, with various concessions. Britain has made agreements with about seventy countries whereby she agrees to forgo the right to tax at full rates, in return for concessions of a like nature. The distinction must now be made between a company that has a subsidiary company which is *located, managed and controlled* abroad and other companies. The general rule is that no United Kingdom tax is payable by subsidiary companies in the first group on profits *retained abroad*. Profits that are remitted to the United Kingdom, and *all profits* of other subsidiary companies are subject to United Kingdom tax, but allowance is given for tax paid abroad.

The allowance takes the form, not of a deduction from gross profits to arrive at taxable profit, but as a direct offset to United Kingdom tax liability. Therefore, if foreign tax is no higher than United Kingdom tax, a company pays no more tax than would be the case if the profits were earned in the United Kingdom.

We now come to the core of the argument. The corporation tax in general continued with the arrangements indicated above, whereby tax paid overseas was offset against home company tax. This was deemed to be corporation tax; no offset was allowed against income tax charged to the individual (but collected by the companies) on dividend payments. As a transitional matter, tax relief is being given to companies which pay overseas tax on income from direct investments which is in excess of corporation tax. The relief, which tapers off after two years, comes to an end after five years. See *Corporation Tax* (1965), on which this section draws.

Before the corporation tax a company's United Kingdom tax-bill, if its profits were more than £12,000, amounted to 53¾% (made up of standard rate tax of 7*s*. 9*d*. in the £1, plus 15% profits tax). Corporation tax at 40% means that companies trading overseas who pay taxes in excess of 40% are worse off. They would in this case not have to pay corporation tax, but whereas before the United Kingdom tax incorporated the shareholders' liability to income tax at the standard rate, now it doesn't. An example should make this clearer.

Assume a company which earns a profit overseas of £20,000, on which it pays £10,000 overseas tax and repatriates the remaining £10,000. The standard rate of income tax is taken at the old rate of 7*s*. 9*d*. in the £1 in each case, and corporation tax at the old rate of 40%.

BEFORE CORPORATION TAX

U.K. tax liability, 53¾%, i.e. £10,750, against which it received a credit of £10,000, leaving £750 to pay. Profits after tax thus £9,250. It could pay, say, £6,000 to shareholders tax free, i.e. pay a net dividend of £6,000, which equals a gross dividend of £9,796 (the difference being tax at 7*s*. 9*d*. in the £1 on the gross dividend of £9,796). The company would have £3,250 to retain in the business.

AFTER CORPORATION TAX

U.K. tax liability, 40%, or £8,000. £10,000 already paid overseas, so no further liability for corporation tax in the U.K. Company now has £10,000 profit. If it still wishes to pay a net dividend of £6,000, it must also pay £3,796 to the Inland Revenue. The company would thus have £10,000, less £9,796, i.e. £204 left in the business, compared to the previous figure of £3,250.

Fair or unfair to companies trading overseas?

In the example given above we saw that under the old system of tax, individuals were credited with tax that had been paid, not to the Inland Revenue, but to some overseas government. One argument put forward for changing the system was that (since U.K. tax rates in this respect were higher than most overseas rates) companies had no incentive to take overseas tax rates into consideration when setting up overseas, since so long as overseas tax was below 53¾%, it was offset against U.K. tax. If the view is taken that a tax on dividends is a tax on individuals, then what companies are really complaining about is the fact that tax on companies is now lower in the United Kingdom than it was! Or, put the other way, that overseas taxes have not been reduced in line with U.K. taxes. We come back once more to the paradox: that we have no clear concept in use to judge the taxation of companies. Should we be thinking in terms of tax on the individual shareholder or tax on the company as an entity in its own right?

The concept of taxable profit

So far in this chapter it has been assumed that the 'taxable profit' of a company is a just and equitable one, and we have been looking at ways of taxing this sum. It is now necessary to look at this assumption and find out how taxable profits are determined. It should be stated at the outset that this question is even more controversial than the matters of company tax just discussed. It is just as fundamental: a correct method of taxing companies would give incorrect results if the tax was applied to an incorrect figure of company profit. The divisions on this subject are sometimes between accountants and economists, but not infrequently there are wide differences within each group. The subject is a complex one, and no more is attempted in this book than an outline of some of the most important features.

Profit and taxable profit

A company incurs costs in making a commodity or in providing a service and receives revenue when the product or service is sold. The difference between costs and revenue (which can be positive or negative) during a specified period of time is profit or loss. Profit or loss, being a residual figure, depends on what the tax authorities allow to be called 'costs', and what they allow to be called 'revenue'.

A convenient division of costs is into *fixed* and *variable*. Fixed refers to items which are necessary to carry on business, but are not completely used up in the process, e.g. buildings and machinery. The problem arises of how the costs of these fixed items are to be apportioned to each year's output. Variable refers to costs which cease if output ceases, e.g. labour and raw material costs. These variable costs are more easily apportioned to annual output, but even here doubts can arise. Should advertising, which is partly aimed at selling current output and partly aimed at building up the long-term goodwill of the firm, be allocated to the one or the other, or both? If both, how is it possible to separate the one kind of expenditure from the other? These, and a large number of other definitional points must be decided. In what follows we shall try and concentrate on the most important aspects. Depreciation will be discussed first. Investment allowances will be treated separately, although perhaps the two should be regarded together. A case can be made for separate treatment on the grounds that depreciation allowances take care of the equity aspect, while investment allowances are primarily concerned to increase the level of real investment; although the practical use of these measures may not accord with this simple division.

Depreciation

It is not generally realized how recent is the relief for the using up of assets in the course of business. To quote from the *Royal Commission on Tax*, 1955:

> The conception of depreciation allowances for fixed assets to which the first Tucker Committee gave their support illustrates how far expert views on the tax system had moved since 1920. In that year the Royal Commission were able to assert that income for purposes of taxation should in general be computed without regard to the amortisation of wasting assets. In contrast, in 1951 the Report of the expert committee accepted as a guiding principle '. . . the general proposition that the Income Tax system should give relief in respect of the wastage of all assets that are used up or consumed in the course of carrying on a business' (para. 322).

A little later the Commission says:

One thing must be said in this connection. The practical result of the changes since 1920 has been to afford a scheme of protection to 'material' capital that is not available to 'personal' capital. Our predecessors were apprehensive about this possibility when they wrote of the risk of creating 'grave inequalities between different classes of income'; and we have seen that it was on this ground, amongst others, that they rejected proposals for a general allowance for the amortisation of wasting assets (para. 325).

The precise details of current depreciation allowances is the concern of the accountant rather than ourselves. The broad system is to lay down the method of depreciation, the amount or the percentage of the cost of the asset which can be written off, and the number of years over which it is to be written off. These agreed sums may be deducted from gross profit before tax-liability is calculated. The agreed system of depreciation varies for different assets. The main categories are:

1. Industrial buildings and structures.
2. Plant and machinery.
3. Exploration, development and construction work in connection with mines, oil wells and other mineral sources.
4. Agricultural buildings and works.
5. Patent rights.
6. Expenditure on scientific research.

A business may adopt any system of depreciation that it wishes, but it is only allowed to offset against tax on the agreed scale.

Almost every aspect of the depreciation allowances is subject to some amount of controversy. Does depreciation cover the right items? Should more flexibility be allowed to companies to write off assets against tax as they wish, or should more uniformity be imposed? What is the correct treatment for an asset that is sold before it is fully depreciated? And so on. The reader is referred to the *Royal Commission on the Taxation of Profits and Income* (1955), for a discussion on these matters. Below a brief look is given to the principle of depreciation and depreciation and inflation.

THE PRINCIPLE OF DEPRECIATION

On the question of whether or not depreciation should be deductible from profits before tax, no clear principle seems to emerge. The Majority Report of the Royal Commission fell back on the argument: '. . . Whatever be the right rationalization, it is clear to us that they [capital allowances] have come to stay and they must be taken as an integral part of our system of taxing business profits. We are content to accept them on this basis . . .' (para. 328).

The Minority Report of the Royal Commission was more positive. They granted that an anomalous position was created because allowances are not given in respect of the wastage of human capital, but thought it would be impractical to try to introduce human capital into the system of depreciation allowances. The Minority Report put more weight on the anomaly that 'allowance is given for capital wastage, whilst no charge is imposed on capital gains'.

As the Minority rather than the Majority Report was followed in respect of capital gains, and we now have such a tax, this particular anomaly is taken care of. It seems that the general concensus of opinion now is that depreciation provisions should be allowed, the distortions that would be caused by its omission being greater than that due to the omission of human capital from the provisions.

Depreciation and inflation

The present system of depreciation allowances is based on the historic cost (that is, the original money cost) of the asset. In times of rising prices, the replacement cost of an asset may well be higher, and sometimes considerably higher, than the historic cost. Companies and their accountants frequently urge that allowance should be made for the change in the price-level by basing depreciation on replacement cost, or some alternative measure.

This argument, on which so much has been written, is plausible enough, but in the context of the present tax system represents a case of special pleading. It should be noted in this connection that while replacement costs may increase, so also may the receipts from current output of the capital asset, so that a firm is in a position to protect itself from inflation if it can raise prices. The Royal Commission on Tax quoted with approval the findings of the Tucker Committee on the Taxation of Trading Profits (1951): '. . . one objection common to all schemes, namely that they involve giving preferential treatment to all owners of businesses as against other classes of taxpayers' (para. 330). The Royal Commission on Tax summed up their position as follows:

(1) We do not accept that as a matter of principle a trader's profits in times of inflation must be computed with allowance for the cost of replacement of fixed assets or the fall in the purchasing power of money.
(2) We think that for the purposes of taxation a system of computing his profits that does not make allowance for these factors is preferable to one that does (para. 368).

The grounds for the rejection of depreciation based on other than historic cost is thus clear: inflationary and deflationary conditions affect all sectors of the community in different degrees; there is no case in equity for trying to compensate one sector. As will be seen in the section on investment incentives, this has the effect of making investment cheaper and can be considered as making some allowance for inflation. It seems better in principle to regard these allowances, not as attempts to allow for changes in the value of money, but as devices whereby the government can attempt to influence investment. They violate equity between different classes of taxpayers, but are accepted on grounds of investment criteria.

Investment incentives

INITIAL ALLOWANCES

Initial allowances were introduced with effect from April, 1946, as part of a new scheme of taxation designed to encourage re-equipment and modernization in productive industry. The scheme was one of accelerated depreciation. In addition to the allowance for depreciation that could be offset against profit before tax, a further allowance was granted in the year of purchase. However, over the remaining period allowed for depreciation, lower depreciation was given, so that over the whole period the same benefit was received. They can be looked on as a device to defer tax-liability or, the same thing, as a tax-free loan from the government.

The rates at the beginning were 20% for plant and machinery, 10% for industrial buildings and 10% for mining works. In 1949 the rate for plant and machinery was raised to 40%. They were suspended from April, 1952, because it was thought that the heavy calls which the defence programme would make on the engineering industry made it desirable to reduce the pressure of civilian demand for plant and machinery. In 1953 they were restored for the purpose of increasing investment in the assets selected: 20% was given for plant and machinery, 10% for industrial buildings and 40% for mining works. In 1954 they were changed by investment allowances.

As an inducement to invest, the initial allowance made only a small impact. Dow, J. C. R. (1964), 205, has estimated that it was equivalent to 'something like a reduction in the rate of interest by ½%. Its importance lay in providing an internal source of finance for the firm undertaking investment, providing the firm was paying taxes'.

INVESTMENT ALLOWANCES

In 1954 investment allowances were given on a range of assets. Initial allowances were not discontinued for those assets that formally received them and were not given the new allowance. The allowances were given in the year of purchase in a similar manner to the initial allowances, but, unlike them, they were not recouped in later years. Industrial and agricultural buildings and works were given a 10% investment allowance, machinery and plant, mining works, and scientific research assets 20%.

The system of initial and investment allowances continued with several switches and changes until 1966, when they were largely superseded by a system of grants.

ASSESSMENT OF INITIAL AND INVESTMENT ALLOWANCES

The Royal Commission on Taxation in 1955 expressed strongly the opinion that these allowances violate the principle that persons with equal incomes should bear an equal burden of tax. They go on:

> For these reasons we think that instruments of this kind will require to be justified in due course by convincing evidence that they are not only effective in achieving the results anticipated but also worth-while in the value of the results contrasted with the revenue foregone . . . (para. 421).

The evidence in 1966 as given in a White Paper on 'Investment Incentives' is that these measures have largely failed in their objectives:

> The National Plan makes it plain that the overriding need during the next few years is to give priority to those sectors of industry which can make the greatest contribution to strengthening the balance of payments. The benefits of the present system are too widely dispersed to be fully effective. Investment allowances are given for some items which have little or no relation to productive investment. For example, purchases of furniture, curtains and carpets in offices or cutlery in dining-rooms or canteens qualify for investment allowances. Television sets rented by the public do so too, since the purchase of the set by the rental firm qualifies (para. 14).

The White Paper goes on to list other defects; the fact that the allowances take an average eighteen months to be felt, that they are spread over a long period and uncertain because of the uncertainty about future tax rates; also firms with small profits get little benefit.

A more fundamental criticism is mentioned as a result of a survey carried out by the Confederation of British Industry. It appears that a substantial number of firms still do not take tax allowances fully into account in investment decisions. In many cases firms seem to have no rational policy of making investment decisions, but proceed 'by God and by guess'.

The remedy carried out to meet these criticisms was not to stop the incentives or to confine them to firms who could present a reasoned case for the allowances, but to convert them into cash grants. No mention was made in the White Paper of the equity aspects that had troubled the Royal Commission. The whole emphasis was on the need to provide an effective investment incentive.

INVESTMENT GRANTS

From January 17th, 1966, the system of investment allowances was swept away and replaced by a system of grants. Initial allowances continued on some assets.

The system of grants applies in respect of expenditure on new plant and machinery used in manufacturing or extraction industries, but excluding furniture and similar items mentioned above, which were criticized as making no contribution to productive investment. Manufacturing covers all the processes of making articles, including the intermediate stages of processing materials. Extraction covers quarrying, mining and the extraction of natural mineral deposits. Excluded from the grants are service industries and construction industries. Special arrangements were made in respect of ships, hovercraft and computers. In addition, the new legislation swept aside the old development districts (areas of the country that were deemed to need special measures) and introduced 'development areas'.

The development areas cover much wider tracts of country. In these areas investment grants are given on a more generous scale. The table on p. 172 shows the main items qualifying for grants with the rates of grant that applied during 1967 and 1968. The most usual grant was 25% in a non-development area and 45% in a development area. In 1969 these rates reverted back to their previous levels of 20 and 40% respectively.

The Development Areas are, as indicated in Chapter 10, now defined to include, except for small areas deemed to be sufficiently developed, Scotland, Northern England (i.e. the four northernmost counties of England plus the North Riding of Yorkshire), Wales, Merseyside and the South-western area, which takes in much of Devon and Cornwall.

Table 2

Rates of Investment Grants and Initial Allowances applicable to capital expenditure between January 1st, 1967, and December 31st, 1968

	Non-development Areas Grant	Initial Allowances, etc.	*Development Areas* Grant	Initial Allowances, etc.
	%	%	%	%
New plant and machinery for manufacturing, extraction or construction	25	—	45	—
Other plant and machinery, including second-hand and most vehicles	—	30	—	30
Plant and machinery for scientific research relating to qualifying processes	25	100 write-off[1]	45	100 write-off[1]
New buildings and structures				
Industrial	—	15	25 or 35[2]	15
Non-industrial	—	—	25 or 35[2]	—
Computers				
New	25	—	43[3]	—
Second-hand	—	30	—	30
Mining Works	25	—	45	—
Ships[5]	25	Free depreciation[4]	25	Free depreciation[4]
Hovercraft	25	—	25	—
Hotels from April, 1968[6]	20	—	25	—

[1] 100% write-off means that assets may be completely written-off against profits in the first year.

[2] These grants are conditional on an adequate provision of employment. The 35% rate is given to certain new undertakings where the Board of Trade consider that the problems involved justify additional assistance.

[3] A 45% grant is paid in a development area for computers if it is solely or primarily (*a*) for integration with machinery or plant which is or is to be used for carrying on a qualifying industrial process, (*b*) for carrying on qualifying research.

[4] 'Free depreciation' means that the taxpayer can claim depreciation allowance for tax purposes at whatever rate suits him, instead of at the rates prescribed under the ordinary rules.

[5] Except for fishing vessels, which receive separate and normally larger grants.

WHAT DO THESE GRANTS MEAN TO BUSINESSES?

Grants will not be treated as part of the taxable income of a business, but are assumed to reduce the capital cost of the assets to which they relate. Thus an asset costing £1,000 that qualifies for a grant of 45% will be deemed to cost the business £550. Depreciation is allowed on the net cost of £550. Future depreciation allowances against tax will be smaller to this extent, but if the allowances continue unchanged, so also will the effective replacement cost of the asset be reduced.

EVALUATION OF INVESTMENT GRANTS

Since the war the government has been evolving a new fiscal weapon to try to influence real private investment. The current system of grants (and initial allowances) gives a weapon that is free from most of the defects noted in connection with investment allowances. Once the scheme of grants is properly in operation, the grants should be paid within six months of the investment taking place. The grant is not dependent on the amount of profits being made, so that, for example, new businesses which have not yet begun to make profits will benefit. The system could be very flexible: it remains to be seen how flexibly it will be operated. It is flexible in the sense that grants differentiate between different geographical regions and different types of real investment. Finally, cash grants are more easily taken into account by firms when making their investment decisions.

Taken together with the depreciation allowances, there is no doubt that in manufacturing and extractive industries firms have been placed on a favourable footing *vis-à-vis* other firms and individuals. In time the benefits are likely to be fairly widely spread over the community in the form of better goods or goods cheaper than they would have been in the absence of grants, and in a better export performance. In the short run it should not be forgotten that these grants create an opportunity for the owners of these businesses to take most of the gain to themselves by not passing on the benefits to the consumer. Time alone will show which path has been taken.

There are strong arguments for modernizing these sectors of British industry, and the arguments as to whether investment grants are the best way to achieve this will go on for a long while. The Board

[6] From April, 1968, hotels qualify for grants towards the capital cost of new hotels and extensions and improvements. These are conditional on certain requirements being met as to the number of rooms available and to the accommodation not being made solely against advanced bookings. Hotels that satisfy these conditions also qualify for loan assistance.

of Trade has been given certain discretionary powers under the Act, and it may be that in future a case can be made for more rigorous selection amongst firms. The granting of allowances to all firms will undoubtedly help the progressive firm to keep in the forefront of developments; it will also have the effect of propping up the inefficient firm for a period of time. If minimum requirements were drawn up for each industry on criteria to be taken into account when making investment decisions, the receipt of an investment grant could be made conditional on these requirements being met. The working out of these criteria would be likely to stimulate fruitful discussion in the industries concerned as well as spreading existing knowledge, a process that can do little but good.

Summary

The taxation of companies raises many contentious problems and conflicts between the aims of equity and the aims of incentive to investment.

If, on the grounds that it will act as a disincentive to investment, the owners of companies are not to have the whole of business profits attributable to them, the adoption of the total-accretion principle would go a long way to achieving equity between shareholders and other taxpayers without seriously weakening investment in business.

On the general question of tax-discrimination against distributed profits, it was concluded that there is no clear evidence that this is likely to have marked effects on overall investment. While such discrimination is likely to help the company relying on ploughed-back profits for investment capital, it hinders rather than helps the company which relies on raising new equity capital. No simple answer can be given as to whether discrimination is desirable on equity considerations, since this depends both on the dividend policy of the company concerned and the recipient's own tax position.

The evidence of previous Royal Commissions on Tax is unanimous that the granting of depreciation allowances puts companies in a privileged tax position *vis-à-vis* the individual taxpayer. The system of initial allowances and investment grants further substantially favours some companies. These tax privileges are generally accepted as desirable in order to achieve investment and growth in the economy, and it is likely that at least some of the benefits will in time be spread more evenly through the economy in the form of prices lower than they would be in the absence of these privileges.

The most serious criticism of the system of allowances, and in particular of investment grants, is that, in spite of clear evidence that many firms were not using sensible investment criteria, the grants were nevertheless given to any firm which invested in the designated assets. They thus serve to prop up the inefficient firm as well as to help the progressive firm. A highly desirable reform would be the recognition that grants are a tax privilege, to be given only to those firms who have evaluated their investment projects on approved lines. The working out of investment criteria between industries and an appropriate government body—perhaps the Economic Development Council—is likely to do more than polite exhortation to see that rational investment policies are widely and quickly adopted by all firms.

14
Value-added tax

Reactions to new taxes conform to a clear pattern: shock, opposition, understanding, acceptance.

The Times editorial, May 7th, 1966.

Introduction

The merits or otherwise of the value-added tax (abbreviated to V.A.T.) are worth considering, whatever the political future of Great Britain, but they are posed in urgent form by British approaches to join the European Common Market.

The Common Market countries agreed in February, 1967, that a single type of turnover tax based on the French T.V.A. (*taxe sur la valeur ajoutée*) system shall come into effect from 1970. This means the other five countries of the Common Market will have to adjust their turnover taxes to conform to the principles of T.V.A. although the rate of tax can be at different levels. A V.A.T. can take different forms: in what follows attention is mainly concentrated on the Common Market type of tax.

The National Economic Development Council in *Conditions Favourable to Faster Growth* (1963), paras. 165-70, suggested that a V.A.T. might be more conducive to economic growth and that it would have benefits for the balance of payments because the tax could, under the rules of the General Agreement on Tariffs and Trade (G.A.T.T.), be rebated on exports and charged on imports. The *Committee on Turnover Tax* (1964), considered such a tax and advised against a change in 1964. This decision was considered controversial at the time and the government has said that it is being reconsidered in the light of new circumstances.

The French system

Before the tax changes that came into force on January 1st, 1968, between a quarter and a fifth of all tax revenue in France came from turnover and sales taxes, of which T.V.A. provided the bulk. The tax is charged comprehensively on all goods, subject only to defined exceptions. Thus it covers consumer goods, many foodstuffs, industrial materials and intermediate products.

The changes in 1968 extend the tax to wholesale and retail trade and to services. The normal rate of tax has been set at 16·66% of the tax-inclusive value. Certain products will be charged at 20%, services at 13% and basic necessities at 6%.

The tax at the appropriate rate is levied at each stage of production, but is levied only on the value added at that particular stage. This is achieved administratively by allowing each stage to deduct the tax paid by previous stages, *as shown on the invoices of their suppliers*. Since the sum of values added at successive stages is equal to the final wholesale price of the product, the amount of tax paid will be the same as if the tax was charged once on this final value.

An example of a value-added tax

An example taken from the *Committee on Turnover Tax* (1964), para. 17, should make this clear:

Suppose the manufacture of a product which requires materials, fuel, and containers (but nothing else) to be brought in from outside suppliers, and suppose that the making of the product is costed as follows, and that there is a value-added tax at the uniform rate of 20% of tax-inclusive values [i.e. 25% of the tax-exclusive values]:

	Tax-inclusive Invoice Price	Amount of Tax included in Price	Price exclusive of Tax
	£	£	£
Purchases:			
Materials	100	20	80
Fuel	45	9	36
Containers	10	2	8
	155	31	124
Value added by the manufacturer by way of salaries, wages, profit, etc.	100		100
Tax payable by the manufacturer	25	25	
Selling price of product	280	56	224

In this example the manufacturer purchases materials, fuel and containers, which cost him £155, of which £31 is tax. The manufacturer adds £100 to the value (his salaries, wages, profit, etc.) and pays £25 tax on this value. So the final wholesale price of the product is £280, of which £56 is tax.

In France firms must send in returns showing the amount of tax payable within a given number of days of the end of the month, and they then pay tax on purchases of the previous month. Firms paying small amounts of tax are allowed to make quarterly returns.

The V.A.T. is, as the example already given shows, basically a tax on sales less purchases. This figure can be arrived at directly by an inspection of the sales and purchases figures or by adding up the money spent on wages and salaries, depreciation, interest and profit. Problems arise from stocks on hand at the start and finish of a tax period, and from purchases of capital equipment. Stocks present an accounting problem, but no problem of principle. With capital equipment the decision has to be made if this is to be subject to the tax or not. The most usual suggestion, on the grounds that investment should be encouraged, is that net capital expenditure should not be taxed. If this is to be the case a firm would be assessed to tax on value added calculated either

(a) upon the difference between the total of its sales; and the total of its purchases, including purchases of capital equipment;
(*b*) upon the sum of its wages and salaries, depreciation, trading profits and interest payments; minus its purchases of capital equipment.

In both cases exports of products would be excepted and imports taxed so that the tax is one based on final expenditure.[1]

Is a value-added tax an incentive to exports?

Purchase tax is also allowed to be rebated on exports and charged on imports. The significance of the change to a V.A.T. would lie in what other taxes were reduced or abolished. If, for example, employers' National Insurance contributions, which cannot be rebated at present, were lowered as a result of the introduction of a V.A.T., export prices would be lower and import prices higher. There are two advantages: one that follows from this price-change and the incentive this gives to exports; the other follows from the possible

[1] If in (*a*) purchases of capital equipment are excluded and depreciation charges are deducted from sales and in (*b*) capital equipment is excluded and profits taken net of depreciation, the tax becomes one on final expenditure and investment.

advantage to profits if a firm exports. Once again the benefit to profits (since firms are not charged purchase tax on exports) lies in the significance to the firm of the alternative taxes which are rebated.

However, the assumption that the present system, whereby all of the V.A.T. can be imposed on imports and rebated on exports, may be unrealistic. At present a country which imposes taxes on companies for social services, in a form which can not be imposed on imported goods, may complain that it is being discriminated against, since its exports will have to bear the V.A.T. of the country to which it is exporting, part of which is used for social service payments. On the other hand, imports to the country do not bear this social service tax. The question is complicated and one that is likely to lead to international retaliation if international agreement cannot be reached. A United States Congressional Foreign Trade Committee has voiced criticism on these lines and has called for an international review of all non-tariff barriers. And the United States Administration has said it may impose retaliatory 'border taxes' to offset the effect of the European Economic Community's use of the V.A.T.

Is the value-added tax a tax on costs or a tax on the consumer?

It is worth looking briefly at the incidence of a profits tax before the incidence of a V.A.T. is taken up. It is generally accepted that, at least in the short run, a tax on profits does not affect prices. The theoretical case is that if a firm is already charging prices that are maximizing profits, an increase in profits tax will not alter the optimum price and output decisions of the firm. There may be exceptions to this rule if a firm is in a monopolistic or oligopolistic position. If an industry's pricing structure is maintained by a firm, or a small number of firms, acting as a price-leader, or if the firms in an industry act together on pricing, and if they look to a level of return on capital *calculated after taxation is taken into account*, then a change in profits tax could be reflected fairly quickly in a change of prices. The consumer is in this case bearing all or part of the tax. In the long run, it is generally accepted that a profits tax is more likely to be passed on to the consumer. For a selection of articles on incidence refer to Musgrave, R. A. and Shoup, C. S. (1959).

Should a V.A.T. be regarded as a tax on consumption which will be paid by consumers or as a tax on business costs which will be paid by firms? The Richardson Committee considered that the former would be the case.

The procedure of invoicing that has been outlined leads to the expectation that the amount of tax will be carried through each stage of processing to the retail level, in the same way that purchase tax is invoiced through to the retailer and thence to the consumer. The question then arises whether or not firms will reduce the price of commodities in line with any tax-reductions that may come about with the introduction of a V.A.T. On the assumptions that both the V.A.T. and the cost savings that result from other tax reductions are passed on to the consumer, differential effects on retail prices can be expected. These are likely because the change in taxation, even if it is designed to bring in the same aggregate tax revenue, will have a different impact on different firms.[2]

On these assumptions the V.A.T. is primarily a tax on consumption, although it can be conceded that some firms faced with an elastic demand for their products may be forced to bear part of the cost themselves.

Is the value-added tax an incentive to efficiency?

If the V.A.T. is, by and large, a tax on consumers, can it at the same time be claimed that it is a spur to business efficiency? The grounds for arguing that this can be the case run on the following lines: A firm will find that its tax bill will be higher than its competitors if its costs are higher than theirs. Attempts to pass on this tax in excess of the amount the most efficient firm in the industry passes on will therefore result in loss of sales, and act as a direct incentive to the firm to reduce its costs by increasing its efficiency. This argument will now be examined.

500 175
600 1?.

The tax position in the competitive case

Let us take two firms producing for a competitive market, so that

	Firm A	Firm B
	£	£
Wages and salaries	400,000	500,000
Depreciation	200,000	200,000
Materials	100,000	100,000
Interest	100,000	100,000
Trading profit	200,000	100,000
Total sales	1,000,000	1,000,000

[2] For example, if government services are to be subject to the V.A.T. it makes a good deal of difference whether corporation tax or employers' Insurance and Health Contributions are remitted. In general, government services do not make profits, so that they would not benefit from a reduction in corporation tax.

the pricing policy of the firms is the same. Firm A is assumed to be the more efficient, its labour costs are lower and trading profits higher than firm B and other costs are assumed to be the same.

In this situation, with no capital expenditure, firm A pays more tax under corporation tax, since its trading profit is higher than firm B. However, despite the fact that firm B has lower profit, each would pay the same amount of V.A.T. (other taxes are ignored for the moment). The amount of V.A.T. can be calculated either as: sales, less purchases (£1,000,000, less £100,000), or as the sum of its wages and salaries, depreciation, interest and trading profit. In both cases, for both firms, this leaves £900,000 as the sum subject to the V.A.T. It is not necessarily correct to say therefore that because firm A has lower costs than firm B it will pay less tax. This is so because the tax base given here includes not only costs, but also trading profit, since profit forms part of the value added by the firm. The case where profits are excluded from the base is considered further below.

The 'incentive' to investment comes about firstly because firm B will have the same amount of V.A.T. to pay as firm A. In the competitive situation outlined firm B cannot increase its prices to improve its profits; it needs to reduce costs, or it may find itself insolvent. The direct incentive to investment comes about as a consequence of allowing capital purchases to be deducted from total sales. If firm B invests £500,000 in capital equipment to bring it up to the efficiency of firm A, its tax liability, in the year in which it undertakes the investment, will be reduced by £500,000. This provision does not reward the existing efficient firm, but gives an inducement to the less efficient firm to invest.

It is sometimes suggested that trading profit be excluded from the tax so that it would be calculated as sales, less purchases and profits or as the sum of its wages and salaries, depreciation and interest. In this case firm A would be liable to V.A.T. on £700,000; firm B on £800,000. This form of the tax obviously favours the efficient firm more than the previous example. *However, in both cases, this is looking only at the firms liability for V.A.T.* without taking into account liability for other taxes. The critical consideration is what other taxes will firms have to pay. The combinations of possible reductions in other taxes are endless, and the taxes to be paid have to be specified before it can be known how favourable or unfavourable the whole tax position is to one company or the other.

The imperfectly competitive situation

If the case is now taken where the firms are working in a market which is less than perfect, the situation changes a little. If firm B is able to maintain its profits by charging a higher price, the following situation emerges:

	Firm A	Firm B
	£	£
Wages and salaries	400,000	500,000
Depreciation	200,000	200,000
Materials	100,000	100,000
Interest	100,000	100,000
Trading profit	200,000	200,000
Total sales	1,000,000	1,100,000

Firm B's sales are higher because its final prices are higher. Taking the case where profits are included in the tax base, firm B will pay tax on £1,000,000 as opposed to firm A on £900,000. If firm B passes the tax on to the consumer, its prices and tax bill will diverge even further from firm A. The inducement to firm B to reduce its costs thus depends on two things. Firstly, the amount of tax paid on the difference in cost and profit between itself and the most efficient firm in the industry. Secondly, on the degree of monopoly power it can exercise. While the tax, in these circumstances, is an inducement to reduce prices and improve efficiency, it seems easy to overstate the benefits that can be expected from it. As in the previous example, the main inducement still lies in the tax-reduction that comes about in the year in which capital investment is undertaken.

As in the previous example, if profits are excluded from the base, the situation becomes more favourable, so far as V.A.T. is concerned, to the more efficient firm. Firm A would then be liable to tax on £700,000; firm B on £800,000. The previous reservations about other taxes that firms may be liable for still applies.

A value-added tax and equity

Speaking generally, it is very difficult to devise a tax which is borne by a company. The reason for this is that companies are often in a position to alter their price and output policies and shift all or part of the tax on to the consumer.[3]

Adopting the position that a V.A.T. is a tax on consumers collected by companies, an equity problem arises. It is concerned with the regressive nature of indirect tax. Although (assuming a comprehensive

[3] Part of the tax may, in effect, be shifted on to the employees if the employer is able to use the tax as a counter to resist wage-claims.

tax) the actual amount of tax paid will increase with the amount of expenditure, the tax is regressive because as a rule consumption expenditure represents a decreasing proportion of income, as income levels rise, e.g. with a V.A.T. at 10% a person earning £10 a week will probably have to spend the whole of his income; in this case he will pay £1 in tax or 10% of his income. If a man earning £40 a week can save £10, he will pay £3 tax on his purchases of £30, or 7½% of his income.[4] This question will be taken up in Chapter 18.

Summary

Britain will have to adopt a V.A.T. if she enters the Common Market. In any case, the tax has advantages in its own right. At present the price system is distorted because some goods are subject to purchase tax and other goods and all services are not. (The S.E.T., which was dealt with in a previous chapter, was seen to be a very imperfect way of subjecting service industries to tax.)

V.A.T. could raise large sums in revenue, and the important question is which taxes will be abolished or reduced as a result of bringing in a V.A.T. Speculation as to which taxes should be reduced has been avoided. A 10% V.A.T. would, it has been estimated, bring in something like £2,000 million. If purchase taxes and S.E.T. were abolished, this will still leave a substantial sum, which could be applied to tax-reductions elsewhere.

The claim that a V.A.T. will encourage exports may be true under certain circumstances, but it is subject to important reservations about the reactions of other countries. A clarification of existing international agreements on tax rebates on exports and levies on imports is posed in urgent form by this tax if international retaliation is to be avoided.

If net capital formation is to be excluded from the scope of the tax, it forms a strong incentive to undertake capital investment.

A V.A.T. is a regressive tax. The problem this poses for equity will be considered in Chapter 18.

[4] Some of these expenditures are likely to be ways that do not attract the tax, such as the payment of rates; this does not alter the principle.

15
Wealth

Having regard to all the evidence presented here, it seems fair to conclude that there was no very marked change in the relative importance of inheritance in the creation of the personal fortunes of the top wealth-leavers of the generations of the mid-twenties and the mid-fifties of this century. For either, the chance of leaving an estate valued at over £100,000 or even £50,000 was outstandingly enhanced if one's father had been at least moderately well off.

HARBURY, C. D., 'Inheritance in the Distribution of Personal Wealth', *Economic Journal*, December, 1962.

Anybody that's got money can hire somebody who's smart to make them money. It's a son of a bitch that hasn't got any money that has to be smart.

HIBBARD, R., a self-made multi-millionaire, quoted by Bainbridge, J., *The Super-Americans*.

Apart from minor stamp duties, which may fall on wealth-transfers, the only continuing tax on wealth in Great Britain is that brought about by estate duties. There were legacy and successive duties until they were abolished in 1949. These duties were not important quantitatively, but important in principle, as an example of what is possible. They will be looked at briefly before details of estate duty are given. Estate duty is, then, related to the accretion principle of income. This section continues with a look at the special investment charge in the year 1967-8, and concludes with a brief look at some of the changes that have been proposed from time to time in taxing wealth.

Legacy and successive duties

Legacy and successive duties were minor duties, complementary to estate duties. The rate at which duties were charged was determined solely by the relationship of the beneficiary to the donor. They varied according to whether:

(1) The beneficiary was the husband, wife or lineal issue or ancestor of the donor.
(2) The beneficiary was a brother or sister or a descendant of a brother or sister.
(3) All other cases.

The lowest duty was payable in case (1); the highest in case (3).

The duties were based on the idea that a person who comes into an inheritance may justly be asked for a special contribution to the needs of the State, and that, if the inheritance has in it something of the nature of a windfall, the contribution should on that account be at a higher rate. These duties were abolished in 1949, when estate duty was increased.

Outline of existing estate duties

Estate or death duties were introduced in 1894, although since that time there have been many changes in detail and in the rates which have been applied. The current rates of tax are given in Table 1, and were introduced in 1969 when the size of estates on which duty is payable was raised from £5,000 to £10,000. The system prior to this had been to subject the whole of an estate to duty at a rate which progressed in 24 steps from 1% on an estate between £5,000 and £6,000 to 80% on an estate exceeding £1,000,000. The current system is that the rates of duty quoted are payable only on the appropriate tranche, or slice, of the estate. Thus from Table 1, an estate worth £30,000 will pay tax at 30% on £12,500 (£30,000 less £17,500) and 25% on the lower tranche of £7,500, the first £10,000 of the estate being free of duty. This was not primarily a revenue change, the

Table 1

Rates of estate duty in Great Britain applying 1969

Tranche of net capital value		
Exceeding	*Not Exceeding*	*Rate*
£	£	%
10,000	17,500	25
17,500	30,000	30
30,000	40,000	45
80,000	150,000	65
150,000	300,000	70
300,000	500,000	75
500,000	750,000	80
over 750,000		85*

* with a ceiling of 80% overall

estimated loss of revenue of £8 million a year is mainly due to raising the limit at which duty becomes payable. The adoption of the tranche system avoids the difficulty under the old scale of an estate which just came into a higher category of duty which needed 'marginal relief' so as not to be penalized compared to an estate which was slightly smaller. The change results in some sizes of estate paying a little more duty than under the old system and some a little less but the difference is not very great in either case.

These rates, if they were effective, might be considered unduly harsh. As Chapter 8 pointed out, the yield from this source is comparatively small, accounting for about 3% of government revenue. A system of high but ineffective rates has been described by Simons, H. (1938), 11 as:

> . . . a subtle kind of moral and intellectual dishonesty . . . a grand scheme of deception, whereby enormous surtaxes are voted in exchange for promises that they will not be made effective. Thus, the politicians may point with pride to the rates, while quietly reminding their wealthy constituents of the loopholes.

That the rates quoted in Table 1 are nominal, rather than effective rates, is due to two main causes: one, the extensive concessions that the legislature has granted, and two, the ease of avoidance.

Duty is charged on property passing on death of the individual, less various estate liabilities, which in general are limited to debts created for value. The meaning of debts created for value is to ensure that an estate is not reduced in value by the deceased having created IOU's for which he had not received full value in money or money's worth. We need not enter here into legal niceties of what constitutes property passing at death, except to note that the device of the trust, particularly the discretionary trust, has become increasingly important as a means of avoidance. (A discretionary trust enables the trustee to distribute income or capital to a specified list of beneficiaries. When a beneficiary dies, no property is deemed to pass, so long as at least two beneficiaries are left. An estate may, in favourable circumstances, be isolated from the revenue for up to 100 years, and duty can be minimized at the close of the trust by suitable distributions.[1]) The net value of the property is then usually aggregated to form one value, on which estate duty is levied at the appropriate rate. To this rule of aggregation there are exceptions, which can substantially reduce the amount of tax.

The general rule is that property in which the deceased never had an interest is treated as a separate estate. This is an easy and

[1] In 1969 this loophole was partly closed by a provision that there should be a charge on the capital of such a trust on the death of a beneficiary.

popular way to lessen estate duties. It could be achieved, for example, by taking out an insurance policy vested absolutely and irrevocably, from the start of the policy, in another person—for example, policies by a man in favour of his wife under the Married Women's Property Act, 1882. This loophole was closed in March, 1968.

Aggregation is also not carried out between 'settled' and 'unsettled' property when the 'unsettled' property of the deceased does not exceed £10,000. In lay terms, unsettled property covers the assets of the deceased, while settled property covers property in which the deceased had a limited or life interest only. Thus, if a deceased's estate was worth £6,000 and he was life tenant of a fund worth £25,000, each would be treated as a separate estate. However, if in the above example, the deceased's estate was worth £10,000 or more, the two would be aggregated for estate duty purposes.

Rapid succession relief is available to reduce estate duty if it becomes liable to duty for a second time within five years, e.g. in the case of the husband dying, followed by the death of his wife within five years. Duty is reduced by up to one-half, according to the length of time involved between the deaths.

A significant and curious provision is the relief granted to agricultural land and appropriate property thereon. Relief was first granted in 1925, and since 1949 it has taken the form of abatement of duty of 45%. A minor provision is that timber is not taken into account until the timber is sold. These provisions take no account of when the property was acquired, so that a death-bed purchase qualifies for relief; the distortion which this introduces into land prices is likely to be significant.

This legislation was further extended in 1954 to industrial premises, plant and machinery used by the deceased or by a company under his control where there is no Stock Exchange quotation. In general, valuation of these assets takes place and a reduction of 45% in duty is made. This class of business may well be faced with special difficulties on the death of an individual, but this form of exemption seems an inequitable way to deal with the problem. It encourages more individuals to arrange their affairs under the protection of this form of ownership, to the detriment of the revenue and of individuals who cannot so arrange their affairs in this form.

In Britain the simplest way to avoid estate duty is to give one's wealth away. There is in Britain, unlike many other countries, no gifts tax as such, although gifts within seven years of death are aggregated and taxed with the deceased person's estate. However, even in this case, reduced rates are payable if the donor dies in the last three years of the period. The period for which gifts are caught for estate duties was increased from three to five years in 1946 and from five to seven years in 1968. The reductions allowed are 15% if the donor dies in the fifth year after the gift was made, 30% if he dies in the sixth year, and 60% in the seventh year.

In the words of Grundy, J. M. (1956), 7, 'as far as estate duty is concerned, the Revenue benefit almost exclusively from the unlucky, the ungenerous and the unwise'.

As illustrations, the unlucky would be those who gave away much of their wealth and died within four years, or those who on their death-bed negotiate to buy a farm or woodland (which has an abatement of duty of 45%) and who die before the transaction can be ratified; the ungenerous, those who refuse to part with any of their wealth before they die or to make other provision; the unwise, those who refuse to pay for competent professional advice in setting up their affairs, particularly in setting up discretionary trusts.

Estate duty and the accretion of income principle

The setting up of the total-accretion principle is an attempt, as we have seen, to tax persons on the increment of spending power that accrues to them per period of time. It is immaterial whether the increment comes in the form of earned or unearned receipts, gifts, bequests, or a change in value of assets held.

The adoption of such an approach to taxation does not change the *existing* pattern of wealth ownership. A person with assets of £1 million, which do not change in value, has had no net accretion of income from capital appreciation (he may, of course, have had an income from these assets, which will be taxed), and he, therefore, will pay no more tax than a person with no wealth but the same income.

However, the *future* pattern of wealth ownership will be changed since any disposal of wealth by way of gift, or bequest at death, will be taxed as the income of the recipient of the gift or bequest.

The community may decide to impose an additional tax on wealth in order to secure more equality in the ownership of wealth. The simplest form of such a wealth tax would be one imposed at death. More complicated will be the imposition of an annual or periodic net wealth tax.

An intrinsic part of any form of wealth tax, whether at death or a periodic tax, is that gifts must also be brought into the tax net, otherwise the wealth tax becomes, at least in part, a discretionary tax, which can be escaped by 'giving away' one's wealth. This is one of the loopholes which makes a mockery of death duties in their present form. The effect of the adoption of gifts as part of the income of the beneficiary with death duties imposed in addition on wealth at death is to give a person the possible option of reducing his tax liability by spreading his gifts out over a number of years and thereby reducing both his own liability for estate duties and the recipient's tax liability. This may not, it itself, be undesirable on social grounds, and averaging of income would greatly reduce the magnitude of the problem.

Special charge on investment income

The Finance Bill in 1968 made a special charge on the investment income of individuals for 1967-8, imposed for one year only. Although this is a charge on income, it can be treated in a chapter on wealth, since when income tax, surtax and the special charge are taken into account the tax will be greater than the income on high investment incomes, and will thus tend to lead to some redistribution of wealth. Disregarding the effect of personal allowances, an individual will surrender more in tax than he receives in investment income when that income has passed £18,580. A sum of approximately £411,000, invested to produce the average yield on *The Times* share index, would produce this sum.

The first £3,000 of investment income, after deduction of personal allowances as allowed for surtax, is exempt from the charge. The remainder is charged at the following rates: between £3,000 and £4,000 2*s*. in the £1 between £4,000 and £5,000 at 3*s*., between £5,000 and £8,000 at 6*s*., and above £8,000 at 9*s*. The yield is estimated at £100 million and about 90,000 people are affected.

This tax was seen at the time as a temporary expedient which would not preclude the introduction of a wealth tax in the future. The problems of taxing wealth are now briefly taken up.

Estate duty or net wealth tax?

The chief difficulty with having an annual wealth tax is the administrative problem of valuation. In contrast, valuation at death normally has to take place in any case. On other grounds, a tax at death comes out well; it is likely to cause less disincentive to effort than most other taxes. Also, the tax has the effect of lessening the inheritance of the beneficiaries, which, because they are unearned by their own efforts, is usually preferred on ethical considerations.

An annual wealth tax, by most of those who propose such a tax, attempts to lessen the problems of valuation by reducing the effectiveness of this tax. They do this by proposing that the tax starts only at high wealth levels, or proposing a very low rate of tax, or limiting the tax to selected assets. These are serious limitations, and because of this in what follows a net wealth tax will not be further elaborated.

Alternatives to a net wealth tax

A frequently advocated alternative is that receipts not subject to income tax and other gifts and bequests should be cumulated over the beneficiaries' lifetime and subject to some form of progressive tax (see Sandford, C. T. (1965) and (April, 1967)). The tax to be paid on a particular bequest would thus depend on the total sum already received. A minor difficulty of such a tax is that the position may arise where the tax due on a gift or bequest is greater (because of past accumulation) than the gift or bequest received. In such cases, the tax could be limited to the sum of the gift or bequest. These proposals can be seen as a way of supplementing death duties or as a substitute for them.

A further complication can be introduced if the proposal to tax gifts and legacies is based on the wealth already possessed by the the recipient, as well as the size of the gift or legacy.

It should be stressed that, in spite of administrative difficulties, taxes on wealth have been introduced in other countries. The Scandinavian countries operate a net wealth tax. Australia, Canada, and the U.S.A. operate gifts taxes of various forms.

Summary

Apart from minor stamp duties which may fall on wealth-transfers, the only tax on wealth in Great Britain is that imposed by estate duties. In their present form, estate duties exhibit most of the disadvantages of a bad tax. Yields are low and administrative costs high. High nominal rates of duty are largely ineffective and lead to the channelling of a good deal of time, money and effort into tax-avoidance.

On the assumption that wealth, as well as income, forms a proper component to tax, a wide variety of suggestions has been made as to the form such a tax should take. The question is not independent of the receipts that are counted as income, and therefore subject to income tax.

The argument adopted in this book is that as much as possible of 'current purchasing power' should be brought into the income tax net. Changes in 'net wealth' due to an inheritance or a gift would therefore be treated as income as well as all capital gains: averaging of income will be necessary to cover the problem of exceptional receipts in any one year, causing an excessive tax burden. The chief benefit to be derived from this change is that an overhaul of the existing tax and surtax rates can be undertaken. Death duties in a modified form should continue with legislative changes to counter the present evasion by way of discretionary trusts and other devices.

As an alternative, it has been suggested that inheritances, gifts and capital gains should be subject to a progressive tax, and that these receipts should be cumulated over a person's lifetime. Such a tax could be extended to lump-sum gratuities and other receipts not subject to income tax.

No attempt has been made to go into the many administrative complexities of taxing wealth more equitably. The problems may appear formidable, but they are not insurmountable if other countries' experience is relevant to Britain.

16
Land

The real property laws of this country, from the period immediately succeeding the Conquest down to the present time, presents a history consistent with itself in one particular, that of a perpetual struggle of rival interests.

C. WREN HOSKYNS (1881), *The Land-laws of England in Systems of Land Tenure in Various Countries.*

Introduction: the meanings attached to 'ownership'

Mankind, even at a primitive stage of development, shows an acute interest in land and territorial rights. Ownership itself is not a simple issue: it presents a highly complex tangle of privileges, rights and duties. By way of illustration, does ownership confer—

The right of alienation, that is, to sell or give it away?
The right of bequest?
The right of franchise?
The right to mineral wealth below ground?
The right to hunt and fish?
The right to erect buildings on it?
The right to neglect land to the detriment of neighbours and future generations?
Rights above ground?
What happens on intestacy?
Are services or taxes required of the owner?
Does it accord social status?
Are improvements made by a tenant the property of the owner, or must the tenant be compensated?
Are improvements to land by acts of the community chargeable to the owner, and is spoilation compensated, e.g. acts such as sea-defences, drainage, town-expansion, siting of airports, roads, etc.?
Does the community reserve any public rights, e.g. of access?

Has the community the right to acquire the land for the public good?

'Ownership' is the rag-bag into which all aspects are bundled. The history of land and of the privileges, rights and duties that attach thereto exhibits a rich variety of solutions to be found at different times and in different places. Much history is a record of this changing nexus of privilege and responsibility.

The subject of land abounds in legal subtleties. A short summary or outline is hardly possible, and certainly cannot do justice to the niceties that have developed. In Great Britain the Norman Conquest of 1066 brought great changes. After the Conquest the normal position was for the Crown to *own* land, and others to hold an estate under various forms of tenure, either directly from the Crown or from an intermediate holder, who himself had tenure directly or indirectly from the Crown.[1] Feudal tenure involved the granting of an estate for services. These were in the form of military, spiritual or agricultural obligations. Wills of land were not permitted; descent in the male line predominated.

This situation was gradually changed in a number of ways. Feudal services tended to be commuted into annual money payments or 'rents'. The trust device came to be used to get around the ban on bequeathing land; this right was not legally established until 1540. The freehold, as a freely marketable commodity unencumbered by onerous feudal rights, was achieved by statute in 1660. The system thus established is, speaking very broadly, the one existing until 1947, although there were numerous alterations in the laws affecting land during this time, some of considerable importance. Developments since 1947 will be looked at in more detail later in this chapter.

The economics of land

David Ricardo, an economist of the early nineteenth century, developed the idea that land is in a separate category from other factors of production, since its supply could neither be diminished or reduced. He argued that a tax on land could not reduce the available supply,

[1] 'He who held land as tenant of the royal lord could himself become lord by granting the land to another. The primary rung in the feudal tenurial ladder was the tenant in actual possession of the tenement, the tenant *in dominico*. The ultimate rung was the king, the one man in all the realm who was never tenant. Between the two extremes the rungs were either an ascending series of lordships or a descending series of tenures, according to the view taken. There is no land unowned in all England. Land can be without a tenant where he who is in possession is the king; but land without a lord there cannot be——*nulle terre sans seigneur*' (Denman, D. R. (1958), 80).

and hence could have no adverse effect on production: therefore 'rent' should be treated differently from other factor payments. Fundamentally, the quantity of land is limited in supply. A community with a growing population is likely to experience an increasing demand for the limited amount of land available—for food-growing, dwellings, transport and amenities—which will raise its real value. This 'unearned income' may not accrue to every landowner, but it will accrue to landowners *en masse*. We have here the germ of later ideas developed by 'single-taxers', such as Henry George, that land need be the only item to bear tax, an idea which today, even if acceptable, would not yield the amount of revenue required.

Ricardo's ideas have been modified on two fronts. The supply of services from land can be increased by, for example, better agricultural methods or increasing the height of buildings; it can also be reduced by, for example, soil erosion. Secondly, other factors may be akin to land, in that the supply cannot immediately be changed in response to an increase in demand, and these factors will also enjoy an enhanced price, or 'quasi-rent', for a period.

Land has one other attribute which is sufficient to mark it off from most other assets: that is the degree to which the price of land is affected by socially created values.

There is no novelty in proposals to secure for the community at least a share in the values it has itself created. An Act of 1427 sought to recover increases in the value of property attributable to public expenditure on works for sea-defence, and in the reign of Charles II there was statutory appropriation of a part of landowners' unearned enhancement or 'melioration' assessed upon the benefits of street widening in London (*Land Commission* (1965), para. 2).

With increased government activity today, the scope for great changes in land values which accrue without effort on the landowners' part is very much increased. Proposals to build new towns, the reconstruction of existing towns, new road links, the closing of railway lines, siting of power stations, airports and seaports, the planning regulations which permit or prohibit certain types of development are but a few of the more obvious examples of community decisions, which can greatly increase, and less often decrease, the value of land.

Should land be treated differently from other assets?

From the fiscal viewpoint, it is necessary to decide whether the relative uniqueness of land—that is, its 'fixed quantity' and change in value which can occur through public action—is sufficiently marked to call for special tax treatment. In a country which is sparsely populated, the question may seem an academic one; in a well-populated country like Britain it becomes more acute. The problem, as has been indicated, is made more complex since a wide variety of planning regulations have grown up. The redesignation of land from 'green belt'—that is, land that shall not be built upon—to a housing area can increase the price of land many hundred-fold. In a similar way, the price may be adversely affected by planning permission, which goes the other way.[2]

The authors' opinion is that the factors indicated provide clear evidence that land should be taxed. From the account given below of the period since 1947, it will be seen that the tax on land has taken various forms.

The period 1947-67

Land was considered in the *Report of the Expert Committee on Compensation and Betterment* (1942) under the Chairmanship of Mr Justice Uthwatt. The *Land Commission* (1965) White Paper reported as follows:

The main recommendations of the Uthwatt Committee were implemented by the Labour government in the Town and Country Planning Act, 1947, which vested in the State all development rights in land. Anyone wishing to develop land had to recover the right to develop by payment of a development charge to the Central Land Board. A capital sum of £300 million was available for payments to those who established claims that the value of their land had depreciated as a result of the Act.

The Central Land Board were also given powers to buy land compulsorily for the purpose of disposing of it for development. The Uthwatt Committee had considered that public acquisition, if need be by compulsion, was the only satisfactory answer to the problem of comprehensive development and of securing betterment. In practice, doubts arose about the validity of the powers given to the Central Land Board and they had not been widely used when the Conservative government changed the situation by abolishing development charges in the Town and Country Planning Act, 1953.

The 1953 Act, a stop-gap measure, was followed by the Town and County Planning Act, 1954, which removed the restrictions on private sales, so that those sales took place at market prices. A two-price system was thereby created: prices paid when land with development value was sold privately were higher than those paid when such land was acquired compulsorily for public purposes. This two-price system was so clearly inequitable that the government was forced to eliminate it, and

[2] It was reported in the *Sunday Times* of July 12th, 1964, that 30 acres of land at Mill Hill bought in 1954 for £3,000 was saleable for £700,000 in 1964.

this they chose to do by the Town and County Planning Act, 1959, which restored market value as the basis for compensation on compulsory purchase.

Since the removal in 1959 of the last restraints on the market in land for development, land with planning permission for development or even with the hope of such planning permission, whether stimulated by a development plan or not, has been fetching ever-increasing prices. These prices, which must be paid by public authorities buying land for their essential purposes, place a heavy burden on their financial resources; they are also a deterrent to people wishing to buy their own homes (paras. 3, 4, 5, 6).

1947, therefore, sees an attempt to implement some of the recommendations of the Uthwatt Committee *Report* and secure for the State the betterment value of land. This attempt fails because of legislative shortcomings, the complexity of the Act and probably also resentment of a 100% tax on betterment values, and lead to the gradual abandonment of the attempt: by 1959 a return to free market pricing had taken place.

This period was one in general of steeply rising prices of land. Gains made in this way were, unless caught by the 1947 Act, untaxed until 1962, unless they were undertaken 'by way of trade' and fell to be taxed under normal company taxation. In 1962 capital gains in land and building were taxed, as we have seen, if realized within three years. The 1965 Act charged all gains either to the short-term or the long-term tax.

Land Commission Act, April, 1967

The Land Commission Act, 1967, is an attempt to re-establish some of the recommendations of the Uthwatt Committee of 1942, but to achieve the aims of the Committee in a different way from the Act of 1947.

The Land Commission has a head office in Newcastle and eleven regional offices, which administer a tax known as the 'betterment levy', and it is invested with wide powers to acquire land compulsorily. Compulsory purchase will be based on current market values (less the betterment levy), so it should be a matter of indifference to a landowner whether he sells to the Land Commission, a public authority or a private purchaser.

The betterment levy is at an initial rate of 40% and the stated intention of the government is to increase the rate progressively to 45% and then to 50% at reasonably short intervals. The question of increasing the rate further is not ruled out. The levy thus presents an important change from the Act of 1947, which sought to obtain the whole of the betterment value. Further, the charge is only on the increase in the value for a new use, less the current value in its old one.

Thus if a piece of agricultural land were originally bought for £300, and is currently worth £1,000 if sold as agricultural land, but worth £3,000 if sold as housing land, no betterment levy is imposed in the case of continuing agricultural use; it is payable on £2,000 if sold as housing land (current value in existing use deducted from current value in new use). Where the betterment levy is charged, the capital gains tax will not apply, but this tax will continue to apply where land is sold for existing use.

The betterment levy is charged on the person who has actually realized the gain. This would normally be the seller. In the above example, the seller would pay the 40% levy on £2,000. If, however, the purchaser defers development and the value of the land rises to £4,000, he will be liable to a betterment levy on the difference of £1,000.

In the case of development of land, the levy may be payable even though no sale takes place, but only *material* development as defined by the Act ranks for levy. Thus a person can rebuild his house and increase its size up to 1,000 square feet, erect a garage, or turn his house into flats without incurring a levy. In a like manner, a factory may be rebuilt and enlarged without incurring a levy, provided neither the floor area or the cubic content is enlarged more than 10%. No levy will be imposed on the development or disposal of land held by local authorities for their social services, including comprehensive development and town development, but it will apply to land held by them for commercial purposes. Similarly, the levy will not be payable by statutory undertakings or endowed charities.

An amendment in 1969 exempted from levy cases where the market value of the land does not exceed £1,500. This was expected to reduce by half the number of cases subject to levy. Provision was also made to deal with hardship in cases where a plot of land has been received as a gift and in which the recipient is building a house for his own occupation.

The financial provisions of the Act probably have the effect of taxing gains on land at a higher rate than for other capital gains, since long-term gains accruing to the individual attract tax at a top rate of 30%. However, this is not necessarily the case. It should be borne in mind in looking at the levy of 40% that this is a charge only on the change between its current value in its new use and the current value in its old use. Any capital appreciation of the land in its existing use is untaxed. When the land is sold, appreciation is only taxed to capital gains if the land retains its present use when sold. There seems little justification for this curious anomaly. The argument that it is difficult to establish the value of land at April 6th, 1965, doesn't deter this date being used for capital gains. As an illustration, we can use the figures given in the example above. If we assume that a piece of agricultural land had a value of £300 on April 6th, 1965, and is now worth £1,000 in its existing use as agricultural land, or £3,000 as housing land, the betterment levy takes the difference between £3,000 and £1,000 as the sum to tax; at 40% this yields £800. If we take the difference in value as £2,700 (the difference between its value in 1965 and now), this effectively reduces the betterment levy to a little below 30%.

Probably of more practical importance than the yield of the tax on land, if the intentions of the Act are carried out, are the powers of compulsory purchase given to the Land Commission. It seems to be envisaged that the Land Commission shall be an active body, not just acquiring land piecemeal as the need arises, but ensuring 'that the right land is made available at the right time'. It is envisaged that the Commission will buy, hold, manage and sell land to developers. These powers are to be gradually given to the Commission.

One by-product of the Act is that the government intends local authorities to benefit from the levy:

> It would, however, be impractical and inequitable to relate this assistance directly to the levy arising on conveyances of land purchased by each local authority, since the benefit could vary between local authorities in an arbitrary fashion. Without prejudice to the discussions which are to take place during the current review of local government finance, it is the intention of the government to ensure that the gain to the Exchequer from the operations of the Land Commission will in one way or another be reflected in the new arrangements under which local authorities will receive financial assistance from government. *Land Commission* (1965), para. 35.

Evaluation of the Land Commission Act, 1967

The Act, as we have seen, has two aims: one to secure the better use of land and, secondly, to tax the increment of betterment value. We shall confine ourselves to consideration of the second point.

Although the Act links these two points together, this is not logically necessary. The Land Commission could continue with its powers for the better use of land while the tax is dealt with separately.

The criticism was made earlier that the long-term capital gains tax is a flat-rate tax, while 'income' is subject to very progressive tax rates. The same criticism applies to the betterment levy. If capital gains were counted as part of personal income, as current short-term gains are, the case for a separate tax on land (with its administrative complexities) could be reconsidered. The case for the community securing at least a large part of socially created values is strong. Whether more revenue would be gained by treating betterment on land as part of a person's income depends on the rate of tax to which a person's income is subject, compared to the rate at which the betterment levy finally comes to rest. The wealthy taxpayer would almost certainly pay more if it is assessed to income, unless the betterment levy is raised to 70% or 80%.

Effect on the price of land

The intention of the 1947 Act was to secure for the government the whole of the increment in the price of land. The 1967 Act subjects this to, at present, a tax of 40%. This difference makes it very difficult to discuss the effects of the tax on land prices. With a tax of 100%, the seller has, at least theoretically, no incentive to hold out for a higher price, since only the revenue will benefit.[3] With a tax at a lower rate, the seller may try to hold out for a higher price, so that his gain after tax has been paid is bigger. The extent to which a seller is able to gain a higher price, and so effectively pass the tax on to the buyer, depends on the strength of demand and supply for the land.

The stated intention to increase the rate to 45% and then to 50% and perhaps higher is a partial inducement not to hold out for too long. However, because the tax is on the difference in the value of the land between its existing use and its new use, too much should not be made of this point. This anomaly, already referred to, whereby land, unlike other capital gains, escapes any tax on the increase in value for existing use when it is sold for a new use may create serious distortions. It is likely to lessen the supply of land coming on to the market, since the effect of higher rates of betterment levy is to some extent mollified. It is also likely to increase the demand for land by those who see a chance to make a capital gain which is partly tax-free. It is true that this advantage will be wiped out if the betterment levy is set at a sufficiently high rate, but there are obvious disadvantages in giving the appearance of high rates without, in practice, taxing at these rates. The rates of the betterment levy are, as shown by the example given in this chapter, not the effective

[3] The intention not to interfere with the market in land clearly failed in the case of the 1947 Act. Land was held back by owners in the hope (subsequently fulfilled) that the levy would be abandoned. Also, land was sold at prices higher than its value in 1947.

rates which will apply. It is possible for the rate of 40% to be a lighter tax than a capital gains tax of 30%, because gains on existing use escape the tax net when land is sold for a different use.

In Chapter 15, on 'Wealth', a more serious distortion is pointed out. Agricultural land and property, even if purchased from the deathbed, is entitled to a 45% rebate of estate duty. While such a tax haven remains open, the demand for agricultural land—and therefore its price—can be expected to be artificially inflated, and this in turn is likely to affect the price of other land.

No very firm conclusions can be drawn, so recently after the passing of the Act, on the effects of the levy on the price of land and the supply coming on to the market. Removal of the levy concession and estate duty rebate would go a long way towards creating a more realistic market in land. Their presence is only likely to inflate the price of land. Of crucial importance is how soon it is intended to increase the levy above the present level of 40% and the level at which it is expected to finally come to rest.

Summary

Land in a developed community is a scarce resource, and can by actions of the community be subject to very wide fluctuations in price.

The Land Commission Act, 1967, set out to secure the better use of land by giving the Land Commission powers to purchase land, if necessary by compulsory purchase, and, secondly, to tax the increase in land values. This tax carries on the tradition of imposing a nominal rate of tax (at present 40%) which is not the effective rate, because gains on the existing use of land escape tax when the land is sold for a different use.

The tax on land in its present form seems a needless complication of the tax structure; the difference in yield if land were taxed to capital gains cannot be very large. As with capital gains, treating gains made on land as income seems to be the equitable solution.

17
The national debt

Although the National Debt, in the sense in which we are using the term, is of such great importance for economic policy, there is in existing publications no adequate statistical analysis of it, nor indeed is there any statement of its size, either in published documents or in any official papers that have been brought to our notice. The great advance in official statistical knowledge of national income has not been matched by any comparable advance in knowledge of national assets and liabilities. We have therefore had to piece together, as best we could, a great deal of scattered information, which has been very substantially increased by figures produced specially for us, both by the authorities and by non-official bodies . . .

(*Radcliffe Committee* (1959), para. 536.)

Meaning of national debt

When the government spends more than it receives, this results in the issue of some sort of security to cover the deficiency. In like manner, a surplus results in a reduction of securities. The aggregate of securities issued over time is called the 'national debt'.

In earlier chapters, when looking at government spending and revenue, it was found necessary to define 'government' carefully in order to avoid misunderstanding. We there included central and local government, but excluded the nationalized industries. Likewise, in order to try to make sense of the figures over time it was necessary to be clear whether the figures were in money terms or deflated for changes in the price-level, and whether account had or had not been taken of changes in population. The National Debt seems to arouse more misunderstanding and emotion than either government spending or revenue, and these reservations are even more necessary. An added reason for caution is, as the quotation to this chapter shows, the lack of adequate data. More information has become available in recent years, but still the quality and quantity leave much to be desired.

The terminology and concepts used will be those adopted by the Radcliffe Committee as modified by the Bank of England. The major modification is the omission from the concept of national debt of debt payable in overseas currency, amounting to £1,822 million in 1967. Used without further qualification, 'national debt' is taken to mean the *net* debt of the public sector. That is to say, the obligations of the public sector, excluding debt held by the public sector itself. The term 'gross' is used to mean all debt, whether held by the public sector itself, termed 'official holdings', or whether it is held outside the public sector. Official holdings would be holdings by the Bank of England, the Exchange Equalization Account, the National Debt Commissioners, and certain government departments.

The public sector is a combination of central government, local authorities, nationalized industries and other public bodies. The inclusion of nationalized industries thus gives wider coverage than that used for spending and revenue. It will be argued later that the debt of the nationalized industries may be on a different footing to other debt, and for this reason the debt of these industries has been distinguished in the figures.

Table 1 presents figures of the gross debt of the public sector by

Table 1

Gross debt of the public sector by origin

(£ million nominal value)

Year	Central Government		Local Authorities in Great Britain		Public Corporations		Total
	Consolidated Fund	Banknotes and Other Debt	To P.W.L.B.	Other Debt	To Exchequer	Other Debt	
1935	6,760	575	289	1,301	—	161	9,086
1952	23,723	1,961	1,818	1,126	480	2,871	31,978
1955	24,804	2,313	2,828	1,505	776	3,364	35,590
1958	25,069	2,766	3,210	2,390	1,796	3,616	38,848
			Percentages				
1935	81		17		2		100
1952	80		9		11		100
1955	76		12		12		100
1958	72		14		14		100

Source: *Committee on the Working of the Monetary System*, Tables 24, 25.

type of issuing authority. In accordance with the definitions adopted, these figures do not include debt payable in overseas currency. In money terms the debt has increased from £9,086 million in 1935 to £38,848 million in 1958. Prices roughly doubled in this period, the debt increased fourfold, mainly due to the Second World War. In 1935 the central government had issued about 80% of the debt, with local authorities accounting for most of the balance. In 1958 the relative share of the central government had declined to 72%, while local authorities and public corporations have roughly equal responsibility for the remainder. It will be seen from the table that the central government has been a substantial net lender since the war, the increase in its debt being much more than offset by Exchequer advances to public corporations and loans through the Public Works Loan Board to local authorities.

Table 2 shows the composition of the net debt of the public sector —that is, excluding holdings of the public sector held by itself. This will be seen to have increased less rapidly than the gross figures— in other words, the holdings of the public sector of its own debt has increased in this period. One explanation of this has already been noted: the increased lending by the central government to other parts of the public sector. Further holdings will be explained by the development of National Insurance and similar funds. This table also shows that the debt was more liquid post-war. Gilt-edged securities had fallen from 62% of the total to 51%, while notes, Treasury bills and National Savings show big increases. Local authority debt was growing rapidly from 1952, and had important monetary implications, since after 1955 much of it consisted of short-term securities. However, the percentage of local authority debt was still substantially below the pre-war percentage. The line at the bottom of Table 2 is important. It expresses the money values of net debt shown in the table as a percentage of the money national income. It can be seen that, in spite of the large increase in money terms of the debt it has not increased as fast as the national income.

These figures, as most that are published on debt, must be used carefully: they will not bear any but broad conclusions. In particular, it should be noted that the analysis is in terms of nominal values. Nominal values are usually taken as the face value of the security, which is usually the value at which the security is originally sold, although on occasions a security is issued either at a discount or a premium. Long-term gilt-edged securities have for many years stood at a substantial discount on the Stock Exchange on their nominal values, and for many purposes details in market values would provide more meaningful information. In many other respects the figures have to be treated as little more than estimates of the true position;

Table 2

Composition of the net debt of the public sector at 31st March

	£ million nominal value				Percentages			
	1935	1952	1955	1958	1935	1952	1955	1958
Notes and Coin	453	1,545	1,858	2,199	6	6	7	8
Treasury bills	371	2,334	3,024	2,938	4	9	11	10
Gilt-edged securities	5,219	13,048	14,024	14,489	62	52	52	51
National Savings plus accrued interest	1,003	5,786	5,735	5,756	12	23	21	20
Tax reserve certificates	—	368	388	346	—	2	1	1
Northern Ireland government and local authorities	34	43	63	87	0	0	0	0
Local authorities in Great Britain	1,301	1,126	1,505	2,390	16	5	6	8
Borrowing from banks or other funds by public bodies	—	281	196	225	—	1	1	1
Overseas loans payable in sterling	—	361	318	134	—	2	1	1
Total	8,381	24,892	27,111	28,564	100	100	100	100
Total as a percentage of national income	204	195	175	154				

Source: *Committee on the Working of the Monetary System*, Tables 24, 25.

most, for example, contain large residual errors.

Of the figure of £25,069 million shown in Table 1 under Consolidated Fund,[1] together with £3,294 million of nationalized industries' stocks guaranteed by the government, in all a figure of £28,363 million, the Bank of England have estimated holders in 1958 as appears on p. 204.

They found in 1958 that official holdings account for a quarter of the total, the banking sector for 16% and official overseas holdings for 11%. Unfortunately, the value of this analysis is lessened by the figure of 'other' holdings, which, besides concealing the holdings of the company sector and the holdings of individuals, contains a large residual item which the Bank was unable to allocate (see below).

	£m.	%
Official Holdings	7,032	25
Public bodies	179	1
Banking sector	4,629	16
Overseas official	3,094	11
Other	13,429	47
	28,363	100

In their evidence to the Radcliffe Committee, the Treasury estimated the time-structure of that part of the debt which consisted of marketable government and government-guaranteed securities as follows:

Year:	1935	1955	1957
Amount in £m.:	5,508	17,521	18,630
	%	%	%
Up to 5 years	3	20	25
5 to 15 years	12	24	25
15 to 25 years	5	21	19
Over 25 years	19	13	11
Undated	61	22	20
Total	100	100	100

[1] The term 'Consolidated Fund' refers to procedure laid down for payment of moneys to or from the State. It is not of practical significance in this context.

This brings out clearly the sharp change in the time-structure of the debt pre-war and post-war. The figures relate to marketable securities of the government or securities under their guarantee. The data for 1958 are not available. Whereas in 1935 80% of this debt was either undated or had more than twenty-five years to run to maturity, the corresponding figure in 1957 was only 31%. It is not surprising that the monetary authorities in the post-war period were concerned about the liquidity of the economy.

Table 3, still largely in terms of nominal values, analyses the gross debt of the Consolidated Fund and government-guaranteed nationalized industries' stocks for the year 1967 in more detail. The debt is broken down into four categories: Treasury bills, stocks which have between nought and five years to run to maturity, stocks with over five years to maturity or that are undated, and non-marketable securities, such as Post Office savings and certificates. These account respectively for 12%, 20%, 48% and 20% of the total. Treasury bills and short-dated stocks thus account for nearly a third of the total.

The breakdown by holders shows: official holdings (29% of the total), public bodies (1%), the banking sector (6%), overseas banks in the U.K. (2%), accepting houses and the discount market (3%), financial institutions (14%), overseas residents, which includes both official and private holdings (14%), individuals (19%), other holders (2%), residual, much of which is believed to belong to individuals (10%). Even if the whole of the residual column is attributed to individuals, we find that less than 29% of the debt is held by United Kingdom individuals.

Within each category of debt besides official holdings, the important holders of Treasury bills are domestic banks, acceptance houses, the discount market and overseas residents. For short-term stocks, the domestic banks, acceptance houses, the discount market, financial institutions, overseas residents and individuals. For long-term or undated stocks, financial institutions, overseas residents and individuals. For non-marketable stock, overseas residents and individuals.

From the point of view of government finance, the sale of non-marketable debt is no different from the sale of marketable debt, e.g. when the public deposits money with the Post Office Savings Bank and the ordinary departments of the Trustee Savings Banks, and when it holds bank-notes, this is in effect lending to the government. Of the official holdings of £9,278 million nearly two-thirds represents securities held for this purpose. That is to say, a deposit by a member of the public at a Post Office Savings Bank has much the same effect as a purchase from the government of a security for the same amount. In the first case the Savings Bank deposit is credited to the government account and the Savings Bank is issued with a government

Table 3

Estimated distribution of the gross debt of the Consolidated Fund and government-guaranteed nationalized industries' stocks, March 31st, 1967

(£ nominal value)

	Treasury Bills	Stocks: Maturity of 0-5 years	Stocks: Maturity over 5 years	Non-market-able	Total	Total holdings as %age of total debt
Official holdings	2,162	1,650	4,487	929	9,228	29
Public bodies	0	56	137		193	1
Domestic banks	425	899	568	68	1,892	6
Overseas banks in U.K.	43	248	267		558	2
Accepting houses and Discount Mkt.	233	715	73		1,021	3
Financial institutions	9	579	3,985	7	4,580	14
Overseas residents	903	860	1,156	1,563	4,482	14
Individuals	0	427	2,251	3,289	5,967	19
Other holders[2]	2	827	2,425	138	750	2
Residual[3]	108			432	3,182	10
Total	3,885	6,261	15,349	6,426	31,921[4]	100
Total as %	12	20	48	20	100	

Source: *Bank of England Quarterly Bulletin*, March, 1968.

Nationalized industries' guaranteed stocks account for £1,757 million of the above.
Debt payable in overseas currencies of £1,822 million not included in the table.
0 Negligible or small holdings.
[2] Public Trustee, non-corporate bodies, companies and friendly societies.
[3] Much of this is believed to belong to individuals.
[4] Includes £68 million of non-marketable debt which cannot be allocated.

security as collateral; in the second case the individual receives the security as collateral directly. The remaining one-third of official holdings is divided between various government funds, mainly the National Insurance and Industrial Injuries Funds and the holdings of the Exchange Equalization Account and of the Banking Department of the Bank of England.

Summary of statistical data

The national debt shows a large money increase in the post-war period compared to the pre-war period. However, the net debt expressed as a percentage of national income shows a marked decrease. The composition of the debt has changed from being primarily long-term or undated to being primarily short- or medium-term.

Greater detail is now available for that part of the debt that comes under the Consolidated Fund and government-guaranteed securities of the nationalized industries.[5]

Official holdings have increased in recent years, and in 1967 accounted for 29% of the total, domestic banks show a decline in holdings and now account for about 6%, other financial institutions in the economy hold 13%, 14% is held overseas, while it is estimated that individuals hold between 18% and 29%.

The relevance of the national debt

The total amount of the debt has now been looked at, and it has been shown how much of this is issued by the central government and how much by local authorities and by nationalized industries. The time-structure of the debt has been given and a broad classification shown of the main holders. With this information we are in a position to take up some of the important implications of the national debt.

Can any valid comparisons be drawn between the debt of a nation and the debt of a company? Briefly, the answer is 'yes'; but there are also pitfalls to be avoided.

A company balance-sheet over time will normally show an increase in the liabilities of the company, which will be matched by corresponding increases on the asset side. Before a judgment is made that the increase in liabilities is good or bad, it is necessary to know a great deal more about the changes. For example, it makes a difference if it is the issued capital, reserves or bank overdraft which has increased;

[5] Separate details are also available in the financial statistics on local authority debt by type of holder and structure of the debt.

and also it makes a difference how the assets have changed. Has more been put into plant or is it that unwanted stocks are piling up?

It is also necessary, within limits, to take account of both sides of the national balance-sheet. The debt has been primarily incurred as a result of war expenditure. There are no physical assets corresponding to this expenditure. However, the public sector has tangible assets and the public debt in the post-war period is not quite the same thing as the pre-war debt. In particular, the nationalization of industries has resulted in an increase in debt which has been matched by an increase in assets. Much expenditure of local authorities has been on housing, and once again there are corresponding real assets. A reduction in debt could be achieved by selling these assets to the private sector, but, considered solely as a means of reducing the debt, the exercise achieves little. Since the government undertakes 'commercial' activities, there is a case for separating out debt operations of this kind. It may well happen that full commercial criteria should not be applied to all parts of commercial government activity; that, for example, some branch railway lines should be run even though this entails a loss, but separation at least enables a more realistic appraisal of both the national debt and government commercial activities.

The danger inherent in applying company balance-sheet ideas to the national balance-sheet has been labelled the 'cement and steel' concept. The purpose of business finance is to increase its profits and net worth, but this is not the case for government finance (with the possible modification just noted of government commercial activities). Assets held by the firm are the collateral against the firm's debt, but no such reasoning applies to government assets. Applying commercial ideas to the whole of government debt 'reinforces the ancient prejudice in favour of expenditure on hardware as distinct from services': the type of thinking that enjoins the building of schools and hospitals but jibs at paying those who run them adequate salaries. In particular, it has been alleged in recent years that some underdeveloped countries are prone to prestige development rather than undertaking less glamorous but more productive investment.

We can look at this matter from another viewpoint. It is true that the economy will be worse off if the government increases the national debt (i.e. borrows) and uses the money wastefully. But this argument has nothing to do with increasing the national debt. It would be equally valid if the wasteful spending was out of tax revenue.

The technical problems of debt management

So far it has been established that the size of the debt by itself is not a good guide to its economic significance. It nevertheless remains true that a large debt poses problems of debt-management. These were grouped into five by the Radcliffe Committee:

(*a*) The Treasury has to deal with maturities of marketable debt, and to make new issues to replace these and to finance new requirements, beyond current revenue, of the central government.

(*b*) The markets in outstanding liabilities require 'management', both to facilitate (*a*) and to avert undesirable repercussions on the wider financial structure of the economy. This requirement applies both to the very short-term liabilities (management of 'the money market') and to the longer-term liabilities (management of the gilt-edged section of the Stock Exchange).

(*c*) The net capital requirements of the nationalized industries have to be provided; this involves questions of how the money should be raised (which connects with (*a*) above) and the terms on which it should be made available to the industries.

(*d*) Similarly, the net capital requirements of the local government authorities have to be provided.

(*e*) The methods of raising funds by the sale of non-marketable securities (e.g. Tax Reserve Certificates and the 'small savings' instruments) have to be determined. All of these tasks are related to each other, and decisions on any one of them must have regard to repercussions on others. In carrying out these tasks the Treasury has always to have regard to the fact that a considerable proportion of the National Debt is held overseas (para. 532).

The most important problems in the post-war period, it has already been indicated, occurred under headings (*a*) and (*b*) above. As a result of war-time financing, large blocks of debt became due for repayment. The debt was considerably more liquid and presented a threat of inflationary pressure if the assets, as they matured, were spent on consumer goods rather than reinvested. The period has been labelled one of the 'cult of the equity', in other words the market for fixed interest long-term securities, such as gilt-edged, was not buoyant. Clearly these matters impinge on monetary and fiscal policy and affect rates of interest. A related set of problems was the cost of servicing the debt. In so far as the debt is held by residents of Britain the problem is not so serious: high interest costs mean that taxation must be higher than it would otherwise need to be in order to pay the interest charges. The problem may have important considerations concerning the redistribution of income, but this is not our immediate concern in this section. The problem is more serious for that part of the debt which is held by non-residents of Britain (over £4,482 million in 1967). This implies a payment outflow from this country to the foreign holders, and in so far as they are not content to hold sterling, but require their own currencies, this is a factor operating to depress the price of sterling on world markets.

Management of the debt in relation to the economy

In the words of the Radcliffe Committee:

The most elementary problem of debt management is one that is necessarily solved in some way or other day by day. The previously existing debt, plus any current Exchequer cash deficit, or minus any current Exchequer cash surplus, has to be and is absorbed. Each day the vast majority of holders of government securities continue to hold those securities at the end of the day, but a fraction of the securities is unloaded during the day: this unloaded fraction, and any currently accruing deficit, must be absorbed either by new holders in the private sector or against release of cash by the monetary authorities. And the same is true of a year's operations: in some way or other the government's needs are met, and the debt existing at the end of the year must be held by someone, even if this result can only be achieved by allowing cash to constitute a greater part of the debt than before. If the achievement of this result threatens to entail growth of cash or other highly liquid liabilities to a degree thought dangerous, because of the repercussions of this growth of liquidity in the private sector, the authorities have in theory three courses open to them:

(1) they can make long-term securities so much more attractive that the threat is averted (i.e. 'funding' succeeds);
(2) they can increase taxation, so enabling themselves to get the real resources they want without adding so much to, and perhaps even bringing about some reduction of, the National Debt;
(3) they can cut the use of real resources by the public sector (cutting either government expenditure or investment in the public sector) so reducing the amount of debt to be placed with the private sector in the period.

There have been in the last decade examples of all three methods of adjustment (para. 558).

This quotation brings out clearly one problem: that the management of the debt may result in a growth of unwanted liquidity of the debt in which case a number of alternative (but unpleasant) choices are available. Not brought out quite so clearly is the allied problem that, if the debt is changing in total as well as in maturity structure; this implies a different use of real resources. As an example, consider the case of an Exchequer cash deficit (i.e. a need to increase the debt) in a year in which the economy is fully employed.

Even if in these circumstances the most favourable case is taken where the government is able to make good the deficiency by the sale of long-term securities, it is unlikely that private expenditure will be cut back by the whole amount of the deficiency. Unless additional action is taken on one or more of the ways suggested in (1) to (3) above, inflationary pressure will result.

Similar considerations apply if the economy is not fully employed and the government is running a surplus (i.e. reducing the national debt). It is unlikely that the whole of the proceeds will be spent by the private sector on consumer goods or investment projects, and in the absence of offsetting action the economy will be further run down.

It is now possible to understand the statements of the Radcliffe Committee:

> For the debt ought not to be regarded as a given total, whose structure alone can be manipulated. If all possible courses in manipulating the structure threaten serious disadvantages this can be a reason for aiming at a bigger Exchequer cash surplus (or smaller deficit), so as to lessen the difficulties of management of the debt. . . . The debt is not, that is to say, to be regarded as a residual among the quantities of economy policy. Thus debt management can be regarded neither as something to be, as it were, left to the last and adjusted to all other policy decisions, nor on the other hand as a consideration which should override all other policy decisions; it has to be integrated with a variety of measures in the pursuit of the broad aims of economic policy (para. 535).

To recapitulate, the management of the debt has both monetary implications and implications for the use of the real resources in the economy. Because the propensities to spend of the government and the private sectors will usually differ, the problem in ensuring balance in the economy is not just a simple one of, for example, ensuring that increased government expenditure is equally matched by an increase in taxation or by an increase in debt. In full-employment conditions, a greater sum will normally have to be raised, because private expenditure on goods and services is likely to fall by a smaller magnitude than the changes in revenue brought about by the changes in government spending. Likewise, given a reduction in government spending matched by a cut in taxes, it is unlikely that the whole of this sum will be spent on investment or consumption goods, and it may be necessary for the government to take some action to maintain a balance in the economy.

If we revert back to the three courses of action open to the authorities, we find that restraints are present on each of them. The success of funding depends on the public's willingness to take up government long-term debt; there may be periods during which the public is not willing to do this. It may be possible to induce the public to hold more debt at a higher rate of interest (the Radcliffe Committee express some doubt on this), but even so an increase in interest rates has other implications which must be considered. In particular, rates of interest in Britain that are out of line with other developed countries may result in undesirable flows of money (so called 'hot money') into and out of the country, which are very disturbing to the balance of payments.

Changes in taxation can be aimed primarily either at changing spending in the company sector or at changing the level of personal spending. The latter is likely to reflect on the company sector if the change continues for any length of time. A variety of other methods can also be used to influence behaviour in these two sectors, e.g. changing investment allowances or grants, and altering hire-purchase regulations on down-payment and length of time over which payments can be made. Much use has been made in the post-war period of such policies, designed to influence the private sector. This will be taken up later.

Changes in the use of real resources by the government also has obvious drawbacks. Much of government expenditure is on essential services, such as roads, hospitals and various kinds of educational establishments. Many people are of the opinion that expenditure on these items should be increased, not decreased. In the words of Professor Galbraith, 'Public squalor is contrasted with private affluence'. The interruption of capital plans, particularly the capital spending of local authorities and nationalized industries, has been a feature on several occasions in the post-war period. It is particularly wasteful and expensive to try to alter capital expenditure once a certain stage of work has been reached, and this type of action is a desperate resort. The recasting of long-term plans is a different matter, but it is the case that planning techniques have not developed to the extent that much reliance can be placed on such forecasts, and altering long-term plans is no remedy for a current imbalance.

Burden of the debt

The phrase 'burden of the debt' is unfortunately one that seems to be embedded in any discussion about the national debt. The implication of the word 'burden' is that life would be better if only the burden could be got rid of. Discussion about the debt is thus biased in advance. Confusion is made worse by difference about the meaning of 'burden'.

WHAT DO WE MEAN BY 'BURDEN'?

Burden is sometimes construed to mean the current amount of goods and services which the private sector gives up in order to enable the public sector to consume. This may be nil in the case of an under-employed economy, where the use of resources by the public sector need not be at the expense of private consumption, but can come from increased production out of previously unused resources. With full employment of resources, by definition, increased consumption by one sector is at the expense of another if imported commodities remain unchanged. To make sense of the 'burden' argument in conditions of full employment, it is necessary, somehow, to evaluate the government's use of resources and its worth to individuals as opposed to leaving the resources as they were. It is clear that while this line of argument poses important issues, these have nothing specifically to do with debt-financing. Tax-financing raises exactly similar problems.

Another concept of burden relates to the amount of goods and services forgone by the people currently living during the period of their lifetimes. Given full employment, capital projects which take a long time to fructify will lessen the amount of currently available consumer goods, but increase the amount available, say, ten or twenty years ahead. Again, it is clear that important issues are involved which have nothing specifically to do with the national debt.

The two concepts of burden dealt with approached the question from the side of the use of resources. They can be argued in terms of the money burden on the existing population or in terms of the money burden on the future. Real economic issues underly the discussion in money terms, which will be taken up shortly. Again, these issues are misleading when confined to a discussion of debt-financing, with the implied assumption that financing by other means does not also have similar implications. This will be looked at in Chapter 19.

Yet another concept of burden relates to the estimated effects that the debt has upon incentives to work, to save, to take risks and so on.

What emerges from our discussion of the meaning of the 'debt burden' is that government spending raises very important issues. We mentioned the current use of real resources, the stock of capital we should aim to bequeath to the future, and the effect on incentives. The important point emerges that however the government sector obtains the use of these resources, whether it is by commandeering them, by taxation or by debt, these important issues remain. To look at the so-called burden of the debt in isolation is a misleading exercise; it is necessary to consider the advantages and disadvantages of alternative methods of obtaining these resources.

Internal and external borrowing

An important distinction to be made is between internal and externally held debt—that is, between internal and external borrowing. Internal borrowing is a rearrangement of assets: citizens surrender current purchasing power in return for government securities. No increase of real resources is directly created as a result. External borrowing, on the other hand, permits an import of real resources, either of consumption or capital goods. Likewise, interest and repayment of internal debt is the transfer of current purchasing power back to holders of the debt. Interest and repayment of external borrowing mean, however, a corresponding outflow of goods and services unless the external holders choose for a time to reinvest in securities of the country making the repayment. From the point of view of interest and repayment of external debt, it can be said that this constitutes a 'burden' on future output of goods and services. However, it must not be lost sight of that if the borrowing is used to increase the productive capacity of the economy, this may create the capacity not only to do both of these things, but also to yield a return over and above this. The application of this to underdeveloped countries is obvious. It may at times be necessary to use foreign loans for purposes of increasing imports of consumption goods; but the use to increase productive capacity is to be preferred, if at all possible, as this will help to create the output to repay and service the loan.

Equity aspects of the debt

Probably the most frequently mentioned aspect of the internally held national debt is the concern which is expressed over its effects on the distribution of income and wealth. The debt represents a transfer of income from those who pay taxes to those who own the securities. Since all citizens pay taxes of one sort or another, it is not easy to work out how much transference in fact takes place. If the debt was abolished overnight by decree, the government would be able to forgo collecting £1,599 million or so in revenue which is at present paid in interest. The distributional effects of this would depend on whether it is assumed that income tax is reduced as a result or whether indirect taxes are reduced or abolished. Objections on these lines, that the payment of interest is unfair, as it represents a transfer from the poor (who pay taxes) to the rich (who own the securities), is, as we have seen, dependent on assumptions about which taxes are relieved as a result of not paying interest. The real objection that seems to be at the back of this type of argument is to the very unequal distribution of wealth and income in the community. This is a question which is worth discussion in its own right. Interest payments on the national debt are of only subsidiary importance to the topic.

Future generations

Similar considerations apply to the argument that government financing by debt imposes a burden on future generations who have to repay the debt. What, however, is frequently not pointed out, is that future generations also benefit by the repayment. The debt existing at the present time has, as we have seen, the effect of redistributing income from existing taxpayers to existing holders of securities. In 100 years from now both the holders of the debt and the taxpayers will be different people. If we take a shorter time-span—say, thirty years—the argument can be looked at in terms of inter-generation equity: that sons will be paying for the debts of their fathers. This point has some validity, but doesn't boil down to anything more than the truism that our actions today will affect the future in a number of ways, some of them calculable and some of them not. In particular, the argument that raising funds by taxation today, instead of by debt, imposes no burden on the future is clearly false. If a person's wealth and income is taxed today, while it is true that no 'burden' is left to future generations, it is also true that the assets of the individual to leave to his dependants will be less. Or, in terms of the father-and-son argument, that the father will have less to spend on his son. In order to make sense of the argument that raising money by debt finance is a burden on the future, the stream of consequences stemming from raising finance in this way has to be compared with the stream of consequences stemming from raising finance in alternative ways. The number of alternative ways is innumerable, as they can take the form of various combinations of different taxes. In a trivial sense, however we raise the money imposes a burden on the future, in the sense that this question is usually phrased: that raising money by debt imposes more of a burden on the future than raising it by taxation, the question is not capable of a precise answer. Different assumptions about future behaviour are likely to yield different answers.

In this question we come back once more to a more fundamental question that appears to underlie much argument on this subject. That is the question of the perpetuation of the existing structure of wealth by inheritance; and once more it seems that discussion of this question directly is more fruitful than a roundabout discussion of imprecise 'burdens' caused by this or that method of financing.[6]

[6] The reader interested in pursuing this topic to its metaphysical heights is referred to a collection of recent writings edited by Ferguson, J. M. (1964).

Monetary and fiscal implications of the debt

In looking at the so-called burden of the debt, it was found that merely looking at money transfers obscured rather than illuminated some of the problems. In considering the fiscal and monetary implications, it will also be found useful to bear 'real' implications in mind. The following will serve as a summary of points that have been raised earlier:

COMPOSITION OF THE DEBT

The importance of the composition of the debt has been raised on several occasions. In particular, the authorities are concerned with the liquidity of the debt, with the ratio of short-term to long-term debt. The importance, it will be remembered, is that, although money can be obtained by selling both types of security on the market, only short-term debt has a fairly certain value. The implications of liquidity are twofold: (1) the fear that the private sector will be tempted to convert their assets into spending power, and (2) that the banks and other financial institutions may use the assets as a base on which to expand credit. In both cases what is important is the relationship between the monetary authorities and the private sector. A sale of assets from a private individual to another individual or a sale from a bank to a private individual is merely a rearrangement of assets within the private sector, not of monetary importance except in so far as this implies changes in interest rates. If, however, the monetary authorities buy the securities, then this is directly increasing the purchasing power of the private sector. They may have to buy the securities because these are repayable on demand, such as deposits at the Post Office Savings Bank or short-term deposits with local authorities. They may buy marketable securities because they wish to maintain the level of interest rates. They may be forced into raising more money on such short-term assets as Treasury bills, because the public are unwilling to subscribe to long-term issues.

TOTAL OF THE DEBT

We have seen that the absolute size of the debt does not as a rule form a big constraint on the government. If interest payments form a large proportion of the Budget, it is possible that this will form a constraint on government spending because they fear to put up taxes. Since interest payments are taxed as unearned income, this problem is not likely to arise out of normal peace-time financing.

An increase in the total of the debt is important in so far as it affects the composition of the debt on the lines indicated in the previous section.[7]

INTEREST RATES

The effect of interest rates on the economy will be discussed in Part III. Changes in interest rates do affect the economy in various ways, but these effects are not felt in any simple or direct manner. The monetary authorities must bear in mind the effect on the demand for money by borrowers, on the supply of money, and more directly the effects on the flow of money into or out of the country from overseas.

Bank Rate is a key rate in the economy because, in particular, the commercial bank rates are by convention tied to it, and the Treasury bill rate moves in sympathy. Movements in these rates are likely to cause similar movements in most other short-term market rates, and in time to spread to the longer-term securities. Debt-management policy has obvious implications also for affecting the structure of interest rates. It would be possible for the monetary authorities to set the general level of long-term interest rates by making new issues of securities at the interest rate they had selected and operating in the market day by day to support that rate. If the authorities try to maintain a rate that is clearly out of line with market expectations, undesirable repercussions may follow which will lead them to revise the rate structure they have set. The 'cheap money' policy pursued after 1945 had this pattern. The authorities had the policy of maintaining low interest rates. An investor who expects the rate of interest to

[7] A more diffused effect of the size and composition of the debt may be apparent from its effect on private wealth. An increase in debts among the public itself does not constitute an increase in wealth when aggregation takes place. The assets of some members of the public are matched by corresponding liabilities of other members. To what extent an increase in national debt is regarded by the public as a net increase in wealth is empirically uncertain. An increase in the national debt does two things: it increases the public's ownership of claims against the monetary sector, and at the same time it increases the tax liability of the public to service the debt. The public's reaction can vary considerably. One extreme is considering the increase in claims it holds as an increase in wealth without making any allowance for the tax liability. At the other extreme, if full offset for tax liability is conceded no net increase in wealth is apparent. Put simply, in the latter case there would be no change in aggregate behaviour, due to the wealth effect, if the national debt was halved or changed by some other fraction.

The wealth effect will be considered in the Appendix to Chapter 19. In the context of the present chapter, while it may be true that the wealth effect is important as a long-run determinant of behaviour, it is unlikely to be important as a short-run determinant.

This question is discussed in relation to the Federal Debt of the United States by Tobin, J. (1963).

increase (i.e. a fall in the market value of existing securities), not only does not subscribe to new low coupon issues for fear of making a capital loss when interest rates change, but also tends to sell securities and keep liquid in order to take advantage of the investment opportunities when interest rates do change. In the late 1940s the authorities were having to acquiesce in the increasing liquidity of the public, which resulted in their eventual abandonment of the cheap money policy.

The policy followed in much of the 1950s was use of Bank Rate and other measures to affect short-term rates and thereby indirectly long-term rates, but no deliberate manipulation of long-term rates. In general, the authorities followed rather than led the rates in the long-term sector. In the words of the Radcliffe Committee: 'Until the last year or so [i.e. 1958-9] the authorities have not regarded management of the national debt as an opportunity for working on the structure of interest rates . . .' (para. 429).

The position today is that the authorities are more willing to pursue their aims for interest rates throughout the economy by seeking to influence the behaviour of prices and yields in the gilt-edged market. Also:

Management of the gilt-edged market, and the outcome in terms both of prices and of the net amounts of stock sold or bought in official dealings, have considerable bearing on credit policy and the liquidity of the banks and others, creating conditions that may help or hinder policy in this field. Neither interest rate policy nor credit policy, however, is the dominant long-term consideration in debt-management; this is rather to ensure so far as possible that suitable finance for the Exchequer is available in the future, so that there be no excessive recourse to short-term borrowing from the banks on Treasury bills and accompanying increase in the money supply ('Official Transactions in the Gilt-edged Market' (June, 1966)).

Summary

Details of the available statistical data on the debt, which are still far from adequate, has been given. Although the debt has increased greatly in money terms, as a percentage of national income it shows a marked decrease since 1935. The debt after 1945 is, however, much more liquid, and this poses problems for the monetary authorities. A particular problem is the need, as well as meeting new borrowing requirements, to replace the debt with fresh borrowing as it comes up for redemption.

The implications of the debt on the use of real resources in the economy are complicated and pose difficult choices.

It is necessary to try to trace the effects caused by the size of the debt, the composition of the debt and the structure of interest rates which are influenced by debt management. These factors affect the liquidity of the economy and the ability of the banks and other financial institutions to create credit, and also have direct effects on individuals and companies. The task is a difficult one, and it is not surprising that differences of opinion exist at many points of the analysis. The conclusion reached is that debt-management should not be considered as an end in itself, but as part of the whole fiscal process.

In discussing the so-called 'burden' of the debt, a distinction should be drawn between debt held internally and debt held by foreigners. The discussion of 'burden' unearthed somc important problems: the use of resources by the public sector, the amount of capital investment being undertaken, the effect on incentives, the distribution of wealth and income, and the perpetuation of the existing structure of wealth by inheritance. In all cases it was found that discussion of these problems solely in terms of debt-financing obscured rather than illuminated the issues.

18
Public finance critique

To restrict our Report completely to an analysis of the revenue-raising side would be equivalent to saying that we think it meaningful to ignore one blade of a pair of scissors. There may be some who would say that our efforts should be directed to spreading more equitably the 'burden' of taxation and that we should not concern ourselves with the results of government expenditure. But in many respects one is essential to the other and it is their joint product that must be our concern. Therefore, while we do not attempt to assess government expenditure programmes, we do not ignore them.

Report of the Canadian Royal Commission on Taxation (1966).

Summary of major faults in present system

This section has outlined the main changes in government spending and revenue during this century. Chapter 11, set up the total-accretion principle as a yardstick to evaluate the current system, which was detailed in the following chapters. A summary follows of the major faults found:

1. The complexity of the tax-and-benefit system.
2. The appearance of high rates of tax which are not in many cases effective rates. Particularly is this so with estate duty. It applies to the recently introduced taxes on capital gains and land and also to income, because of earned income relief, up to a level of income of £9,945, and the form in which allowances against tax are given.
3. High rates of tax on earned incomes with alleged disincentive effects on incentives, the diversion of effort into forms of output attracting low rates of tax, the unproductive use of resources specifically for tax avoidance, and the setting up of residence abroad by high-rate taxpayers.
4. Lower flat-rate taxes, or zero taxes, on most other spending power.

5. Many social benefits channelled via tax allowances which do not help the most needy.
6. The lack of any consistent principles for company taxation.

These faults add up to a formidable indictment of the system which is likely to have serious economic and social consequences. This chapter attempts to suggest remedies. First, the problem of incidence in its traditional form is looked at in more detail. This concept is modified on the grounds that the approach is too narrow. There is a need to look at the total incidence of taxes and benefits. This is carried out for the income groups for which information is at present available. Finally, ways in which the system can be improved are investigated.

Incidence

The classical concept of incidence deals with the problem of trying to sort out who really pays a particular tax, and what are the effects of a tax change. In this book the problem has arisen on several occasions. For example, should taxes on companies be considered as being borne by the shareholders, the employees or the customers of the company? Are capital gains paid by the seller on whom the tax is imposed, or the buyer, or in some measure between them?

This concept of incidence refers to the location of the 'ultimate' as opposed to the 'direct' money burden of the tax. The direct location of a tax is the person on whom the legal liability is imposed; the ultimate location the person who finally pays it. 'Shifting' refers to the process by which the direct money burden is pushed along through price adjustments from the point of impact (i.e. where statutory liability is imposed) to the final resting-place. 'Effects' refer to all other changes that the tax may bring about, e.g. inflation, changes in output or incomes and transfer effects.

It should be noted that we cannot in any case make practical measurements of the 'ultimate' burden of a tax. Take, for example, a tax on cigarettes. We can measure the consumption of cigarettes and, on the assumption that the consumer pays the whole of the tax, say that this individual pays so much tobacco tax compared to that one. But we cannot catch by this measuring-rod the 'burden' on the person who has had to reduce or stop smoking because of the tax.

Incidence in this traditional sense is an academic exercise. Different assumptions—for example, about the degree of monopoly power being exercised and about the ratio of elasticities of supply and demand—lead to different answers. The argument used in this book is that it can be highly misleading to talk about the burden of a particular tax in isolation from the rest of the tax system. That is the distortion that is involved, for example, in judging from our progressive system of income tax and surtax that the system as a whole is progressive. As we have seen, this is as misleading as to judge that because we have high rates of estate duty we are thereby rapidly achieving greater equality of wealth.

As a first rough check on the equity of the tax system it is possible to use the figures from Table 1, Chapter 9, showing the sources of U.K. tax revenue. National Insurance and Health contributions, Customs and Excise, and rates can be classified as regressive taxes, falling more heavily on those with low incomes.[1] Profits tax, motor-vehicle tax and the selective employment tax are deducted from the total revenue in 1967 of £13,337 million, to leave a figure of £11,566 million. These taxes are not easily classified as regressive or progressive. The taxes labelled 'regressive' then amount to £7,112 million, or 61% of the total of £11,566. Most of the years shown in the table in Chapter 9 record a figure of near to 60% for these regressive taxes. From the tax revenue side the fiscal system therefore looks to be regressive on low incomes, and not progressive.

However, this is only looking at one side of the picture: the side of income after tax. It is possible that when the expenditure side of the picture is taken into account, it will be found that the addition to income in cash, or money's worth, more than covers the tax paid by lower incomes. What picture emerges when both the costs (i.e. taxes paid) and the benefits are taken into account?

The term 'cost-benefit' has been pre-empted in economics for a rather different idea.[2] So to describe the process when both sides are taken into account the term 'incidence' will be retained and

[1] The recent scheme of rates rebate to those on very low income and the fact that size of house may be correlated with income make rates difficult to classify definitely into one category or the other. In 1967, if rates are included with profits tax, motor-vehicle tax and the selective employment tax as not easily classifiable, we get a total of £10,091 million that can be classified. Regressive taxes amount to 69% of this. If rates are classified as progressive taxes, this leaves a total of £5,637 million as regressive taxation, or 49% of the total of £11,566 million. The point made—that regressive taxes are a large part of tax revenue—holds, whichever of these classifications is judged the best.

[2] Cost-benefit analysis attempts to assess the costs and the benefits of a particular item, such as a new road, or airport, or a Channel tunnel. Costs and benefits are defined in the broadest possible way to embrace, not only direct costs, such as money costs of construction, but indirect costs, such as loss of amenities. Similarly, benefits take in not only direct benefits, such as quicker travelling time for persons using the proposed new route, but indirect benefits, such as quicker travel for persons on old routes because of less congestion. What is included on the cost-and-benefit side and how these are evaluated are obviously of crucial importance.

qualified, as the 'incidence of taxes and benefits'.

The incidence of taxes and benefits in 1966

Incidence is transformed into a study of costs (that is, who pays) and benefits of the whole fiscal system. Criticism of this approach has been made on a number of grounds (see Prest, A. R. (1968), and Peacock, A. T. and Shannon, R. (1968)). The criticisms concern the

Table 1

Average incomes before and after taxes and benefits, 1966

(£ per year)

RANGE OF

		£260–	£315–	£382–	£460–	£559–	£676–	£816–
1 adult								
1.	£	279	348	412	507	624	743	904
2.	£	405	447	448	479	455	561	629
3.	£	+126	+99	+36	−28	−169	−182	−275
4.	%	+41·2	+28·4	+8·7	−5·5	−27·1	−24·5	−30·4
2 adults								
1.	£	287	347	424	510	621	759	901
2.	£	513	583	611	653	607	669	727
3.	£	+226	+236	+187	+143	−14	−90	−174
4.	%	+78·7	+68·0	+44·1	+28·0	−2·3	−12·0	−19·3
2 adults, 1 child								
1.	£	—	—	—	—	—	753	891
2.	£	—	—	—	—	—	668	701
3.	£	—	—	—	—	—	−85	−190
4.	%	—	—	—	—	—	−11·3	−21·3
2 adults, 2 children								
1.	£	—	—	—	—	—	766	903
2.	£	—	—	—	—	—	836	843
3.	£	—	—	—	—	—	+70	−60
4.	%	—	—	—	—	—	+9·1	−6·6
2 adults, 3 children								
1.	£	—	—	—	—	—	—	891
2.	£	—	—	—	—	—	—	987
3.	£	—	—	—	—	—	—	+96
4.	%	—	—	—	—	—	—	+10·8

Source: *Economic Trends*, No. 172, February, 1968.
1. Original income before taxes and benefits.
2. Income after all taxes and benefits: 'effective income'.

general methodology used, assumptions about the incidence of taxes and the need to improve the data. This method is here put forward as the one that approaches most nearly the concept of the standard of living of a person or family. It does so by taking the income of the unit, adding to it a money value of services received where it is sensible to allocate these, and subtracting taxes paid. The fact that the value of nearly half of government expenditure, on such items as defence and roads, cannot be allocated and is ignored as a benefit to the individual or family, while most taxation can be allocated, is, it is suggested, the right approach in this context. Improvements can and should be made to Budget studies, but this does not stop this

ORIGINAL INCOME

£988–	£1,196–	£1,448–	£1,752–	£2,122–	£2,566–£3,104
1,087	1,282	1,570	—	—	—
751	843	1,063	—	—	—
−336	−439	−507	—	—	—
−30·9	−34·2	−32·3	—	—	—
1,091	1,314	1,600	1,912	2,319	3,945
798	923	1,112	1,306	1,571	2,540
−293	−391	−488	−606	−748	−1,405
−26·9	−29·8	−30·5	−31·7	−32·6	−35·6
1,102	1,328	1,598	1,922	2,321	3,550
902	1,018	1,220	1,454	1,796	2,533
−200	−310	−378	−468	−525	−1,017
−18·1	−23·3	−23·7	−24·3	−22·3	−28·6
1,096	1,326	1,596	1,918	2,341	3,744
976	1,142	1,330	1,538	1,934	2,788
−120	−184	−266	−380	−407	−956
−10·9	−13·9	−16·7	−19·8	−17·4	−25·5
1,102	1,310	1,619	1,899	—	—
1,116	1,285	1,521	1,725	—	—
+14	−25	−96	−174	—	—
+1·3	−1·9	−5·9	−9·2	—	—

3. Difference between 1 and 2.
4. Difference as % of original income.

approach being a fruitful one. There is still the problem of deciding who ultimately pays the tax and receives the benefits. Studies must obviously make assumptions about this and what these benefits are worth. However, these problems can be seen in perspective. The importance or otherwise of a particular tax or benefit in relation to the whole can be judged. In particular, with this approach it would be feasible to set up alternative assumptions about the incidence of various taxes and benefits to see what overall difference this makes to the 'burden'.

This type of analysis then sets out to analyse the overall effect of government spending and revenue in its distributional aspect.[3]

For several years the Central Statistical Office has published in *Economic Trends* detailed tax and benefit figures for particular income categories, divided into single persons and married persons with and without children (see 'Incidence of Taxes and Social Service Benefits' (February, 1968)). The information is of necessity in terms of averages. It is obtained from the Ministry of Labour annual survey of expenditure of about 3,000 persons. Each household included in the survey is asked to provide detailed information about all forms of income, including National Insurance and other cash benefits received from the State, payments of income tax and surtax, the type of dwelling occupied, the kind of education which any member of the household is receiving, and so on.

In any exercise of this nature the inclusion or exclusion of particular taxes or benefits may make a big difference to the result. The following outline is intended as a guide:

Direct taxes included are income tax, surtax, and employers' and employees' contributions to National Insurance and Health—that is, the employers' contribution is regarded as part of the employees' income and as a tax borne by him. Death duties and taxes on undistributed profits are not included. Customs and Excise taxes, including purchase and betting tax, are assumed to be fully reflected in the prices paid by consumers when buying commodities subject to indirect tax.

Benefits included are sub-divided into cash benefits and benefits in

[3] Ideally we need also to know the total impact on other variables, such as consumption, investment, prices and growth of the economy. It will be argued in Part III that the problems involved in doing this are formidable. It has also been suggested in the Preface that too much emphasis has been placed on these aspects in recent years. A developed country has the resources to drastically reduce if not solve its social problems now; it is not necessary to wait until this or that particular rate of growth is achieved in order to do more to improve social conditions than we are doing at the moment.

kind. Cash benefits include family allowances, pensions, National Insurance benefits, national assistance grants, etc., but not scholarships and educational grants. Benefits in kind include the National Health Service, State education, school health services, school meals, milk and welfare foods and scholarships and education grants. The method of allocating the benefits from State education is to impute to each child the average cost per child of education in the particular category of school he or she is attending. Benefits of the National Health Services are allocated in a similar manner, it being assumed that the total value of all the services (except maternity services, which are separately allocated) is the same for all persons in each of six different categories of the population.

The benefits derived from government expenditure on administration, defence, museums, libraries, parks, roads and so on are not allocated. By their nature, allocation of benefits to individuals of these services would be a haphazard affair.[4]

When looking at these statistics, it is important to bear in mind that results are not shown for pensioner households, so defined if at least three-quarters of the income is derived from Old Age or National Insurance pensions and National Assistance. Results are not given for households with an income of less than £260 a year, and the highest income range given is £2,566-£3,104. Mixed households—that is, households where there are more than two adults (here defined as a person over sixteen years)—are not shown because of the limited number in the sample.

Where the number of households in each 'cell' fell below ten, the information was not published, as it was thought to be too unreliable. With a small sample, too much reliance should not be placed on each individual figure. The Central Statistical Office state that from 1967 onwards the sample of households will be doubled. This should make the estimates more reliable, and it would also greatly assist in the interpretation of the results if the figures were presented with estimates of standard deviation (i.e. estimates of variation found in each figure).

What emerges from this sample? Table 1 presents information for the year 1966. Reading down the left-hand margin, we have information on family grouping, first for one adult then for two adults with nought, one, two, or three children. Across the page information on income range is presented. Beneath each family grouping appear lines

[4] It is interesting to note that, as with all Budget surveys, the amount that people say they spend on alcohol and tobacco is underestimated (by half on alcohol and a quarter on tobacco) and the figures have to be grossed up to allow for this.

numbered, 1, 2, 3 and 4. The first line presents the average gross income (termed original income) found in each income range, while the second line gives this income after taxes have been deducted and benefits added (this will be termed 'effective income'). Line 3 gives the difference between original income and effective income, while line 4 expresses this difference as a percentage of original income. Line 4 thus gives an approximate measure of the progressiveness of the system of taxes and benefits for households of each size; it expresses the net benefits received or net taxes paid.

A recapitulation is in order before commenting on these figures. The estimates gather up the diverse strands present in the British system of taxation and government spending. We have noted that indirect taxes (as currently administered) and flat-rate Insurance and Health contributions are regressive, while income and surtax rates are progressive. On the expenditure side benefits will normally be progressive—that is, forming a larger percentage of lower incomes than of higher incomes, with the important exception of benefits via tax allowances.

The picture that emerges is that within the income range considered (£260-3,104) the overall impact of taxing and government spending in each family category (1 adult, 2 adults, etc.), is progressive to some extent. Higher incomes in general pay a bigger proportion than lower incomes, and some lower incomes benefit to a greater extent than they pay out. However, the progression quickly flattens out for two categories: single adults with average income between £816 and £1,752 pay roughly 30%; and two adults with average income between £1,196 and £2,122 also pay about 30%. It is to be hoped that information will soon be collected on higher income ranges, so that the progression at higher incomes can be ascertained.

The table also shows the degree of progressiveness between categories. For example, comparing the original income range £676-816 per annum, an average of about £14 a week, with an income that is a little more than double this, i.e. an income in the range £1,448-1,752 per annum, an average of £31 a week, we find:

	Income £14 per Week, Taken Net in Tax Per Annum		*Income £31 per Week,* Taken Net in Tax Per Annum	
	£	%	£	%
1 adult	182	24·5	507	32·3
2 adults	90	12·0	488	30·5
2 adults, 1 child	85	11·3	378	23·7
2 adults, 2 children	+70	+9·1	266	16·7
2 adults, 3 children	Not available		96	5·9

Should we be complacent about these results? Do they accord with current ideas about equity? It may be questioned, for example, whether it is the general wish to impose on a family with one child earning £14 a week a net tax of over 11% of their rather meagre income. This is a sum that is only £5 less than that paid by a couple without children in the same income range, whereas the difference between these categories in the £31 a week range is £110.

While increasing income from £14 a week to £31 a week means that a single person pays about 2·8 times more in tax (from £182 to £507), the other categories go up more steeply. Two adults pay 5·4 times more (from £90 to £488), a couple with one child 4·4 times more, while a couple with two children move from the position of benefiting from an addition to income of £70 to one where they pay £266. Once again it can be questioned whether these results are intended.

Conclusions

The evidence is overwhelming that our system of taxes and benefits, in spite of a considerable amount of effort, is neither equitable, nor is it succeeding very well in achieving its declared object of relieving poverty. No method is likely to achieve these objects by 100%, but there is no doubt that, given the desire, considerable improvements could be made.

Each writer has his own suggestions for reform, and groups from each of the main political parties have suggested changes. Reformers can be categorized into those who want to patch up the grossest deficiencies and those who believe more fundamental changes are needed. The author belongs to this second category. The mistake should not be made of thinking that the former solution is necessarily the simpler to execute and administer. The structure is already complex because of patching up in the past. One of the advantages to follow from more sweeping proposals is the simplification which this makes possible.

The accretion principle has been used as a yardstick. This may be thought of as a guide-line by which various taxes can be judged, or as a practical system to which we should make our system adhere as far as possible. Proposals to impose a progressive tax on inheritances, gifts and capital gains, and to cumulate these receipts over a person's lifetime fall into the former category. The proposals to tax these receipts as income falls into the latter category. The latter solution has been favoured in this book, but either alternative would be preferable to the present inadequate system. There are advantages in administration in subjecting all receipts to one tax, and no sound arguments have been found for separate treatment of inheritance, gifts or capital gains. Redistribution of wealth, if this is desired by the community, can continue by a modified form of estate duty, in addition to taxing bequests as income in the hands of the recipient.

Proposed reforms

The prime reform therefore that is suggested is a reversal of the process which has been going on for so many years, whereby income that is subject to income tax is more and more narrowly drawn. In particular, capital gains, gains on the sale of land, gifts and inheritance should be taxed at the same rate as other income. Some form of averaging of income will be needed, as it is needed under the present system, to achieve equity.

Averaging was considered in Chapter 11, and the conclusion was reached that, as well as being desirable, averaging is feasible: it is possible to avoid the heavy burden of recalculating tax due for past years of the averaging period. As a provisional step, the Royal Commission suggestion could be implemented, that where a drop in earned income of 50% or more over the previous years' income occurs, the taxpayer should have his tax recalculated over the proceeding year. This could be supplemented by provision for forward spreading of receipts, such as a gift, legacy or exceptional earnings in one year, when this has the effect of increasing income by 50% or more over the previous year. Income in these cases could be spread in equal amounts over the year of receipt and the next two or three years.

Tax could still be collected for the majority of taxpayers, as at present, under P.A.Y.E. The taxpayer could have the option of having his tax coding, which is notified to his employer, increased if he has income from other sources than his employment. If he wished to keep this information from his employer, arrangements could be made to pay the tax due on his non-employment income, directly to the Inland Revenue, similarly to the arrangements which exist at present under Schedule D tax.

Against the initial upheaval likely to be caused by these changes can be set some substantial benefits. The incentive for tax-avoidance by shuffling assets around would be greatly reduced. The existing bias against earned income and the alleged disadvantages that follow from this would be alleviated. A benefit that cannot be documented, but one that in the author's opinion is likely to bring substantial benefits, would be achieved just because an attempt was being made to achieve equity.

If the tax base is enlarged, tax rates can be looked at afresh.

The present system of a flat rate of tax at 8*s*. 3*d*. in the £1 over a wide range of income and progressive rates of surtax starting at £5,000 needs re-examination in any case.

A criterion for equity

A criterion for equity could be set up in terms of effective income. The first step in this direction would be to extend the survey made by the Central Statistical Office to cover high-income individuals and families. Information on low-income households was made available for the first time in *Economic Trends*, No. 177 (July, 1968). With this information to hand, the difference between original income and effective income (that is, after allowing for tax and benefits) is known, i.e. this figure gives the value of the *net* benefits received or the *net* taxes paid. Policy on taxation and benefits might with advantage take the form of an attempt to formulate and then to attain an equitable-percentage relationship between net benefits received or net taxes paid (as the case may be) and original income for incomes of various levels. In terms of Table 1, this would be to ensure the right degree of progression in line 4. Ideally, a smoothly decreasing amount of net benefit as income increases, leading to a smoothly progressive amount of net taxation as income increases still further. No attempt is made here to judge the break-even point for each class of taxpayer (that is, the level of income at which tax and benefit should cancel each other out), nor to determine the right degree of steepness of the progression.

The criterion just outlined takes into account that a person's standard of living consists of his income (defined on total-accretion lines), less taxation paid, plus the addition of the value of benefits that can be allocated to him. This criterion for assessing equity goes a long way to ensuring that taxpayers in equal positions are treated equally. It does not achieve complete equity, because both the taxes paid and benefits received are averages found from a sample of the population. Those with consumption patterns or in receipt of benefits markedly different from the average will be treated differently. For example, it is generally assumed that under any tax system alcohol and tobacco will continue to bear a high tax for social reasons. If this is to be the case, a person who smokes or drinks more than the average will pay more tax than a person in a similar position who does not smoke or drink. In a like manner, a person who is unfortunate enough to require prolonged medical treatment will 'benefit' more than the average from Health expenditure. It was stated at the end of Chapter 11 that principles in tax are set up as guides, not as inflexible rules. The presumption is that exceptions of the kind noted above to the rule that taxpayers in equal positions are treated equally would be generally accepted as desirable by the majority of people.

This criterion could be used to judge tax and benefit changes. Do they bring the system nearer to the agreed equity position?

Reform of tax allowances and other benefits and poverty

Widening the tax base on total-accretion lines and setting up a criterion for equity would mean that a radical reappraisal of the whole system of tax allowances and other benefits would be possible. For example, the abolition of tax allowances for children would make no difference to low-income earners who do not benefit at present and would worsen the position of those who pay tax and do benefit. There is likely to be some combination of change in tax rates and grants, in lieu of tax allowances, that will bring the system nearer to the agreed equity position. Over time a simplification of the fiscal system can be looked for. In particular, the pretence of high tax rates, which nevertheless have their impact greatly softened by tax allowances, can be overhauled. Benefits paid to those who need them rather than to everybody would mean that the great game whereby the rich apparently have large sums taken away from them in tax, and also apparently large sums given to them by tax allowances, need no longer be played.

The simplest tax reform would be the replacement of tax allowances by tax credits. This would not help the poor person who does not receive enough income to pay tax. This group cannot be assisted by income tax concessions, but it would ensure equal benefits to taxpayers. The effect of a tax allowance varies with the marginal rate of tax paid by the individual. This is so because an individual deducts any allowances due to him before tax is calculated. He will therefore either not reach so high a rate of tax or he will have less income to be taxed at his top rate. The benefits can be substantial to a high-rate surtax payer. For example, if we compare two individuals who have earned income only, where A has an income of £5,000 per annum and B an income of £25,000 that takes him into the top rate of surtax of 10*s*. in the £1. The cost to A of borrowing £3,000 for house-purchase at 7% is £210 per annum. Allowing for the two-ninths earned income relief, A is taxed at 6*s*. 5*d*. in the £1, so he obtains tax relief of £67 7*s*. 6*d*. His net cost is £142 12*s*. 6*d*. For the same net cost, the top-rate surtax payer can borrow about £23,000.

A tax credit, on the other hand, is a sum which is deductible from a person's tax bill. If all allowances were replaced by tax credits, each taxpayer would calculate his tax from his gross income level. Deductions on an agreed scale would then be made from the tax due, according to the circumstances of the taxpayer. If the allowance for a child was £50, then a taxpayer with two children would reduce his tax due by £100, whatever the size of his tax bill. No longer would the benefit mean most to those with highest incomes. The tax revenue gained could be used partly to reduce taxes and partly to provide benefits to those with low incomes.

The standard of equity set up envisaged judging a person's standard of living by taking his income on total-accretion lines, less taxes paid, plus the value of benefits received. Inevitably some persons' and families' effective incomes will fall below that deemed necessary to maintain an adequate standard of living. For these persons additional supplementation is needed. To this problem we now turn.

Supplementation of low incomes

A fairly simple procedure administratively would be to pay a supplement based on the previous year's effective income, with allowance for any known adjustments for the current year—for example, due to a wage-change or due to changes in benefits. The supplement could be paid weekly on the lines of the current pension book. Allocating a Post Office Giro account to all citizens would greatly facilitate the transfer of money to and from the government (suggested by Williams, B. R. (1967)). In time a simplification could be carried out. In place of a host of allowances, paid by a multiplicity of public authorities (e.g. child allowance, cheap milk and school meals, rate rebates, pensions and so on), a single payment could be made. Flexibility would be necessary to meet sudden calamities, so that money could be paid out immediately in respect of illness and unemployment.

A social objection is sometimes made to subsuming benefits into a weekly cash payment. This is, that benefits in kind, such as milk tokens and subsidized school meals ensure, as far as this is possible, that the benefits go to the intended recipient in the form in which they were intended, whereas, to put it in its worst light, cash payments may go straight to the betting-shop or on alcohol or tobacco, and the recipient's family be no better off. If this objection is thought to be sufficiently strong to warrant directed assistance, it still leaves a number of cash payments which can economically be paid out in one sum. The payment of this sum to the woman, in the case of married couples is likely to ensure that in the majority of cases it would be the family that benefited. Provision for payment to the husband, rather than the wife, could be made in exceptional circumstances.

The arguments that such a scheme would sap initiative, encourage idleness, subsidize employers who paid poor wages and the other objections, emotive or real, which are raised against any extension of welfare provisions must be weighed against the undoubted hardship and misery which exists at present.

It should be stressed that society at present makes the choice to assist its members not in any very rational manner, but as the end result of a series of tax imposts, tax concessions and other benefits. The scheme outlined sets out to ensure that no person or family falls below some minimum standard of living. It does so largely within the current system, but envisages this being greatly simplified over time. It suffers, if the past is any guide to the future, from the difficulties of defining what is the minimum standard to be aimed at and, perhaps of more practical importance, the lag that occurs in adjusting the standard to changes in the cost of living. There will probably always be disagreement on the first point, but making the standard and the amount of supplementation to be paid subject to the annual review of Parliament, on the lines of farming subsidies, should go a long way to ensuring that, in a society which is in aggregate becoming richer, all sectors of the population will participate in the increase to some extent. An annual review would also be likely to draw Parliament's attention more forcibly to alternative ways of relieving poverty; for example, raising the skill and wages of lower-paid workers.

The above proposals are rather different to suggestions that are put forward from time to time for a negative income tax (Friedman, M. (1962), 190-5, and Lees, D. (October, 1967)). These schemes envisage income tax being extended down the income scale so that poorer persons would receive payment. Let us take the position of a married man with two children under eleven earning an income of £522 per annum. Considering only the personal, child and earned-income allowances he was entitled in 1968 to the following tax relief:

	£
Earned-income relief, two-ninths of £522	116
Married person's allowance	340
Children's allowance (twice £115)	230
Total	686

There is a discrepancy of £164 between his income and allowances. Such a person under a negative income tax (i.e. a subsidy) would be entitled to receive payment of this sum. Proposals on these lines may be coupled with the suggestion that less than the full 100% negative tax, or subsidy, be introduced. For example, if the negative tax were introduced at the rate of 50% the person in the above example would be entitled to half of the sum of £164, i.e. £82. The reason given for having a negative tax on these lines at less than 100% is to lessen the effect on incentive to work. In the above example, under a full negative tax, for every £1 earned above his wage of £522 the person loses £1 of relief. At a rate of 50% the person loses 10*s*., and it is argued that his incentive to work is therefore greater.

There are a number of objections to a scheme on these lines. The first is that under any system of progressive taxation, tax concessions, benefit the most wealthy. The drawbacks of seeming to impose high tax and giving large concessions has been emphasized sufficiently in this book. The corresponding injustice at the other end of the scale, under a negative income tax, is that the smaller a person's ability to earn the smaller is the grant to which he is entitled because of the two-ninths earned-income relief. This is so whether the smaller earnings are due to laziness, ill-health, permanent disability or unavailability of work. In the example previously given, and asssuming a 100% tax, if the person was made redundant from his job and was unable to find alternative employment, his income would drop from £686 (£522 earnings and £164 benefit) to £507 in benefit. This is so because he loses earned-income relief, which was formerly worth £116. The author believes that the disincentive-to-work argument against giving benefits is greatly overrated, and does not warrant the hardship that it imposes on other categories of person who are genuinely unable to work, or the alternative, which would involve administrative complications in sorting out the idle from other categories of poor persons. In its desire to prevent a minority of work-shy people from benefiting, this scheme continues the current system of public vindictiveness to the majority who are poor through ill-health, disability or inability to get work. Again, to achieve a greater degree of equity, all income-tax concessions, and not just the three mentioned in the example, should be extended to all, although this would greatly add to the administrative complexity. Finally, and perhaps most importantly, tying benefits to tax concessions will arbitrarily alter benefits with every change in those concessions and any change in earned income relief.

The alternative proposals outlined in this section differ from the negative income tax scheme just outlined in envisaging a joint reduction in tax allowances and in tax rates, with supplementation paid to those with low effective incomes, to ensure, as far as this is possible, that no person or family falls below some minimum standard. The payment of this supplement could be termed a 'negative income tax', but it is not linked to existing concessions given by way of tax allowances.

On indirect taxes the conclusion was reached earlier that the value added tax is to be preferred to the existing purchase-tax system and selective employment tax. One of the advantages to be gained by adopting the foregoing standard of equity is that the proportion of revenue raised by indirect taxes, as opposed to income tax, need no longer be subject to the constraint that indirect taxes weighs more heavily on poorer persons. If more tax is to be raised from indirect taxes, equity can still be achieved. Equity was set up in terms of the net benefits received, or net taxes paid, expressed as a percentage of original income. Heavy indirect taxes would fall more heavily on low incomes, so that minimum 'effective incomes' will need to be revised upward and supplementation increased accordingly to those who fall below those levels.

Vindictiveness of the current system

It is not the purpose of this book to pick out all the defects in the system of benefits. However, the charge of vindictiveness which was made above against the current system, which is nevertheless real if unintended, can be illustrated from two recent reports, motivated, it should be said, by public concern.

The wage stop is a rule that ensures an unemployed man does not receive greater social security benefits when he is out of work than he would receive as a wage when he is working. We are told:

> The purpose of the wage stop is not to provide an incentive to a man to get work. The wage stop does not require a man to get less when receiving Supplementary Benefit than he would get when working. What it does is to ensure that an unemployed man's income is *no greater* than it would be if he were in full-time employment.
>
> *Administration of the Wage Stop* (1967), (para. 4).

It emerges from the Ministry of Social Security investigation into the *Circumstances of Families* (1967), which investigated families with two or more children, that in the summer of 1966 there were about 7 million families with children. About half a million of these families, containing 1¼ million children, had incomes from earnings, contributory benefits, family allowances or other sources (but excluding National Assistance) amounting to less than would be paid to a family which qualified for Supplementary Benefit. About 145,000 of these families were fatherless, 160,000 were sick or unemployed, 140,000 men were in full-time work, the remaining 55,000 covered a variety of cases—for example, where there was no mother or where the father worked away from home. Our interest is in the group of families, estimated to be about 160,000 with half a million children in them, whose fathers were disqualified because of the wage stop from receiving full benefits: 140,000 of these fathers were in work, 20,000 unemployed. It is presumably the fear that this 140,000 would leave the labour force to take advantage of higher benefits that is the reason for the wage-stop rule. Of this group of 160,000, it was estimated, from a sample of 2,500, that more than one in five had ill-health in the father or mother. Of the ill fathers 14% thought their ill-health limited their earning capacity.

The wage-stop enquiry investigated a (regrettably) small number of families, fifty-two in all in five different areas, who were unemployed and living on wage-stopped Supplementary Benefit. It was found that most had three or more children, and two-thirds were not in good health: of these 36% were registered disabled persons.

This evidence, in both cases, was confined to asking persons about their physical health, not investigating the group clinically, and mental health was not taken into account. Limited as the evidence is, it points to the fact that disability and ill-health play a considerable part in many of these families' poverty. In some of these cases the circle of poverty is complete: a man receives a low wage because of disability or ill-health and the benefit system cannot raise him above this level.

Raising the wages of the lowest-paid workers is desirable, but would not solve the problem for many of these half-million families whose income is below Supplementary Benefit level—for example, the fatherless families and where disability and ill-health impair earning ability. The hard core of the problem is likely to remain, given a system whereby many benefits are channelled by way of tax relief: inability to reach a high enough level of income means these benefits are never received, and loss of earnings by those who do earn enough to benefit means also the loss of these benefits. To take benefits out of the tax system, on the lines suggested in this chapter, is one way of assisting both the working people and the unemployed: it would remove many of these half-million families from the need to seek assistance.

Administration

The provision of benefits which have been referred to results in an enormous amount of duplication of government administration, and also of form-filling that has to be carried out by the citizen. Different means tests are applied for rent rebates, rate rebates, school meals, welfare foods, educational allowances, child help and so on. Details will be found in *Social Services for All* (1968), No. 382. Where tests are locally administered, great variation is found in assistance given to families in similar circumstances. With such diversity, it is perhaps inevitable that many who are eligible to benefit do not do so; this may be due to a natural pride and the fear of being stigmatized as 'on Assistance', or due to ignorance as to their rights, or to the difficulty in establishing whether they are eligible for benefit.

Computerized records are being set up by a number of ministries. A single computerized service could bring large economies in time, money and manpower. Sewill (1966) gives a brief outline. The simplification of benefits which has been advocated would assist these economies. It seems clear that parallel to a study of benefits should be undertaken a study of administration. The United States Commission set up by Congress to study automation was already reporting along these lines in 1966. The Belgian government has announced that by 1970 administrative details of every inhabitant will be centrally recorded and used by every government department and agency. Compared to the known technical possibilities, we are still in the quill-pen stage: we pay for this in terms of frustration, waste and hardship. Those that object on the grounds that they will be 'just a number' seem to overlook the fact that they already have a National Health Service number and a different National Insurance number, as well as a wide variety of codes used in most of their dealings with central or local government agencies.

Improvements and administrative savings could also be made if services were unified under one authority instead of being fragmented over many authorities and departments as at present. Proposals have already been made on these lines. The Ministry of Health issued a Green Paper, *Administrative Structure of the Medical and Related Services in England and Wales* (1968), in which they put forward for discussion the idea of a 'unified administration of the medical and related services in an area by one authority, in place of the multiplicity of authorities concerned in the present arrangements'. The *Report of the Committee on Local Authority and Allied Personal Social Services* (1968), known as the *Seebohm Report*, likewise comes up with similar proposals. They suggest the establishment of one central social welfare department in each local authority to be responsible for the whole welfare structure administered by local authorities.

The individual *vis-à-vis* the company

An individual as we have seen may be at a serious tax disadvantage compared to a company, whether the company is incorporated or unincorporated in form. Put the other way, an individual may be able to reap substantial tax advantages by forming a company, and a shareholder may reap tax advantages. This is so because companies are allowed to deduct for the using up of capital before arriving at a figure of taxable profit, whereas individuals do not have this right. Also a company is in a more advantageous position in being able to claim for expenses. In recent years expense claims have been tightened up, but important differences still remain.

The adoption of the accretion principle would, we have seen, go a long way to achieving equity. Dividends would be taxed as income, retained profits, if they enhanced the value of the business, would also be taxed as income when the gains were realized.

Difficult questions remain on the extent of company taxation. A change to a V.A.T. in place of the S.E.T. might, it has been argued, be beneficial, and is necessary if Britain is to align herself with Europe. Though a V.A.T. is mainly borne by consumers, the regressive nature of the impost can be taken care of on the lines previously indicated in this chapter.

A V.A.T. at 10% would bring in far more revenue than the S.E.T. and purchase tax, which, it is assumed, would be abolished. Important questions are raised as to which taxes should be reduced or abolished if a V.A.T. is introduced. The time is ripe for a Royal Commission to investigate these alternatives and the differences in treatment for tax of persons and companies in the light of the many changes which have occurred since 1955. It will be argued in the final chapter of this book that such a Commission should have wide terms of reference to look at taxes and benefits as a whole. The V.A.T. and treatment of companies would then form part of its brief.

Summary

After listing the major faults found in the current system, incidence of tax in the traditional sense is discussed. This is rejected in favour of looking at the impact, in so far as costs and benefits can sensibly be allocated to individuals, of government spending and revenue as a whole. The advantage of this approach is that the importance of a particular tax or benefit in relation to the whole can be judged. In time, alternative assumptions about the incidence of various taxes and benefits can be made in order to see how great a difference this makes to the 'burden'.

The conclusions reached, from the limited statistical evidence available, is that the present system, in spite of considerable effort, is not equitable. Nor, as we have seen, is it succeeding very well in relieving poverty.

Further patching up of the system would not seem to be the answer. The present very complicated tax and benefit arrangements are a result of past piecemeal tackling of problems.

It is possible to see improvement taking place from the side of taxation and from the side of benefits. These are inseparably interlinked and cannot sensibly be discussed in isolation from one another, in spite of many past attempts to do so. Discussion of tax benefits must take place against some criterion of equity. One possibility outlined is to take the difference between original income and income after allowing for taxes paid and benefits received, termed 'effective income'. This difference gives the figure of *net* benefits received or *net* taxes paid, as the case may be, and can be related to original income to build up a standard of equity. Ways of supplementing those people with effective income below that judged adequate by society were discussed.

While this chapter necessarily concentrates on types of benefit, complementary to it is a study of administration. Because of the very fragmented administrative set-up, a great deal of waste, frustration and hardship occurs at present. Improvement could be expected; by integration of services under one authority, by simplification and by using known technical possibilities of computers.

Part III
Policy

19
Introduction to policy considerations

Policy to deal with inflation is a subject on which a great deal has been written and argued by eminent authorities without adding substantially to knowledge, and in some cases subtracting from it.

JOHNSON, H. G. (1967), *Essays in Monetary Economics.*

In Part I the monetary system was examined, and in Part II government expenditure, revenue and debt. It is now time to attempt to draw these threads together and examine their effects on the economy.

Much has been written about the effects that are likely to flow from different monetary and fiscal changes. The analysis is frequently conducted at great length with an impressive array of geometric and mathematical expertise. Within the assumptions adopted by the author, the conclusions can seldom be faulted. As exercises in logic, this work probably has value, but as a guide to the best policy to adopt at any one time they unfortunately yield few results. It is seldom that the conclusions can be shown to hold once the restrictive assumptions have been removed.

An added difficulty is the lack of general agreement on a theory explaining the variables usually selected as important for study. The usual variables on which it is desired to see the effects of monetary or fiscal changes are: consumption and saving, investment, prices and output, and work effort.

Since the theories explaining these variables are in dispute, it is not surprising that an explanation of the effect of this or that Budgetary change is, at best, imprecise and subject to doubt.

This chapter looks briefly at each of these variables. It attempts no precise answers to the question: what would happen to each of these if, say, a particular tax was changed? In our present state of knowledge, such a precise answer is impossible. Neither does it attempt a detailed assessment of the use of monetary and fiscal methods in the post-war period. A number of recent full-scale assessments have been made, to which the interested reader can refer: Brittan, S. (1964), Dow, J. C. R. (1964) and Caves, R. E. (1968). Rather, it looks at some of the problems involved in getting even approximate estimates.

Personal consumption and saving

We have seen in the post-war period direct measures, such as rationing and price-control, influencing consumption and saving. What of the influence of fiscal and monetary policy?

To get somewhere, it is necessary to have a theory to work with, even if it is no stronger than the feeling that 'consumption and saving can be changed by altering income'. Keynes, J. M. (1936), 96, said:

> The fundamental psychological law upon which we are entitled to rely with great confidence both *a priori* from our knowledge of human nature and from detailed facts of experience, is that men are disposed as a rule and on the average to increase their consumption as their income increases, but not by as much as the increase in income.

Since this was written over thirty years ago, this 'law' has been the subject of much debate and investigation. Attempts have been made to modify the law to take account of the structure of wealth as well as of income (see Appendix to this chapter). It has been suggested that past levels of income need to be taken into account as well as current levels, that it is 'permanent' or normal income which is the relevant concept, or that it is the flow of income over the life-cycle of the individual that matters. Many of these alternative statements are concerned with the long-run trend in consumption and the influences, economic and social, which bear on this. Management of the economy, as we are concerned with it, is largely a matter of year-to-year control, and here we are on safe ground in asserting that a change in income will be of major importance and will change consumption and saving in the same direction as the change in income. An advanced study of the determinants of consumer expenditure is given by Suits, D. B. (1963), 1-57.

The size of the change will depend on many factors. One of the most important is likely to be the way the income change is distributed over different income groups. Budget studies inform us that, as we move up the income scale, out of each addition to income more is likely to be saved: in economic terms, the marginal propensity to save increases with income. It follows that £1 paid in tax by a person with a high income will tend to reduce saving more than £1 paid by a taxpayer with a small income. Thus a progressive income tax is likely to reduce saving more than a flat-rate tax. Put the other way, taxes which fall mainly on the poor are likely to have more impact on consumption than taxes which fall mainly on the rich.

These generalizations are frequently invoked by advocates of tax changes—for example, those who advocate reducing the rates of income tax in order to increase savings.

Unfortunately, there is no clear empirical evidence on the magnitude of the difference on savings or consumption. If the difference is small, then arguments for tax changes on these grounds can be ignored.[1] If they are large, it is necessary to take them into account. American studies (Musgrave, R. A. (1959), 269-70) suggest that although taxes that affect high-income earners are likely to effect saving more than consumption, the result is easily overstated. Dow, J. C. R. (1964), 270-5, lists British investigations which in general give more weight to the effect on savings. In view of the uncertain nature of the data and the assumptions that have to be made, authoritative statements on the relationships of changes in tax and effects on consumption and saving must await further investigation.

Let us consider a fully-employed economy where the need is to increase saving (that is, reduce consumption expenditure) in order that resources may be released from the consumption to the investment sector. Even if the argument is accepted that the effect of taxing high incomes is to affect savings to a significant extent, it does not necessarily follow that flat-rate taxes are to be preferred. There is an obvious clash between the objective of control over the economy and of redistribution of income and wealth. Political judgments here come to the fore. From the point of view of controlling the economy, it does not matter whether the savings are undertaken by individuals or the government. If a decision has been made about the degree of progression of the tax system that is desired, and if it is desired to reduce consumption, then tax rates can be changed. The change can be made so as to leave the degree of progression of the system unchanged. If this results in less private saving or a slower increase in private saving, this affect can be allowed for in the new rates. This results in the desired level of saving being obtained through a government surplus or reduced deficit.

It is possible (but not perhaps very likely) that this increase in savings of the government sector would result in a shortage of funds for private investment. Numerous ways are available whereby

[1] Differences may be small in two senses. The first, that the change makes no perceptible difference to behaviour. The second, that although the change makes a large difference, the numbers affected by the change are so small, or the amount of money involved is so small, as to make no significant change in overall saving, e.g. if only 1,000 people are affected by a change, then even though it is assumed they save the whole of the amount involved, this will have an insignificant effect on total savings. Any reactions of those who are not directly affected by the change must also be considered.

these funds can be channelled back to private investment. The decision is once more primarily a political judgment. The government could undertake direct investment in firms, or the resources of the Finance Corporation for Industry or the Industrial and Commercial Finance Corporation and kindred organizations could be supplemented. Alternatively, taxes on companies could be reduced or investment grants increased.

One further illustration will be given. At first sight, a change in estate duties is a clear-cut case of a change in taxation that will affect saving more than consumption. However, it has already been pointed out that one way of avoiding estate duties is to give away one's wealth at least seven years before death. To the extent that wealth is given away to younger persons sooner than it would otherwise be given, the consumption of these younger persons is likely to increase.

A consideration therefore of the impact of monetary and fiscal changes on consumption and saving should take account of the impact on different income-groups, because they are likely to have different propensities to consume. Ideally, the effects of different amounts of wealth should also be taken into account and allowance made for shifts of money and assets to different age-groups who are likely to have different spending habits. Dow, J. C. R. (1964), 275, has suggested that an important category to separate out is the self-employed, whose propensity to consume is lower than that of comparable income groups because of higher saving to provide investment for their own business.

The above brief discussion shows some of the more important difficulties that have to be faced if 'hunches' about the effects of tax or monetary changes are to be turned into objective facts. In Britain the matter is further bedevilled by a lack of adequate statistical data—in particular, in relation to figures of savings. The figures of savings that appear in the *National Income and Expenditure* tables (the so-called Blue Book) are completely unreliable. This is so because no attempt is made to arrive at independent estimates of saving. The figure is arrived at by taking estimates of income and deducting estimates of consumption. The resulting residual figure is called 'saving'. Since income and consumption are big magnitudes, even small errors in these estimates can make a large difference in the residual figure. Independent estimates of savings are beginning to be built up, but these have yet to be incorporated in the Blue Book. For details of the figures of savings compared year by year refer to 'More Light on Personal Saving' (April, 1965). Uncertainty is therefore present concerning the amount of savings in the community and who undertakes it. There is a need for better statistics of what is actually taking place and for more consideration of the motives for savings, and how these motives change in response to different economic and social pressures.

Public expenditure can affect consumption and saving as well as changes in tax or monetary policy. The most important part in this respect is likely to be the extent of transfer payments. These, as we saw in Chapter 8, have increased in recent years to a greater extent than other forms of government expenditure. The greater provision of social security payments by the government, in the form of pensions, children's allowances and the like, reduces the need for private provision for these needs, although the extent to which the private sector would voluntarily save to provide for these contingencies is uncertain. Similar considerations apply to so-called 'free services', such as medical care, but the effect is weaker in that much would be spent directly on these services by individuals in the absence of schemes financed out of taxation.

Save as you earn scheme

The Budget in 1969 announced a contractual savings scheme whereby a person over sixteen years can invest up to a maximum of £10 a month in National Savings for five years and obtain a tax-free bonus at the end of the period of £12 for each £60 saved. If the savings are retained for a further two years, without making further contributions the bonus is doubled to £24 for each £60 saved. This bonus is equivalent after five years to a tax-free rate of interest of about 7% a year or in gross terms 12% for a standard-rate taxpayer. The seven-year rate is equivalent to a tax-free rate of interest of about 11% or gross rate around 19%. It is possible to cash the accumulated savings after one year in which case a tax-free rate of interest of only 2½% is paid. A feature of the scheme is that payment can be deducted from income by the employer. A similar scheme is being set up for contractual savings through a building society. Because the bonuses on these savings are paid free of all tax the effective yield to a top-rate surtax payer is around 80%. If, as seems likely, high-rate taxpayers avail themselves of the maximum permitted savings this is an expensive way for the government to induce contractual savings, but inevitable so long as blanket tax-free bonuses are given.

The extent to which this scheme will shift the savings schedule of the community, that is result in more savings at the same level of National Income, and the extent to which it will merely change the type of security savers take up, remains to be seen.

Investment

The post-war period has seen a variety of methods used to influence investment, from direct controls, such as licensing and planning permission, to various monetary and fiscal policies. Even if there was agreement about a theory of investment (which there is not), the presence of so many variables makes it very difficult to pin down the effect of any one of them. Investment has been the subject of a good part of recent economic writing. For an advanced study see Eisner, R. and Strotz, R. H. (1963), 61-337, with a selected bibliography of 666 items!

The 'acceleration principle' makes investment a function of changes in demand. The truth in this principle, that a permanent change in demand calls for a different stock of investment goods, should not blind us to the obvious defects of the principle as a guide to short-term investment decisions. An increase in demand can often be met from previous resources that were idle or not working to capacity. The length of time required to adjust the capital stock, up or down, may run into years, and so on. Much investment needs to be planned for a number of years ahead. For example, once a decision has been made in principle to go ahead with a new factory, a suitable site has to be found, planning permission obtained, contractors engaged before work can commence, and the construction itself may take one, two or more years. Under these circumstances, it might be thought that investment of this type would be insensitive to temporary changes in demand, brought about by a government that was pledged to full employment not intending permanently to alter demand patterns.

Present evidence is far from conclusive, but from surveys of British industry it seems that investment plans do fluctuate considerably according to the current condition of the economy, whether, that is, the period is one of expansion or contraction: stop or go. There are several possible explanations for this. The most unfavourable interpretation to British industry would be that not many firms plan very far ahead or calculate their intended investments in a very rational manner. The White Paper on *Investment Incentives* (1966) quoting an enquiry carried out by the Confederation of British Industry among their members, gave some support to these pessimistic conclusions. However, other factors must also play a part. Some forms of investment have a short time to come to fruition, and it is then more realistic to expect fluctuations in investment according to fluctuations in demand. Again, the cut-back during times of low demand may be due to difficulties in obtaining finance rather than deliberate intentions to cut investment. There is also business confidence to take into account, which may be unduly pessimistic about investment prospects at a time of contraction of demand, and unduly optimistic at a time of buoyant demand.

To the extent that investment does fluctuate with demand, the conclusions for getting growth in the economy are perverse. The stated intention in cutting consumer demand during times of full employment is to release resources for the investment sector. If the effect is also to cut investment, the required growth will not be forthcoming and employment will fall. If deliberate manipulation of consumer demand in one or more particular sectors can be engineered without too large an overspill to other sectors of the economy, then the non-suppressed sectors of the economy will be able and willing to proceed with their investments.

Other explanations of investment lay more stress on the availability of particular types of saving, e.g. ploughed-back profits or the buoyancy of the stock market. British policy, by its frequent discrimination against distributed profits, changes in tax allowances and experiments with initial allowances, investment allowances and now investment grants, has developed policy actively in this field. It has been argued in Chapter 13 that the most dubious part of this policy, and also, it would appear, the least successful, has been the discrimination against dividends. Initial and investment allowances suffered from several drawbacks, as we saw, which it is hoped the new system of grants will overcome.

A third theory of investment makes it a function of rate of return on investment compared to the rate of interest. If the return from real investment is above the cost of borrowing (or above the best return that can be obtained from putting surplus funds into financial assets), then the inducement to invest is strong and vice versa. The impact of the rate of interest will be considered in Chapter 21. It is argued there that one way that the rate of interest can be important is via the stock-market and its influence on the willingness and ability of firms to raise fresh capital and on the flow of new money into the market.

Econometric studies approach the problem of investment by trying to unravel the interconnections between industries. That, for example, it is estimated that every £100 of final output in 1963 in the metal manufacturing trades requires a net input of £1·8 from coal, £0·7 from other mining, £3 from chemicals, £44·5 from metal, £4·7 from engineering, and so on (figures given in *National Income and Expenditure*, Table 21 (1968). For details of a model of the British economy see Stone, R. and others (1962).) If therefore decisions are made this year as to how the economy should grow next year, the details can be fed into the model and the requirements on the economy can be calculated. If details of investment for the next year are known, the shortfall or over-expansion of investment can then be seen and attempts made to get firms to alter their plans accordingly. If industrialists can be convinced of the soundness of the calculations, they have a firmer base on which to plan their own investments. The firm is well aware intuitively that the success or otherwise of its own plans depends to a large extent on what is happening in the rest of the economy: the more facts can replace guesswork, the more steady is investment likely to become. Too much should not be expected from what are admittedly crude models of the interactions in the economy. The hope is that more data will be forthcoming, improvements in method made and the predictions made more reliable.

These theories of what determines investment concentrate attention on differing variables that enter into the decision whether or not to invest. They are not independent variables, but interact with each other, and their respective importance is likely to change over time. Bearing these facts in mind, it is not surprising that evidence of the effect of government measures on investment is hard to pin down.

Prices and output

The adjustments in prices and output that businesses make in response to government policy changes are at least as difficult to sort out as any that have so far been considered.

It is clear that if a manufacturer passes on to his customers the whole of an increase in cost (whether this is due to an increase in purchase tax, in company tax or higher interest charges), the demand for his product may be affected. He may be forced therefore to reconsider his price and so in effect bear part of the increase, at least in the short run.[2] In the long run adjustments can be made to the size of the plant. The industry itself can also expand or contract by the movement of firms into and out of the industry.

Nor are the changes that occur in one sector of the economy likely to be confined to that sector. An increase in the price of, for example, fruit may lead to some *substitution* for fruit of other goods that are unchanged in price, i.e. now relatively cheaper. Likewise, a decrease in the price of fruit may lead to the substitution of fruit for other goods. As well as this substitution effect as the relative prices of commodities change, an *income* effect is apparent.

[2] The response of demand to a change in price is measured by the concept of 'elasticity': the percentage change in quantity divided by the percentage change in price. But elasticity is a measure of response: it merely says that for a particular change in price in the commodity being considered, demand changes by this or that amount. There is still a need to explain in each case the reasons for the particular degree of responsiveness.

INCOME AND SUBSTITUTION EFFECT

A simple example will be given to illustrate the distinction between the substitution and the income effect. Consider an individual's choice between fruit and other commodities and what happens when a tax on fruit is reduced. It is assumed that the individual spends all his income on these items.

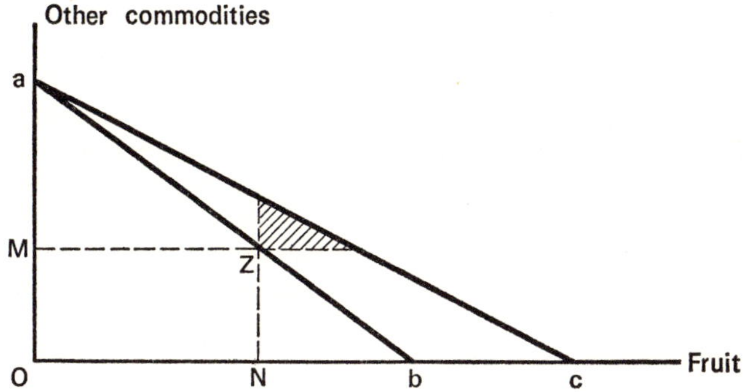

The amount of fruit is plotted along the horizontal axis, the other commodities along the vertical axis. Point *a* represents the amount of commodities other than fruit that could be purchased if the individual spent the whole of his income on these. Likewise, point *b* represents the amount of fruit that could be purchased if the individual spent the whole of his income on fruit. The straight line, joining *a* and *b* indicates the various combinations of each that the individual can purchase with his given income. Let us assume that the individual chooses point Z, which gives him a quantity of OM of other commodities and ON of fruit. Into this picture we now introduce a tax-reduction on fruit; therefore more fruit can be purchased with the same money income as before. Hence we draw the new line, *a*, *c*, to indicate the position after the tax change. Within the shaded area on the diagram the consumer can now, with his same income, have more of both goods—that is, the effect of a price change enables the consumer to have an increase in consumption. The price change has in effect given the consumer an increase in income, hence the name '*income* effect'. Whereabouts on the new budget line *a*, *c* the individual will settle cannot be determined. The price change has altered the relative prices, making fruit cheaper, and *substitution* may well take place—that is, more fruit may be purchased because it is now relatively cheaper. The position taken up by the individual on the budget line *a*, *c*, will depend on the combined results of the income and substitution effects. The strengths of these effects will differ in different cases.

In the simple case considered, a change in the price of fruit, other prices remaining the same, it was concluded that it was not possible as a general rule to pinpoint the exact position that a consumer would take up. The substitution effect would normally be expected to operate to increase demand for the relatively cheaper good, but the income effect is less easy to predict.

AGGREGATE CHANGES IN PRICE AND OUTPUT

The above reasoning deals with the response of an individual manufacturer to a change. In trying to account for aggregate movements in prices and output a number of other considerations need to be borne in mind.

The time element has so far been ignored for exposition purposes. Its presence adds considerable practical difficulties in sorting out the effects of a change. For example, after each recent increase in the tax on tobacco, the consumption of tobacco has fallen for a few weeks or months, only to come back to higher levels. One of the difficulties in sorting out the effects of a change is that the market for tobacco, as for many products, has been an expanding one for many years. Most noticeably, population changes and the spread of smoking among women have increased the market. To say that the consumption of tobacco surpasses its old level is not to say that, in the absence of a tax change, consumption might not be higher than its present level. It is very difficult to separate out statistically the underlying trend in consumption and the change due to the tax measure.

The impact of a change will depend in part on the state of the economy. In conditions of full employment the manufacturer is more likely to pass on increases, reasoning that competitors will follow suit. So relative market shares between himself and competitors in the same industry and also the market share of his industry *vis-à-vis* other industries will be affected slightly or not at all: an increase in price in one sector may lead, that is, to a broad movement in prices over a wide range of goods.

Many countries have experienced a general rise in prices, or inflation, in the post-war period. A number of theories have been developed to try to explain this phenomenon (see Johnson, H. G. (1967), and Bronfenbrenner, M. and Holzman, F. D. (September, 1963), 593-661. Two theories have contended for pride of place: *demand* inflation, which concentrates on the pull which demand can exercise on prices; and *cost* inflation, which lays emphasis on increases in cost forcing up prices. The major emphasis with cost inflation has been put on increases occurring in wages and salaries coming from union pressures. Employers may, however, bid up wages in their demand for labour which tends to blur the distinction between these two theories for practical purposes.

The role assigned to fiscal policy in controlling prices is given different emphasis by these two theories, but both have in common the fact that little emphasis is placed on monetary policy. A reaction against this can be discerned in Johnson, H. G. (1967), and Bronfenbrenner, M. and Holzman, F. D. (September, 1963).

In general, government policy in the post-war period, has been seen as aiding, or hindering, other forces which are moulding prices. British government policy came out of this sheltered position in 1966, when in place of exhortation, control over prices and wages was directly attempted?![3]

Work effort with full employment

The adjustment in the work effort of a community to a fiscal change has been mentioned on several previous occasions.

In order to get a determinate answer, we need to know a great deal. It is worth putting this down, if only to evaluate the exaggerated claims that are sometimes made of the effects on work that will follow from a particular change.

1. It is necessary to know how the change affects each group in the community. A group must be defined in some way to make it economically meaningful, perhaps by occupation or income.
2. The numbers in each group must be determined.
3. The average reactions of each group have to be determined.
4. The weighting to be assigned to each group must be determined, e.g. how should five hours less worked by an accountant be judged in relation to five hours more worked by a dustman?

A determinate answer can only be given if data is available and assumptions are made at the relevant points. Clearly, different assumptions about reactions of each group (e.g. that they will work less hard because they have less income because of the tax change, or that they will work harder to make up for the tax change) will yield different answers. In this context, groups have to take account, not only of the working labour force, but the potential labour force.

[3] A chess-player will recognize the significance of '?!'. In chess notation a '?' is placed after a doubtful move, a '!' after an excellent move. Both signs placed after a move denote a risky move that has the chance of winning or losing the game according to the play of the opponent: signs that could be adopted, with advantage, in economics.

For example, it is frequently asserted that high taxation acts as a disincentive to work, or affects the quality of work, of particular groups. On the other hand, high taxation has been one of the factors leading to married women joining the labour force in order to help out the family income, although in the case where a married couple's joint income brings them into the surtax bracket, tax may be a disincentive to the wife to work (Hockley (May-June, 1967)).

Appendix One of the Royal Commission on the Taxation of Profits and Income (1954) presents the results of an investigation, from a sample of nearly 1,500 persons, of tax on work incentives of industrial workers. It concluded that there was no significant effect on productivity. A bibliography of studies that has been made in the tax-incentive field will be found in Musgrave, R. A. and Shoup, C. S. (1959). Break, G. F. (September, 1957), gives an empirical study amongst solicitors and accountants. Merritt, A. J. and Monk, D. A. G. (1967), and Merritt, A. J. (1968), look at executive remuneration. Titmus, R. M. (1963) (particularly Chapter 11) takes a very broad look at current trends in the economy, and deals *inter alia* with taxation. *The Banker*, March, 1968, contains two articles: one by Cyriax, G., sets out the orthodox case that taxes reduce work incentives; the other, by Daniel, W. W. D., examines evidence against this view. Eisenstein, L. (1961), wittily discusses the art of obtaining a tax system in the interest of particular groups. (Chapter 5 deals with incentive arguments.) Although this book deals with American conditions, the reader should have little difficulty in substituting examples from his own country's institutions and groups.

The difficulties in coming to conclusions in this field can be illustrated from the latest study by Merritt, A. J. (1968). This book gives a valuable look at the remuneration of executives and corporate efficiency.

Merritt argues, among other things, that advantages would follow from higher before-tax executive remuneration, and also advantages would follow from higher net-of-tax benefits. Giving executives, or some of them, the right to stock options on the American pattern is given as one way of increasing net-of-tax benefits.

Higher before-tax remuneration is seen as a way of forcing companies to be more efficient if profitability is not to suffer. However, this is an argument that can be used to justify giving an increase to any category of worker or imposing a swingeing increase in the selective employment tax! Higher after-tax remuneration is recommended on the grounds that it would enable firms to impose stricter work criteria on executives who proved inadequate, since they would have been enabled to provide adequately for this contingency out of their higher net earnings. Again, this argument, if accepted as valid, can be used to justify lower tax on any category of worker. It seems equally plausible to argue that higher remuneration for executives would make it harder for firms to turn out inefficient executives, since it would be known that they would suffer a larger cut in living standards and larger 'golden handshakes' would be needed.

Even if it could be established conclusively that giving stock options would improve the quality and quantity of executives' work, this does not prove that the change is desirable. Before a change can be recommended on these grounds, it is necessary to establish that the reactions of non-executives to this tax privilege would not result in a greater detriment. The change could lead to greater industrial strife by those workers who do not benefit, which would more than outweigh the gain in executive efficiency. This increase in strife could occur through a general feeling that the gulf between 'them' and 'us' had widened, and general antipathy on the part of the ordinary worker to productivity changes which would put more into the pocket of the executive than into his own. It could also occur because the trade unions used this as a lever to be more militant on behalf of their members. The correctness or otherwise of these reactions, whether they are motivated by feelings of vindictiveness or of social justice, is not important in this context. What matters is the strength of the reaction which needs to be measured against the favourable response expected from the change.

Summary

Before it is possible to analyse the effect of a change in government policy, it is necessary to have a theory about how the economy operates.

> When we have no theory about economic affairs, no state of those affairs and no temporal succession of states seems inconceivable. A theory restricts the conceivable states and succession of states to those in which the relations between quantifiable things in the economy conform to some specified rules. Theories differ from each other in the list of quantifiable (not necessarily measurable) things to be considered, and in the precise character of the rules about their interrelation (Shackle, G. L. S. (June, 1961), 200).

In this chapter consumption and saving, investment, prices and output, and work effort have been examined and treated in isolation from each other. In practice they are closely interrelated. A change in government policy may cause significant changes in two or more of them. It is the overall effect that is important. Sometimes changes in different variables will operate in the same direction, e.g. cause a reduction in investment and in work effort, and sometimes changes will tend to cancel each other out.

In judging the implications of economic policy, it has been shown that there is no generally agreed theory to work with. Thus, unfortunately, an analysis even for an observer who is trying to be impartial depends a great deal on which theory is selected and on the weight given to each of the variables. More unfortunately still, it leaves the door wide open for those with special interests to defend to select those theories that serve their cause best. This pessimistic conclusion is not intended as an apologia for inaction. Given the size of the government sector, it is not possible for the government to be neutral. It is an indication of the need for care in accepting the claims put forward for this or that particular measure.

Appendix: wealth effect

In spite of increased attention paid to wealth in recent years, it is still one of the neglected areas in economics. A variety of names have been coined to emphasize one particular aspect of wealth or another, e.g. wealth effect, real balance effect, Pigou effect, Roosa effect. The single term 'wealth effect' will be used here.

It is fairly obvious that, if two persons both have an income of £10,000 after tax, but one person has wealth of £500,000 while the other has wealth of £50,000, then the consumption patterns of the two persons is likely to be very different and the proportions each saves is likely to be different.[4] Unfortunately, we have very little idea how a person's wealth position affects his behaviour. A transfer of income from the wealthy to the less wealthy will have repercussions, but we cannot as yet add in quantitative data.

One aspect of the wealth effect has been looked at, when the idea was examined that a change in the rate of interest may affect capital values, particularly of fixed-interest securities. It is possible that this will deter the holders from selling, but the evidence to date is that this effect is weak. A similarly weak effect may be caused by a general change in the value of money. Supposing there is a deflation, then some assets, e.g. money and government securities, will increase in real value. This may induce some extra spending on behalf of the holders. Once again this effect is likely, in aggregate, to be weak.

[4] The composition of assets in which wealth is held may also be important. Two persons who each have wealth of £100,000, one whose wealth primarily consists of land, the other whose wealth primarily consists of a portfolio of shares, are also likely to have different patterns of consumption and saving.

The extent to which a change in the value of money affects behaviour depends, in part, on the extent *money illusion* is, or is not, present in a community.

In a simple form, money illusion is thinking that one is better off when one's remuneration is increased, although the increase only covers the general increase in prices, or, conversely, thinking that one is worse off because prices are up and ignoring increases in money remuneration.

The problem of money illusion is encountered whenever the price-level changes, whether this is due to changes in indirect taxes or other causes, and likewise is encountered when incomes alter, whether this is due to changes in direct taxes or other causes.

The extent to which consumption alters in response to a price or income change will thus depend on the extent to which money illusion is present in the community. The usual assumption made is to assume that money illusion is absent, or that different people's reactions largely cancel out in the aggregate, but exceptional circumstances may falsify this expectation.

Because economics has in the past built on simple relationships relating consumption and saving to income, largely ignoring the dimension of wealth, it follows that action by the government to regulate the economy based on this simplification can be misleading. It is likely that changes in wealth will proceed fairly gradually over time, and to this extent can be ignored in the short run, but in exceptional circumstances they may be important. For example, most predictions made on how much consumers would spend after the Second World War were too low by a fairly large amount, due to underestimating the build-up of liquid capital during the war. Predictions based on pre-war data were wrong almost certainly because sufficient attention had not been given to the changes in the total and composition of wealth and to changes in its ownership.

20
Policy (continued)

> The state of balance of the conventional budget, judged by the eternal knife-edge precepts of Mr Micawber, is the badge of fiscal success or failure. From the economist's point of view, the focus of attention on the size and state of balance of the conventional budget is quite misplaced. Its size does not measure the government's draft on the productive resources of the economy. Its balance does not measure the effect of the government's transactions with the public on the overall economic balance between supply and demand.
>
> TOBIN, J. (1963), 'An Essay on Principles of Debt Management'.

Introduction

Ideally we set out to ask: if a given change is put into effect, what will be the resulting changes and adjustments in the economy? Or, alternatively, what must be changed in order to achieve some desired objective? The change can be in monetary policy, in government spending, revenue and debt, or in direct types of controls, such as hire-purchase regulations. Our ideal has been called 'a state of bliss' and, like most states of bliss, it is difficult to obtain. The complexity, as the previous chapter indicated, nearly defeats us. There is so much to take into account; so little agreed theory and empirical knowledge to work with.

A recognition of this complexity is in itself an important point. The criticism that, given a group of ten economists, there will be *at least* ten different opinions is not so damaging a remark as it at first appears. Given an objective—say, to increase productive investment—there are usually countless ways of achieving this. There is first of all the decision, a political one, whether it is public or private investment, or both, which shall be increased. If some measure of encouragement of private investment is required, consumer spending could be encouraged, which in turn would be expected to feed back a demand for investment, or investment could be encouraged directly. In either case there are numerous combinations of tax changes, monetary changes, or changes in regulations which can bring this about. No two combinations are likely to have exactly the same repercussions on other parts of the economy. Under these circumstances, it would be surprising if a unique 'best' method could be agreed on. A search for a unique solution is likely to be misleading in other ways. For example it is unlikely that a solution which yields a satisfactory result, given full employment of labour, will be satisfactory, given a large measure of unemployment.

One approach to this problem has been indicated previously: the construction of a model of the economy, which can be put in mathematical terms and programmed on to a computer. Alternatives—for example, different tax changes—can then be fed into the model and results compared. Economic models of this type offer exciting possibilities for the future, but their usefulness is at present limited.

Our approach to this problem is necessarily less ambitious. In this chapter an attempt is made to provide a useful analytical framework. Within this framework regulation of the economy is looked at. This leads to a complete rejection of the idea of a 'balanced Budget'. Finally, problems of control and the effects of control are taken up. Monetary and debt policy is left to the next chapter.

Framework

A basically Keynesian framework will be adopted. The national income or national product account will be used. These terms are synonymous, and merely refer to the fact that it is possible to arrive at the same total estimate of a country's activity either by adding up total expenditure in a year or by adding up the incomes received from producing those goods and services.

Looking at it from the expenditure side, the aggregate sought comprises expenditure on consumption goods and expenditure on investment goods. In both cases there is a mixture of private expenditure and of government expenditure. To complete the picture, allowance must be made for the export and import of goods and services and flows of money into and out of the country. The picture in greater detail for the year 1967 is given in Table 1.

From Table 1 we see that out of gross domestic[1] expenditure of £34,320 million, 61% was accounted for by private expenditure, 18% by public expenditure and the remaining 21% went to investment. Of this investment companies and individuals invested about

[1] 'Domestic' refers to the fact that exports, imports and net flows of money into the economy have not been taken into account. When these magnitudes are incorporated the term 'national' is used.

half, the balance being accounted for chiefly by public corporations and local government. In the second part of the table it can be seen that in 1967 rather more goods were imported and property income paid abroad than was exported and received as income from property held abroad.

The word 'gross' in the table refers to the fact that investment relates to the total undertaken in the year, regardless of the fact that some of it was to replace old equipment. If to the sums of private and public expenditures at the top of the table had been added the amount of indirect taxes paid, less subsidies, a figure of £5,211 million, the aggregates would be at market prices instead of factor prices.

Table 1

Gross National Product 1967

			£m	%
Private expenditure on goods and services[2]			21,039	61
Public expenditure on goods and services[2]			6,136	18
	£m	%		
Gross investment:				
Persons	986	(3)		
Companies	2,519	(7)		
Public corporations	1,661	(5)		
Central government	392	(1)		
Local government	1,587	(5)	7,145	21
Total gross domestic expenditure at factor cost			34,320	100
Add: Exports and property income from abroad	8,736			
Deduct: imports and property income paid abroad	8,894		−158	
Add in: value of stock adjustment			130	
Gross national product at factor cost			34,292	

Source: *National Income and Expenditure*, 1968, Tables, 1, 6, 29.

[2] Prices at factor cost, i.e. with indirect taxes subtracted and subsidies added back. In all, taxes less subsidies amounted to £5,211.

Regulation of the economy: the concept of compensatory finance

The figures just given were all in money terms. The government, in its role of regulating the economy, is concerned with the impact of these money flows on the real resources of the economy. It is usual in these days to consider that labour provides the upper limit to the amount of goods and services that can be obtained from the economy, but in other circumstances the limit may be provided by other factors of production. For example, for several years after 1945 the supply of goods and services was chiefly limited by the amount of coal and electricity that could be produced. The aim of the government will be therefore to keep the economy near the level of full employment, with a large enough proportion of the working population producing investment goods to maintain the appropriate ratio of physical capital to output.

If the spending estimates of the various sectors for the next period when added together amount to more goods and services than can be produced after allowance has been made for a certain level of imports and exports, then the authorities will attempt to cut back these plans. Similarly, a shortfall is an indication that in the absence of action to stimulate the economy there will be unemployment and the economy will be producing less than it could. Failure to reduce over-ambitious plans results in inflationary pressure as each group tries to carry out its plans; moreover, there is a spill-over effect into imports and consequently pressure on the balance of payments. A shortfall in spending results in unemployment and deflationary pressure as producers find that some of the goods and services produced remain unsold.

Let us suppose Budget plans for the next year indicate an inflationary gap (plans exceed, at current prices, the output that is possible, allowing for a certain level of imports and exports). The following alternatives are open:

1. (a) Increase income tax to reduce disposable incomes and thereby reduce consumption expenditure.
   (b) Achieve the same result as in (a) by raising indirect taxes or cutting subsidies.

Both of these may be upset by successful attempts to increase incomes.

   (c) An increase in company tax, hoping to reduce dividends or investment or both, or a cut in investment grants.
2. (a) The gap may be closed by cutting the demands of the public sector for goods and services, either on current or capital account.
   (b) By cutting transfer payments.
3. The use of monetary policy by itself or in conjunction with any

of these measures to try to reduce private consumption or private investment.

In every case the impact on the balance of payments must be taken into account, and assumptions made as to whether or not persons and companies are able to compensate for the change.

In the absence of compensating changes, raising income tax does not alter the price-level. The impact falls on income-tax-payers. Indirect taxes raise the price-level to the extent that the tax is passed on in higher prices to those who buy the taxed goods (with the same money incomes, a reduction in real incomes results). To the extent that prices are not increased, this will result in a reduction in profits. In practice, post-war policy has largely failed to prevent compensatory increases either of wages or of profits.

It is necessary to note that the amount needed to be raised under alternative types of taxes is not the same, because the taxes are likely to affect taxpayers with different marginal propensities to consume. The substitution effect of indirect taxes also has to be taken into account, e.g. some demand may spill over to untaxed commodities. Also, the timing of the measures has to be allowed for.

Using the data of Table 1, we will suppose the inflationary gap for 1967 was estimated in 1966 to be £500 million. A cut of this magnitude on consumers' expenditure of £21,039 million is a cut of 2·4%. The same reduction on public expenditure of £6,136 is a cut of 8·1%. Likewise, if private investment is to bear the whole adjustment this amounts to a cut of 14·3%. Correspondingly, if the public sector investment is to bear the whole of the cut, this would amount to a reduction of 13·7%. This simple illustration goes a long way to explain why adjustments are in the main usually carried out on private expenditure: because it is by far the largest component of the national product, a cut of a given magnitude is a smaller proportion of the total, and hence is likely to have a less disturbing effect. There are other reasons for attempting to regulate private expenditure rather than the other components of national income. One is the speed at which measures can be put into effect: investment must be planned for some time ahead and cutting back can prove a very costly process. Another is the argument we have met before that can be summed up by the phrase, 'public squalor, private affluence'. Public spending, whether on current or capital account is often held to be of an essential nature. There is no need to take this statement at its face value: government spending needs examining in the same way as other magnitudes, but also the germ of truth in this statement is obvious. Finally, since the investment is likely to increase the national product in the future, a cut in current consumption is usually preferred to a cut in investment.

When we come to examine the ways in which adjustments can be imposed, it will be found the problem is much more complicated than the above would imply. Whatever measures are used to reduce consumers' expenditure, these are likely to have differential effects on different commodities. Thus to talk of a cut of £500 million on consumers' expenditure only amounting to a reduction of 2·4% is misleading. The impact on particular products and services may be very severe. Also, of course, there are likely to be repercussions on the other components of the national product.

Political factors must also realistically be taken into account. At times this may weigh against cutting private consumption. A cut in private consumption is obvious and may be actively resented. A cut in public expenditure may be less obvious. A cut in investment (private or public) is followed by consequences that are both remote and not easily related to the original cut.

The balanced budget

The idea that a government is virtuous if it matches expenditure with revenue is still a popular one, and one that receives support from a few economists. It will be clear from this chapter so far that this view is rejected. Our starting-point is that the government has a role to play in regulating the economy. The size of the government sector today is such that a neutral policy is in any case not possible. Seen in this context, there may be strong economic reasons for having either a surplus or a deficit on any particular Budget.

Political reasons appear to underly many objections to departing from a balanced Budget. It is argued that government expenditure is too large already, and anything which induces caution in government spending is to be welcomed. Give the government power to spend more than it raises in taxes, so it is argued, and any discipline over its spending is forfeited

Some time has already been spent on looking at government expenditure in detail. The inadequacy of talking of government expenditure as a total, without considering the components of that total, has already been argued. Useful service may be performed by attacking this or that component of government spending as being too high or too low, judging the grounds of the attack on their merits. To argue that there is some fixed percentage of government spending above which inflation or some other evil or evils set in, as well as being a dubious statistical exercise, is not necessarily an argument for cutting government expenditure, any more than it is an argument for cutting private consumption. What matters, for stabilization purposes, is the total demands on the economy in relation to the real resources of the economy; if the former is above the latter, it is an indication that the demands from all sectors should be looked at anew. The decision that it is best to cut expenditure in one sector or the other does not emerge from the statistics.

It is argued that unbalanced Budgets can lead to currency depreciation. The argument is undoubtedly true: there are many examples of governments, unable or unwilling to tax adequately, resorting to the printing press. To argue that a certain consequence *can* happen is not to argue that it *must* happen. If it is feared that the increase in the level of demand causes inflationary pressure, this only points to the fact that offsetting action is required. If it is feared that deficits over a number of years will so add to the money supply as to be inflationary, a similar reply can be made. This is a pointer to the need for offsetting action—for example, to tighten control of the monetary sector, to fund, or to take action to reduce the deficit, which can be done either by increased taxation or by reducing government expenditure. The latter solution of reducing the deficit does not automatically emerge as the best solution.

A further assertion is that deficits are less painful than current taxes in the sense that people take account of current taxes and discount future taxes to service debt. It is argued that this leads to over-expansion of government services. A counter-assertion is also put forward, that traditional concepts of Budgeting have hindered the provision of much-needed services and that failure to separate the debt of the nationalized industries and local authorities (which debt will normally result in the creation of real assets) accentuates this trend to under-provision. While either of these assertions may be true for a particular historical time period, they become increasingly hard to demonstrate in a modern Budgetary setting. Parliamentary procedures are the same whether the source of finance is loans or taxes, and with the growth of Keynesian ideas, whether a government has a deficit or surplus is likely to be dictated by the claims of all sectors on the real resources of the economy.

The argument is sometimes presented in the form of under- or over-pricing in the public sector leading to a misuse of resources. The 'price' of public services is, as indicated earlier, of real economic and social significance: but its connection with the overall Budget surplus or deficit is remote.

The concept of the balanced Budget has an intuitive appeal to the individual because of the analogy with the economy of the private household. But it has no validity in the accounts of a nation. It is dangerous because it conceals the real issues. In the trite phrase the real issue is 'the best use of the nation's resources'. The injection of the dogma, 'Balance the Budget', merely helps to cloud these real issues.

BRITISH OFFICIAL OPINION ON A BALANCED BUDGET

Official British opinion as expressed in White Papers has shifted a great deal. First is a quotation from a paper on *Employment Policy* published in 1944.

The Government accepts as one of their primary aims and responsibilities the maintenance of a high and stable level of employment after the war . . . to the extent that the policies proposed in this Paper affect the balancing of the Budget in a particular year, they certainly do not contemplate any departure from the principle that the Budget must be balanced over a longer period (foreword and para. 77).

The second quotation is from the *Reform of the Exchequer Accounts*, published in 1963:

The Chancellor's Budget judgment, as embodied in his tax proposals, takes into account, not only the Government's own direct expenditure on current goods and services and on capital formation, but also the level of demand in other sectors of the economy and the balance of payments. These will be influenced by the Government's own activities—by withdrawal of spending power through taxation and by additions to spending power through grants and other forms of assistance. If the prospective growth of productive resources in the period ahead and the growth of demand upon them at the existing level of taxation are in balance, then the Budget will be a neutral one, with either no changes in taxation or offsetting increases and reductions. If the forecasts show demand to be insufficient, then the object of the Budget will normally be to stimulate demand by reducing taxes. If the demand is expected to be excessive the Budget will normally set out to restrict it by increases in taxation. Although forecasts of the developments of the economy and calculations of the effect of particular tax changes are inevitably imprecise, a judgment has still to be made to decide the general direction of the Budget. The judgment will determine the Government's net borrowing or 'financing' requirements, which then has to be considered in itself from the point of view of debt management and monetary policy.

The proper level of the Government's capital expenditure depends on quite separate considerations (e.g. the building programmes of the social services); and therefore it cannot be linked to the Government's borrowing without artificiality (paras. 33-4).

The contrast between these statements is quite clear. From the first it seems that while the unbalanced Budget could be used for war, it could not be used to fight unemployment, poverty and for the social good. Fortunately, nobody seems to have taken a great deal of notice. The second statement omits all reference to a balanced Budget. The balance that matters in the economy is that between real resources and demands on those real resources. The Budget has a part to play because it influences demands on those resources and also influences the amount of real investment that will be undertaken.

Problems of control

In trying to regulate the economy, the fundamental problem is to *diagnose* the trends in the economy. Has employment, private investment, consumer buying or some other economic magnitude changed? Once a change has been spotted, its importance to the economy must be assessed, and a judgment made on whether the change is a temporary one or if it is likely to continue for some time. In the latter event an assessment is needed on whether the change in question —say, a decrease in employment—will increase in intensity or gradually correct itself.

On the factual side of obtaining information about changes in the economy, much has been done to improve the position, although it remains true that a great deal more can and should be done to improve it still further. The question involves not only obtaining information, but of obtaining it in time for it to be economically useful. The deficiencies in information make it difficult to evaluate government measures since the war. It is not easy to decide whether the correct measures were applied in the wrong situation because of faulty information, or whether other elements in the picture were wrong.

After the prognostication, if action is thought to be necessary, the type of action to be taken must be decided on. Enough has been said to indicate that in most cases a number of alternatives are open which will effect a remedy. The choice of which course of action offers the 'best' solution involves both political and economic judgment. In both cases differences of opinion can legitimately occur. Of particular importance in assessing alternative measures is the *time* scale needed to put the measures into effect, and once put into effect the *time* for them to affect the economy. The position today is better than it used to be. The Chancellor has power to vary purchase tax by 10% between Budgets, company tax has been put on a current-year basis and, so on. Another important consideration is how *flexible* the proposed action is. If the prognostication is wrong because it has either underestimated the effects or overestimated the effects, can the action be changed so as to allow for these revised estimates?

Consideration of the pitfalls of economic management has led a number of people to reject altogether the idea that management of the economy should be attempted. They point to mistakes in the past which have had the effect of the remedy making the situation worse. Since the record of the economy when it was 'unregulated' was one of slumps and booms, with long periods of high unemployment, the attempt at management seems likely to be more fruitful in the long run. As improvement takes place both in our knowledge of what is occurring in the economy and of our understanding of its working, we can hope for better results in the future. The moral to be drawn is not that control of the economy is wrong in principle, but that too much should not be expected from what at present are relatively crude methods. The attempt is worth making because improvements can be expected in the future as we learn from past mistakes.

A different attitude is taken by some persons who do not argue against attempts at regulation as such, but wish to see the building up of new, and the strengthening of existing, 'automatic stabilizers'. An example of an automatic stabilizer is provided by a progressive tax on income. A reduction in aggregate wages paid in a period (due to some of the labour force being unemployed) will result in an automatic reduction in tax from income. Whereas, of course, indirect taxes are paid whether the person buying the goods is employed or unemployed. National Insurance contributions, which are not payable when the person is unemployed, and unemployment benefit, which is paid when a person is out of work, both act as automatic stabilizers. A few writers have suggested that the amount of currency in the economy should be automatically regulated and increased by a small regular percentage each year.

The idea behind the concept of automatic stabilizers is an attractive one. However, in the present state of knowledge of the economy, we cannot hope to dispense with deliberate action to aid the economy. Whether, and under what circumstances, it would be possible to make our economy run smoothly by such automatic stabilizers is beyond the scope of this book.

To summarize this section, a flow diagram is useful. The steps outlined above involve:

Identification of change

↓

Assessment of the likely trends in the changes

↓

Assessment of change and trends on the economy

↙ ↘

No action required

Action required, and need to assess what kind of action should be undertaken

The arrows point out the steps involved in the decision, starting from the top. The third step 'Assessment of change and trends on the economy', leads either to no action being required or to an assessment of what kind of action should be put into effect.

Effect of changes on the economy

In trying to assess the relative merits of alternative policies, it has been shown that it is useful to ask a number of questions—namely, how long before the measure can be put into effect; how long before it then makes its impact on the economy; and: is it flexible?

Management of the economy, however, is only one aim of government, labelled *stabilization* in Chapter 9. Policies need also to be judged in relation to their effects on the *allocation* and *distribution* of resources.

Different policies will almost certainly affect the allocation of resources between private and public goods, between investment and consumption goods, and between types of good in each category. A tax on labour—for example, the selective employment tax—is likely to lead to the substitution of capital for labour in the service sector: indeed, this was one of the reasons for introducing it. Tracing the effects of different policies is likely to be difficult because not only is the stock—that is, the amount already in existence—likely to be affected, but also the flow—that is, the additional amount demanded or supplied over time. Thus, as we have seen, one of the effects of the selective employment tax in its original form was to reduce the demand for part-time workers. Again, a change in tax rates may cause the existing labour force to work less hard or more hard, and may also encourage or discourage married women into the labour force.

Different policies will also almost certainly affect the distribution of resources and move the economy towards, or away from, whatever degree of equity is considered desirable. For example, consumers' expenditure could be regulated by much greater use of purchase tax or the adoption of a value-added tax, but unless compensating action is taken considerable hardship is likely to poorer persons.

When the aims of government are considered as a whole, this limits the extent to which any one measure can be used. Favourable effects in one direction tend to be counterbalanced by unfavourable effects in other directions.

The steps outlined can be continued on a flow diagram:

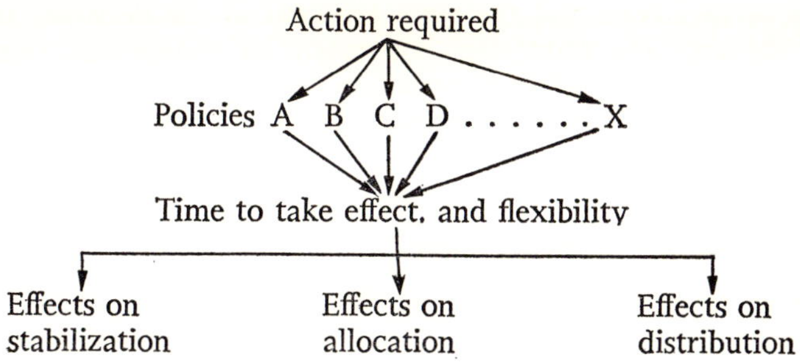

Once it has been decided that action is required, this leads to a consideration of alternative policies indicated by A, B, C, D, ... X. For each policy it is necessary to weigh the time and flexibility elements and their effects on stabilization, allocation and distribution.

Summary

Using the national income figures for 1967, the problem was posed: what alternatives were open to the government if expenditure plans for the following year, of the private and public sectors taken together, exceeded expected output?

The alternatives imply different amounts to be raised by different taxes, different use of resources between public and private goods and different use of resources between consumption and investment goods. The alternatives have only two things in common: they involve unpleasant choices and they require estimates as to whether or not persons and companies are able to compensate for the changes and so nullify the action taken. In practice post-war policy has largely failed to prevent compensatory changes against the increased taxes of either profits or of incomes.

Ideas about a balanced Budget were examined. These ideas have an intuitive appeal to the individual because of the false analogy often made between the economy of the State and of the private household. As is often the case, a number of important issues underlie the discussion about a balanced Budget, and are worth discussing in their own right. To discuss them in the dogmatic context of 'Balance the Budget' obscures rather than illuminates the real issues.

Finally, practical difficulties in establishing just what is happening in the economy, and what measures should be taken if something needs correcting, were outlined and summarized.

21
Monetary and debt policy

. . . economists have had little difficulty in verifying that monetary policy can influence interest rates and credit conditions, and great difficulty in detecting the influences of the latter, or of the quantity of money itself, on economic activity. Nevertheless, very few economists would be prepared to assert, and certainly none has ever attempted to prove, that monetary policy has no influence whatever on the economy.

JOHNSON, H. G. (1967), *Essays in Monetary Economics.*

Introduction

Monetary and debt policy aims at influencing the economic activity of the community by acting on the quantity and composition of money and assets. Indissolubly linked with this is the policy on interest rates. Initially this chapter will be concerned with internal aspects; balance of payments considerations will then be taken up. The last ten years has seen much work in this field at both the empirical and theoretical level. This book attempts no more than to state some of the main issues, many of which have still to be resolved.

Monetary and debt policy

The definition of money as comprising coin, notes and bank deposits was adopted in Part 1. There it was stressed that it must be borne in mind that money has close substitutes in liquid assets, such as Treasury bills. Questions on the quantity of money fall into those dealing with how this quantity can be controlled, and if control can be achieved, is it successful, or does the presence of liquid assets nullify in whole or in part the attempt at control? From a different standpoint, questions were posed on the relation of the quantity of money to prices. Once the simple, but incorrect, idea that there is a direct relation between the two is rejected, it is necessary to look at the reasons for holding money and the effect of other assets on money holdings.

The importance of the composition of assets has been commented on several times. The monetary authorities for much of the post-war period were concerned to reduce the liquidity of the banks for fear that they would use this as a base for extending loans. Also they aimed to reduce the liquidity of the public in general so as to reduce the potential spending power in the economy. The quantity of assets—that is, whether the total is increasing or decreasing—will have repercussions on liquidity, and make it easier or harder for the authorities to maintain the level of liquidity and structure of rates they require.

Monetary policy therefore involves a study of money, assets and interest rates. It is not possible, without drastic simplification, to separate out one of these components for separate study independently of the other components. Indeed, by trying to do so we may obscure the effects we are trying to trace. Monetary and debt analysis thus becomes an attempt to trace the impact on the economy of money, assets and interest rates. An important part of this impact is the action of each of these components on the other.

Money

Working with the definition of money as coin, notes and bank deposits, the conclusion was reached in Part I that the quantity of coin and notes in the British system is not an important policy variable. Control of bank deposits is open to the authorities by a variety of means; the limitations of each measure was dealt with in Chapter 4. These methods were:

1. Open-market operations. } Have direct effects on other
2. Changing Bank Rate. } rates of interest.
3. Use of directives or requests.
4. Special deposits.

1. Open-market sales to the public will tend to depress prices and so drive up the yields on existing securities; conversely, open-market buying will lower yields. Also the issue of new securities will have to take account of the change in yield on old securities. Open-market operations are concerned with government fixed-interest securities and will not thus automatically affect company finance. However, if the change in yield on government securities is expected to be one that will last for some time, it is usual to expect sympathetic changes in other rates, otherwise money will tend to flow to that sector which now offers better terms. As with most relationships, this can be a two-way affair. The yield on existing securities may be used as a

guide by the authorities as to the interest rates to be charged on new government debt. In the words of the *Radcliffe Report*, 'Over much of the period (1945-59), the authorities were therefore entirely passive, indeed fatalistic, in their attitude to the movement of long-term interest rates' (para. 552).

The dilemma is clear: the authorities can set out to control the rates of interest by being willing to buy and sell on the market as required, in which case they cannot have control over the quantity of assets. Or they can control the quantity of assets, in which case they have to forgo control over the rate of interest and let this find the level at which the quantity of assets they have decided on will be held.

2. Changing Bank Rate operates initially on the short end of the market. Given a change in Bank Rate that is expected to continue for some time, it is likely that the long end of the market will be influenced to some extent.

Neither of these two measures as outlined operates directly to change the *quantity* or *supply* of money, as opposed to the *cost* of borrowing. However, it may be the case that open-market operations are undertaken in an attempt to reduce bank deposits and enforce a contraction on banks. By selling securities to the public, the authorities cause the public to exchange some of their bank deposits for government securities—a leakage as far as the banking system is concerned if the authorities do not return the money to the system. The success of this policy depends, as shown earlier, on the willingness of the public to take up new government issues, how they finance these purchases, and on the ease with which the banks can recoup themselves.

Changing interest rates may influence the amount of money people are willing to hold, i.e. the *demand* for money. The higher the rates of interest the more is forgone by keeping a balance in a current banking account. This effect is not thought generally to be very strong. This is the same conclusion that was reached earlier, when the influence of the rate of interest on decision to spend on consumption or investment goods was discussed.

Items 3 and 4. The use of requests and of special deposits do not directly act on interest rates: they are an attempt to restrict the supply of credit that the banks can extend. In Britain it is clear that sufficient pressure can be brought on the banks to make a credit squeeze on the banks effective. The critical question is whether this means an effective squeeze or whether other institutions take up the running.

The conclusion reached earlier was that the presence of other financial institutions with quasi-money assets does to some extent nullify the attempt to limit credit; the expansion that can take place in trade credit and economizing on money balances also helps to limit the effectiveness of a squeeze. However, this is not to say that a squeeze on the banks can be completely counteracted. In particular, certain sectors of the economy—those that traditionally rely on bank credit—are likely to be more seriously affected and to find it more difficult to find substitute finance. In general, small firms and private individuals will be squeezed more than large firms—for example, house purchase, where bridging loans from a bank play an important role, will be affected. Monetary policy has in the past been recommended because its effects were thought to be impersonal, compared to, say, changing indirect taxes, where a decision has to be made as to which articles shall bear the tax. This is seen to be false. A monetary squeeze no less than other measures has directional effects which may be desired or not desired, but cannot be avoided. It remains true, however, that monetary policy has widespread effects on the economy; these are hard to quantify and depend on a number of circumstances—for example, how long the credit squeeze is expected to last.

Monetary assets and rates of interest

We have seen that the monetary authorities are concerned with both the quantity of monetary assets and the composition of them. They are concerned because of the effect on their ability to control the banks and the financial sector, rates of interest, and consumption and investment generally.

The line marked 1 in the diagram below represents the so-called

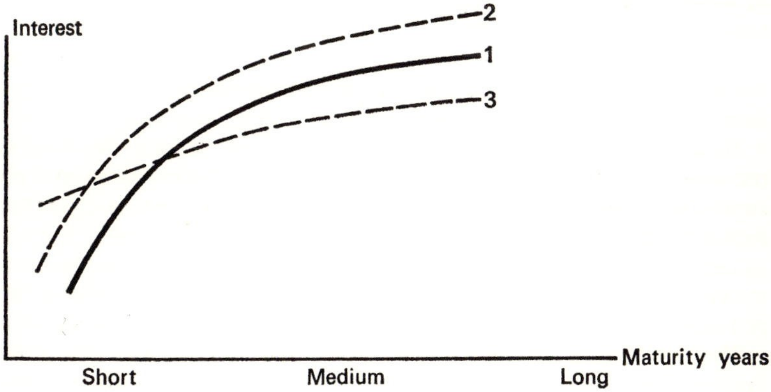

normal-yield curve. It shows the relationship that is usually found between yields and issues of securities of varying maturity, with a similar coupon rate and similar risk in respect of default, e.g. it represents the normal relationship of yield on 6% government securities of varying maturity: other fixed-interest securities will again, as a rule, stand in some stable relationship to yield on government securities.

The yield curve moves sharply up at the short end and then tends to flatten out. The nearer the security is to maturity the more certain is the capital value of the security, the higher yield on longer securities reflects the greater uncertainty as to capital value. An increase in interest rates from say 4% to 6% is not going to make all that difference to the value of a Treasury bill that in any case will be worth its face value in three months. It will make a substantial difference to the market price of a security that is not redeemable for a number of years. Nobody is going to purchase an old security at £100 that yields 4% when a new security that gives 6% can be purchased for £100. The market value of the old security will fall so as to bring its yield into line.

It has already been shown that the monetary authorities can influence the rates of interest in various ways. Here we are talking of a *shift* in the yield curve—say, from curve 1 to curve 2 in the diagram. They can confine their attention to the short end of the market by changing Bank Rate, letting their influence work its way to the longer end of the market. They can conduct open-market operations in longer-term securities and so influence the longer-term direct. Thus selling long-term securities will tend to depress the price and raise the yield; if this is accompanied by an increase in Bank Rate, the yield curve will shift in the direction of curve 2 in the diagram. Selling short-term debt and buying long-term debt will tend to increase the yield on short-term and decrease it on long-term in the manner indicated by curve 3.

One reason why it is necessary to say 'tend to' in any account of influences affecting interest rates is the impossibility of knowing in advance the affect of the influence on expectations and confidence. If a change in Bank Rate, for example, is expected to be reversed in the near future, it is likely to have different results than if it is expected to remain at its new level for some time, and different results again if it is expected to be changed soon in the same direction as the original move.

Other fixed-interest securities, e.g. company debentures, will normally have a slightly higher yield than government securities in order to provide a premium for the risk of default. Again, the action of the market can be expected to keep the yield on government securities and other fixed-interest securities more or less moving together.

When we move to ordinary equity shares of companies, it may be felt intuitively that there should be some connection between yields on fixed-interest securities and yields on equities; but so many other factors play their part in determining the market price of equities that a simple stable relationship is unlikely. In general, we should expect a change in long-term rates on government securities that is expected to last for some time to be reflected in the market for equities by the channelling of some new money, and the channelling of some of the proceeds from the sale of existing securities towards the fixed-interest sector of the market rather than towards the equity market. If such a movement does take place, we have lower prices (i.e. greater yields) in the equity market and the opposite movement in the fixed-interest market. Because risk of default and hopes of gain in the form of dividends paid out by the company and capital value of the equity shares vary so much between companies, and because these hopes and fears need not be linked to (although they may at times be related to) changes in fixed-interest rates, the relationship between equity prices and other security prices is not a direct one. This should not be taken as saying that prices in the two markets are independent of each other. The long-term trend in fixed-interest yields and equity yields will be in the same direction for the reasons indicated: this does not preclude perverse short-term movements in the two kinds of rates.

Influence of interest rates

It has been established so far that the monetary authorities can influence the structure of interest rates in the economy. They do this primarily by Bank Rate and by market operations in their own debt. These effects are fed back by the market and move other fixed-interest rates and perhaps equity rates in the same direction as the movement in government security rates.

It has now to be decided what influence the level of interest rates has on the economy. Here we enter controversial territory. At one extreme we have the view that interest rates are unimportant.

'It seems likely that the interest rates, or the system of rates, will continue to receive from theoreticians the homage due to a ceremonial monarch, without in fact counting for more than such a monarch in the real affairs of western nations' (Shackle, G. L. S. (1961), 252).

Those that hold that interest rates are important have to demonstrate not only a connection between various interest rates (on the lines of the previous section), but a connection between interest rates and real variables in the economy, i.e. between consumption and/or investment.

At several points we have discussed the influence of interest rates, only to conclude that these effects are, at best, very weak ones. Thus both consumption and investment seem relatively insensitive to changes in interest rates. Consumers are affected by changes in down-payment of hire-purchase agreements, but little change is noticed if the interest element of the agreement changes. Many factors are present in a decision whether or not to undertake real investment, and because many investments are required to pay for themselves over a period of a few years a change in interest rates is not likely to change many investment plans. Changes in interest rates are also softened because some fixed-interest charges such as debenture interest and bank overdraft charges, can be offset against tax. If other factors that influence the investment decision change adversely, in addition to an increase in interest rates, an investment project may well be abandoned. For example, if the cost of the investment goes up due to an increase in prices and the expected returns from the investment decrease due to a change in demand for the particular end product of the investment concerned, then these adverse factors will be weighed with the increase in interest rates. In these circumstances it appears to be stretching the use of language and logic to ascribe the investment decision as depending on the rate of interest. As the projected life of the investment goes up the rate of interest plays an increasingly important part: the weight given to this factor has to be increased, but still a variety of factors play their part in the final decision whether to go ahead or not with the investment. Attempts to link changes in the rate of interest with changes in the supply of money via the liquidity effect were also discounted.

Thus far, with the important exception of investments involving long-lived capital installations, we do appear to be dealing with a 'ceremonial monarch' with little real power to influence real variables in the economy. Let us approach this question from a different angle. The stock of financial assets in the economy is very large, and is very large in relation to the flow of new financial assets coming on to the market in any financial period—say, a year. Now the stock of assets must be held by somebody or some institution. Securities can only be sold if somebody else is willing to purchase them. The prices of existing securities will affect the price at which new securities will find willing holders.

It is submitted that, because the amount of existing securities is very large in relation to new issues in a year, the causation runs from the yield on existing securities determining the conditions under which a new issue can be successful rather than from new issues influencing to any great extent the yield on old securities. It is now possible to distinguish two important ways that current yields can influence investment.

Firstly, if current holders of existing securities are content with low yields (i.e. prices of securities are 'high'), firms find the stock market buoyant, and issues of new securities are easier and more profitable. Easier because the market is buoyant, and more profitable because the securities can be issued at a higher price (lower yield). The reverse situation also holds: a depressed market makes it harder and more costly to raise new money by the issue of securities. Thus investment which has to be financed by the issue of securities can be influenced if the stock market can be influenced.[1] It has been argued in the previous section that a change in interest rates on government securities which compete on the market with company issues can have this effect.[2] As an example, the case of an increase in Bank Rate will be taken. Two strands of influence can be picked out: (1) The relative effect: that, because rates on government securities have increased, rates on company securities will have to adjust in the same direction; and (2) effects on confidence. If raising Bank Rate is taken as a sign that a period of restriction is on hand (and particularly if it is accompanied by other measures which depress the

[1] The crucial assumption in this sentence is 'investment which has to be financed by the issue of securities'. Little evidence is available on the extent to which investment, intended to be financed by an issue of securities, is deferred or abandoned, when the stock market becomes unfavourable. The alternative is to go ahead with the investment, if temporary finance is available, with the intention of repaying this when an issue can be made on more favourable terms. Temporary finance is usually costly and is likely to deter the use of this method.

[2] The oral evidence of the representatives of the Issuing Houses Association to the Radcliffe Committee, Minutes of Evidence, Questions 4001-167, is germane. Three strands can be distinguished. Did a change in interest rates affect new issues (1) by freezing the market for technical reasons, i.e. because of interruption of the mechanism for making new issues, (2) by affecting the supply of capital, or (3) by affecting the demand for capital? The effects under (1) and (2) were generally discounted, but the third heading raised some interesting replies: 'The whole terms of an issue depend on the Bank Rate and gilt-edged prices, and if we thought there were likely to be very wide or large fluctuations in the Bank Rate we should just have to be more careful' (Question 4039).

'Presumably it is part of the job of the issuing house, advising their clients, to consider that economic climate, and they would be considering their assessment, in the light of that and of the possibility of a movement in the Bank Rate' (Question 4044).

'But, generally speaking, I would think that the actual mechanical fact of raising the Bank Rate merely means a mechanical adjustment of rates. It might in certain cases make borrowing too expensive; and some people might say that they would not go ahead' (Question 4045).

economy or particular sectors of it), then (1) and (2), taken together, may operate to have a sizeable affect on Stock Exchange prices as a whole or of the particular sectors concerned. In addition, the authorities can influence the market in other ways, e.g. by asking for dividend restraint or altering company tax or allowances.

Secondly, if the return which a firm is receiving from its existing real investment is below the average yield on financial assets, incentive to undertake further real investment will be low. The prudent firm will hold any funds it has in financial assets which will give it a greater return than putting it into real assets. Also it will not attempt to raise money on the market at a cost which exceeds the expected return. This reasoning will not hold in every individual case: it is not difficult, for example, to imagine circumstances where a firm can find profitable real investment outlets even though the yield from its existing real capital is low. However, as an explanation of aggregate behaviour of the real investment market, this influence is likely to be a powerful one.

It may be questioned whether the above reasoning is sufficient to reinstate the influence of interest rates as an important force in the economy. Because it is not possible to point to immediate and direct effects of changes in rates, it is not necessarily correct to assume either that influences are absent or, if present, that they must be weak. Empirical investigations yield as yet no conclusive results. Trying to measure the influence of the rate of interest has much in common with trying to measure the influence of love. We may be quite certain in our minds that both exercise a powerful influence on human affairs, but it is beyond our capacity to demonstrate this conclusively to the sceptic.

External considerations

Monetary and debt policy has major implications for the balance of payments. This is particularly true of a country like Great Britain, which is one of the world's financial centres. One effect follows from the fact that part of the national debt is held by other than British residents. Servicing this part of the debt therefore results in a flow of payments overseas and pressure on the balance of payments. There is thus a possibility that rates of interest considered desirable for internal purposes clash with rates considered desirable for external reasons. The effect on the balance of payments of the external debt depends on a number of considerations. In particular, it depends on whether the overseas holder is prepared (for a time) to hold sterling balances—that is, in effect, to reinvest in sterling securities—or whether these holders convert into gold or foreign currencies. The only official estimate of the effect was given in the *Radcliffe Report* (para. 438). They estimated that a 1% increase in Bank Rate, on the assumption that other short-term rates rise by the same amount, affects the balance of payments adversely to the extent of £15 million a year. This figure can vary a great deal, depending on the amount and type of debt held abroad, the reactions of these holders, and the extent to which transactions are covered in the forward exchange market.

A relative change in interest rates between countries, or changes in confidence, may cause flows of money between financial centres. So-called 'hot' money is money invested short-term for speculative reasons and in order to take advantage of differentials in interest rates. A change in confidence or in interest differentials will reverse the flow. The danger of these flows of short-term money is that they may cause (taking Great Britain as an example) a 'run on the £1'. Since there is nothing to distinguish 'hot' money from other sterling balances (although some idea of the magnitudes involved may be built up from a knowledge of the lenders), an adverse balance of payments caused by the outflow of these volatile funds may so unsettle other foreign holders that they too seek to convert their sterling holdings into gold or foreign currencies, and a run on the £1 is under way. The primary fear is that a devaluation of sterling will take place, which would reduce the value of sterling balances in terms of gold and other currencies. We have therefore an added reason why rates of interest in one country need to take account of rates ruling in other financial centres.

Flows of money between countries depend on much more than differential interest rates; these other influences are usually summed up by the word 'confidence'. In the post-war period Bank Rate has usually been changed only as part of a 'package deal'. That is to say, other things are altered at the same time. For example, an increase in Bank Rate may be accompanied by all, or some, of the following measures: restrictions on the banks; hire purchase made less attractive by increasing the down-payment and decreasing the period over which payments can be spread; restrictions on currency movements; and tax increases. In these circumstances the 'package deal' of which Bank Rate forms a part may restore confidence that sterling is not going to be devalued and result in a substantial improvement in the reserve position—that is, foreign holders are willing to retain their sterling holdings and many of those who caused the adverse outflow by exchanging sterling for gold or other currencies are induced to return to sterling.

This section has confined itself to looking at the main implications of monetary and debt policy on the balance of payments. The subject of the balance of payments is complex: students interested in pursuing it should refer to the literature on the subject. In particular, this book assumes throughout that the present system of fixed exchange rates will be maintained, and policy is looked at in the light of this constraint. There are a few economists who advocate flexible exchange rates and many more who have indicated the need for improvements in the system of international payments. These are important issues which lie outside the scope of this book. From a policy point of view, it is clear that if a satisfactory balance of payments could be achieved by internal means or by international co-operation this would leave more scope for monetary and debt policy to be used to influence the home economy.

Conclusion

The monetary authorities, because of the size and importance of their operations, are not in a position to adopt a 'neutral' policy, where they can leave market forces to determine interest rates and the size and composition of money and assets.

Although policy changes in this field have effects on the internal economy, these effects are not precise, nor can their magnitude be predicted very accurately. Reasons for this stressed the part played by expectations and the effects on confidence. Thus rates of interest above traditional levels may yet stimulate, rather than depress, economic activity, if it is generally thought that rates will shortly go higher and remain higher for some time. Similarly, rates of interest below traditional levels may depress rather than stimulate activity if it is thought rates will shortly go lower and remain lower for some time.

External effects of changes in policy are, unlike internal effects, often very quick to take effect, but they share with internal effects the difficulty of predicting the magnitude of the change. Maintaining confidence that the currency will not be devalued is the most important external role of monetary and debt policy, but monetary and debt policy is only one (although an important one) of the factors affecting confidence.

The conclusions that emerge from consideration of the internal and external effects of monetary and debt policy are contradictory. Internal considerations point to its use as a long-term rather than a short-term instrument of control. External considerations point to its usefulness, particularly in the short-term. This clash goes some way to explain the contradictions that are found in post-war policy.

Given this contradiction, it is possible for purposes of exposition to extract three alternative policies:

At one extreme, policy in this field could concentrate on internal effects. Monetary and debt policies would be pursued with long-term internal economic considerations in mind. Of necessity, this would leave fiscal and other policies to take care of short-term fluctuations and the balance of payments. The chief difficulties are presented by the latter. Control in the short-term was dealt with at length in the previous chapter. Control of the balance of payments is only briefly looked at in this volume. Short-term control by means of capital movements and exchange restrictions are subject to international agreement. More fundamental long-term improvements to the balance of payments by improving Britain's export performance have largely been sought in vain. Fundamental changes in the world's system of international payments require international co-operation and agreement of a kind which has been most conspicuous by its absence.

At the other extreme, policy could concentrate on the external repercussions of monetary and debt policy, leaving internal regulation to be largely carried out by other means. This policy leaves a wide variety of methods open for the achievement of this aim. Thus firms could be at least partially isolated from the effects of high interest rates (set for external reasons) by appropriate tax measures or cheap lending policies. If the structure of the debt judged right for external reasons differed from the structure judged right for purposes of internal control over the monetary system, the banks and other financial institutions could likewise be partially screened by appropriate reserve requirements and other measures.

The third policy makes no attempt to separate the domestic economy from the international economy, considering each as part of an indivisible whole. Monetary and debt policy, where internal and external considerations differ, would compromise, and fiscal and other methods would be used to reinforce the policy where it fell short.

It is not the purpose of this volume to canvass one of these policies over the others. It should be clear from the previous analysis that what is the best policy in one set of circumstances may not be so in another set of circumstances. In economics there is no golden rule that can be applied that allows escape from the long and exhausting examination and evaluation of current and expected conditions.

Summary

This chapter started with a résumé of how effectively the monetary authorities can control the supply of money and credit. The authorities are in the dilemma of being able to influence *either* rates of interest *or* the quantity of assets. Their main influence on rates of interest is by changing Bank Rate and by open-market operations.

The influence of interest rates on the economy is important because it will attract or repel funds from abroad, and is likely to have some effect on long-lived capital investment. Other effects on the economy are harder to pinpoint, although if the stock market can be influenced this is likely to affect companies thinking of raising new money by a stock or share issue. The impact of a change in interest rates is difficult to measure because it depends so much on whether the change affects, and in what direction it affects, confidence and business expectations.

This section of the book set out with the limited aim of showing just how difficult management of the economy is, whether this is attempted by fiscal or monetary means. It is not just that our theories about how the economy operates are imperfect and our knowledge of the facts imprecise: given perfection in both cases, there would still be disagreement because value judgments enter as to which way should be selected out of numerous possible ways to achieve any particular object. This has important policy implications which are developed in the next and final chapter.

22
Conclusions

There are times when some aspects of our economic situation have what is almost a Biblical quality: 'And life becomes harder in those times, and the people refused to co-operate one with another. Citizen was pitched against citizen, and there was disarray in that country's market-place. Few were content with their lot, and none could determine how the fruits of the land should be shared. Whereupon there came unto the midst of the people, a prophet who told them: "There is much waste in the land because the people are divided." And the queen of that country did summon the prophet to the palace, and did charge him to bring peace and prosperity unto the land.'

WILLIAM KEEGAN, *Financial Times*, October 9th, 1967. Commenting on the Prices and Incomes Board.

Part III of this book sets out to analyse the problems of managing the economy via fiscal and monetary policies. The conclusions are pessimistic: that within the existing state of knowledge effects of policy are frequently uncertain and always difficult to quantify. The need for better data, collected more quickly, seems self-evident. To the author these facts lead to an important positive result: that the first priority of a fiscal system should be equity. Inevitably objectives that include equity, full employment, stability of the value of money, a satisfactory balance of payments, and emphasis on growth will show conflicts. Without equity, the achievement of these other objectives are likely to be harmed. The morale of taxpayers is at a low ebb, as has been brought out at numerous points of this book. The fact is that large numbers of citizens *feel* the current system to be unjust. The most frequent complaints are made about high marginal rates of tax at one extreme, and at the other extreme the existence of large pockets of poverty, particularly amongst the old, the young, and the disabled.

This book has attempted to show that both of these criticisms are largely justified and they follow inevitably from the structure of tax and benefits that has been adopted. Piecemeal adaptation of the system has been ruled out as a solution, since this has resulted in the past in yet more anomalies and complexities in the system. The solution has been envisaged basically in terms of recasting the tax base.

It is clear that a solution on these lines needs to be backed by a full-scale study, with detailed facts and figures; it is equally clear that such a study is beyond the scope of this book and of a single person. One country has recently undertaken such an investigation in depth, and a brief summary of the main recommendations and results follow. It is not suggested that the tax conditions in the two countries are identical, but they do have a lot in common. In particular, there are common problems of high marginal rates of tax that are easily avoided, harsh treatment of low-income families and disincentives that follow from the existing tax structure.

The Report of the Royal Commission on Taxation of Canada, produced in 1966, is a lengthy, complex report in six volumes. The Commission was appointed in 1962 and the inquiry cost nearly $3,500,000: Its major proposals were:

The ability-to-pay principle would be reflected in a new 'comprehensive tax base' that would include, for tax purposes, all net gains in purchasing power, including capital gains and windfalls and many other forms of real income that now are tax-exempt.

Rates of personal income tax would be greatly reduced from the present top rate of 80% to 50%.

New tax-paying units would be created and a different rate schedule would apply to each: families (parents and children under twenty-one, or twenty-five if receiving education) and individuals. Families must aggregate income. Gifts within the family would not count for tax purposes until a child was eligible for tax treatment on his own, when tax adjustments would be made.

Anyone with large fluctuations in income would be permitted to average that income over a five-year period, provided the tax saving amounted to more than $50 (to avoid numerous claims), and provided that income in the lowest year of the average period is less than 75% of income of the highest year. Special averaging rate schedules would be available, so that only one computation of tax needs to be made, instead of a new computation for each year averaged.

Corporations would be taxed at 50%, but the shareholder would receive credit for this. The shareholder, that is, would be liable at his personal rate for gross dividends and capital gains on his shares, but would be credited with the 50% tax paid by corporations.

Studies indicated that as a result of their recommendations and assuming the same amount of revenue raised, 46% of the country's

7 million taxpayers would get income cuts of more than 15%.

The Commission emphasized that their proposals should be considered as part of a 'package deal' and that to select some of their proposals and reject others would probably wreck the intentions of their proposals.

The Commission paid much attention to other objectives besides equity; particularly to the effects on growth. They said that the principal objective was to design a tax system that would be fair, but one that would not erode future sources of income simply in order to redistribute current income. They believe that this goal has been achieved while providing for more Canadian ownership of Canadian industry without discriminating against foreign investors, and also achieving an improved allocation of savings.

> We hope Canadians will accept the challenge implicit in our recommendations. And there can be no doubt that our recommendations constitute a great challenge. Preconceived opinions about taxation are deeply and firmly held. Many will find it difficult to take a new look at old questions. Because some facts cannot be readily ascertained, honest differences of opinion are inevitable. There is a danger that the debate about these minor factual questions will divert attention from the major issues (Vol. I, 2).

There is therefore evidence, backed by detailed investigations, from a country with a tax system not so very different from Britain's and faced with similar problems and inequities, that a tax system can be devised that would overcome many of these problems. The author feels that the time is now overdue for a full-scale investigation on comprehensive lines in this country. The proposed entry to the Common Market already dictates, because they have adopted a system of value-added tax, that this area of taxation be investigated. But yet another Commission with limited terms of reference is not the answer; nothing short of a comprehensive look at the whole field of tax and benefits is likely to be able to come to grips with the problems that have been outlined.

The difficulties of controlling the economy have been stressed. If equity was achieved in the tax and benefit structure, these problems would still remain, but equity could be achieved without harmful effects on other objectives.

Income tax changes would probably still remain the chief method of affecting consumption expenditures. Management would be easier with a wider tax base with a smoother progression and lower marginal rates of tax. Britain has developed over the years a new fiscal weapon in the form of investment allowances and grants to industry, which, despite their drawbacks, can be used to influence investment. If investment grants and allowances are used in this way, the taxation of companies on the lines indicated in Chapter 13 would go a long way to ensuring more equitable treatment between individuals and companies. The shareholder pays income tax both on his gross dividends and any capital gains on the sale of his shares, and can be credited with tax paid by the company. The public at large gain if the investment results in a better or cheaper product. Finally, an indispensable prerequisite for the control of inflation by means of a prices and incomes policy is, it has been argued, a fiscal system that tries to achieve equity.

Society in Britain is fortunate in having reached a stage where it can afford to think, not only in terms of growth, but also in terms of the quality of life of its citizens. The means are available if we have the will.

Works cited

ABEL-SMITH, B. and TOWNSEND, P. (1965), *The Poor and the Poorest*, Bell.
'Administration of the Wage Stop' (1967), Ministry of Social Security.
'Administrative Structure of the Medical and Related Services in England and Wales' (1968), Ministry of Health.
'Annual Report of the Ministry of Health' (1967), H.M.S.O.
'Annual Report of the Ministry of Social Security' (1967), H.M.S.O.
ARTIS, M. J. (1965), *Foundations of British Monetary Policy*, Blackwell.
'Bank Charges' (1967), Report No. 34, National Board for Prices and Incomes.
'Bank Liquidity in the United Kingdom' (December, 1962), *Bank of England Quarterly Bulletin*.
BEVERIDGE, W. H. (1944), *Full Employment in a Free Society*, George Allen & Unwin.
BREAK, G. F. (September, 1957), 'Income Taxes and Incentives to Work', *American Economic Review*, XLVII.
BRITTAN, S. (1964), *The Treasury under the Tories, 1951-1964*, Pelican.
BRONFENBRENNER, M. and HOLZMAN, F. D. (September, 1963), 'Survey of Inflation Theory', *American Economic Review*, LIII, No. 4.
CAVES, R. E. (1968), ed. for the Brookings Institute of Washington, *Britain's Economic Prospects*, George Allen & Unwin.
'Circumstances of Families' (1967), Ministry of Social Security.
COLE, D. and UTTING, J. (1962), *The Economic Circumstances of Old People*, Codicote Press.
'Commentary' (March, 1966), *Bank of England Quarterly Bulletin*.
'Committee on the Working of the Monetary System' (1959), Cmnd. 827.
'Committee on Turnover Tax' (1964), Cmnd. 2300.
'Conditions Favourable to Faster Growth' (1963), National Economic Development Council.
'Control of Bank Lending: the Cash Deposits Scheme' (June, 1968), *Bank of England Quarterly Bulletin*.
'Corporation Tax' (1965), Cmnd. 2646.
CRAMP, A. B. (February, 1963), 'Banks and Their Competitors', *The Banker*.
—— (June, 1966), 'Control of the Money Supply', *Economic Journal*.
—— (October, 1967), 'The Control of Bank Deposits', *Lloyds Bank Review*.
CROUCH, R. L. (December, 1964), 'The Inadequacy of "New Orthodox" Methods of Monetary Control', *Economic Journal*.

—— (August, 1965), 'The Genesis of Bank Deposits, New English Version', *Bulletin of the Oxford Institute of Statistics.*

CYRIAX, G. (March, 1968), 'Tax Incentives—A New Urgency', *The Banker.*

DALTON, H. (1959), *The Inequality of Incomes,* Routledge & Kegan Paul.

DANIEL, W. W. D. (March, 1968), 'Personal Taxation and Occupational Incentives', *The Banker.*

DENMAN, D. R. (1958), *Origins of Ownership,* George Allen & Unwin.

'Development Areas Regional Employment Premium' (1967), Cmnd. 3310.

'Distribution of the National Debt' (March, 1967), *Bank of England Quarterly Bulletin.*

DOW, J. C. R. (1964), *The Management of the British Economy, 1945-60,* C.U.P.

DREES, W., JR. (1967), 'Efficiency in Government Spending', *Public Finance,* XXII, Nos. 1-2/1967.

EISENSTEIN, L. (1961). *The Ideologies of Taxation,* New York: The Ronald Press.

EISNER, R. and STROTZ, R. H. (1963), 'Determinants of Business Investment', contained in *Impacts of Monetary Policy,* Prentice-Hall.

'Employment Policy' (1944), Cmnd. 6527.

'Expert Committee on Compensation and Betterment' (1942), Cmnd. 6386.

FELDSTEIN, M. S. (December, 1967), 'The Effectiveness of the British Differential Profits Tax', *Economic Journal.*

FERGUSON, J. M., ed. (1964), *Public Debt and Future Generations,* University of North Carolina Press.

Financial Accounts of the U.K. H.M.S.O.

'Financial Institutions' (June, 1965), *Bank of England Quarterly Bulletin.*

Financial Statistics (Monthly publication), Central Statistical Office.

FRIEDMAN, M. (1962), *Capitalism and Freedom,* University of Chicago Press.

GRUNDY, J. M. (1956), *Tax Problems of the Family Company,* Sweet & Maxwell.

HARBURY, C. D. (December, 1962), 'Inheritance in the Distribution of Personal Wealth', *Economic Journal.*

HARCOURT, G. C. and WHITTINGTON, G. (June, 1965), 'A Comment on the Irrelevancy of the British Differential Profits Tax', *Economic Journal.*

HEMMING, M. F. W. (August, 1965), 'Social Security in Britain and Certain Other Countries', *National Institute Economic Review,* No. 33.

—— and DUFFY, H. (August, 1964), 'The Price of Accommodation', *National Institute Economic Review,* No. 29.

HOCKLEY, G. C. (May/June, 1967), 'Taxation and the Employment of Married Women', *British Tax Review.*

—— (January/February, 1968), 'Capital Gains and Inflation' and a 'Rejoinder', *British Tax Review.*

—— (March, 1968), 'Incentives under a Value-added Tax', *The Banker.*

'How the Banks Compete for Deposits' (July, 1967), *The Banker.*

'Incidence of Taxes and Social Service Benefits' (February, 1968 and July, 1968), *Economic Trends,* Nos. 172 and 177.

'Inflows and Outflows of Foreign Funds' (June, 1962), *Bank of England Quarterly Bulletin.*

'Investment Incentives' (1966), Cmnd. 2874.
JOHNSON, H. G. (1967), *Essays in Monetary Economics,* George Allen & Unwin.
KALDOR, N. (1955), *An Expenditure Tax,* George Allen & Unwin.
KEYNES, J. M. (1936), *The General Theory of Employment, Interest and Money,* Macmillan.
—— (1940), *How to Pay for the War,* Macmillan.
'Land Commission' (1965), Cmnd. 2771.
LEES, D. (October, 1967), 'Families and Fiscal Reform', *Lloyds Bank Review.*
'London Money Market' (May, 1966), *Midland Bank Review.*
'Management of Money Day by Day' (March, 1963), *Bank of England Quarterly Bulletin.*
MEADE, J. E. (1964), *Efficiency, Equality and the Ownership of Property,* George Allen & Unwin.
MERRITT, A. J. (1968), *Executive Remuneration in the* U.K., Longmans.
—— and MONK, D. A. G. (1967), *Inflation Taxation and Executive Remuneration,* Hallam Press.
MISHAN, E. J. (1967), *The Costs of Economic Growth,* Staples Press.
'More Light on Personal Saving' (April, 1965), *Economic Trends.*
MUSGRAVE, R. A. (1959), *The Theory of Public Finance,* McGraw-Hill.
—— and SHOUP, C. S., eds. (1959), *Readings in the Economics of Taxation,* George Allen & Unwin.
MYRDAL, G. (1960), *Beyond the Welfare State,* Duckworth.
'National Income and Expenditure' (1968), Central Statistical Office.
'Nationalized Industries: A Review of Economic and Financial Objectives', (November, 1967), Cmnd. 3437.
'National Superannuation & Social Insurance Proposals for Earnings-Related Social Security' (1969), Cmnd. 3883.
NEWLYN, W. T. (June, 1964), 'The Supply of Money and Its Control', *Economic Journal.*
'Note Circulation' (March, 1965), *Bank of England Quarterly Bulletin.*
'Official Transactions in the Gilt-edged Market' (June, 1966), *Bank of England Quarterly Bulletin.*
'Overseas and Foreign Banks in London' (September, 1961 and June, 1968), *Bank of England Quarterly Bulletin.*
PEACOCK, A. T. and SHANNON, R. (August, 1968) 'The Welfare State and the Redistribution of Income', *Westminster Bank Review.*
PEACOCK, A. T. (January, 1964), 'Problems of Government Budgetary Reform', *Lloyds Bank Review.*
—— and WISEMAN, J. (1961), *The Growth of Public Expenditure in the United Kingdom,* O.U.P.
'Post Office Giro' (1965), Cmnd. 2751.
PREST, A. R. (1968), 'The Budget and Interpersonal Distribution', *Public Finance,* XXIII, Nos. 1-2/1968.
'Radcliffe Report'. Refer to 'Committee on the Working of the Monetary System' (1959).
'Railway Policy' (November, 1967), Cmnd. 3439.
'Reform of the Exchequer Accounts' (1963), Cmnd. 2014.

'Report of the Canadian Royal Commission on Taxation' (1966). Queen's Printer, Ottawa, Canada.

'Report on the U.S. Commission on Money and Credit (1961), Prentice-Hall.

'Report of the Committee on Local Authority and Allied Personal Social Services' (1968), Cmnd. 3703.

'Report of the Committee on the Taxation of Trading Profits' (1951), Cmnd. 8189.

REVELL, J. R. S. and HOCKLEY, G. C. (July and December, 1960), 'A Survey of the Holders of Local Authority Debt', *Local Government Finance.*

ROBINSON, J. (1962), *Economic Philosophy*, Pelican.

'Royal Commission on the Taxation of Profits and Income' (1954), Second Report, Cmnd. 9105, and (1955) Final Report, Cmnd. 9474.

RUBNER, A. (June, 1964), 'The Irrelevancy of the British Differential Profits Tax', *Economic Journal.*

SANDFORD, C. T. (1965), 'Taxing Inheritance and Capital Gains', Hobart Paper, No. 32.

—— (April, 1967), 'The Swedes can do It, why can't We?' *The Banker.*

'Selective Employment Tax' (1966), Cmnd. 2986.

SEWILL, H. (November, 1966), 'Automatic Unit for National Taxation and Insurance,' Conservative New Techniques, No. 6.

SHACKLE, G. L. S. (June, 1961), 'Recent Theories concerning the Nature and Role of Interest', *Economic Journal.*

SHULTZ, W. J. and HARRISS, C. L. (1965), *American Public Finance*, 8th edition, Prentice-Hall.

SIMONS, H. (1938), *Personal Income Taxation*, Chicago.

'Social Insurance and Allied Services' (1942), Cmnd. 6404.

'Social Services for All?' (1968), various authors, Fabian Society Tracts, Nos. 382-5.

Statistical Abstracts of the U.K., H.M.S.O.

STONE, R. and others (1962), *A Computable Model of Economic Growth*, Chapman & Hall.

SUITS, D. B. (1963), 'The Determinants of Consumer Expenditure: a Review of Present Knowledge', contained in *Impacts of Monetary Policy*, 1-57, Prentice-Hall.

'Taxation of Trading Profits' (1951), Cmnd. 8189.

TEW, B. and HENDERSON, R. F. (1959), eds., *Company Income and Finance, 1949-53*, C.U.P.

TITMUS, R. M. (1962), *Income Distribution and Social Change*, Unwin University Books.

—— (1963), *Essays on 'the Welfare State'*, Unwin University Books.

TOBIN, J. (1963), 'An Essay on Principles of Debt Management', contained in *Fiscal and Debt Management Policies*, Prentice-Hall.

VICKRAY, W. (1947), *Agenda for Progressive Taxation*, New York: The Ronald Press.

WHEATCROFT, G. S. A. (January/February, 1968), 'A Reply to "Capital Gains and Inflation"', *British Tax Review.*

WILLIAMS, B. R. (1967), 'The New Social Contract', Conservative Political Centre.

Further reading

The following is intended as an introduction to books for further reading. The list is far from exhaustive: more specialized references can be obtained from the list of 'Works Cited' in this volume.

THE MONETARY SYSTEM

Committee on the Working of the Monetary System (1959), Cmd. 827.

Day, A. C. L., *The Economics of Money*, 2nd edition 1968, O.U.P.

Sayers, R. S., *Modern Banking*, 7th edition 1967, O.U.P.

PUBLIC FINANCE Texts with U.K. emphasis

Hicks, U. K., *Public Finance*, 3rd edition 1968, C.U.P.

Prest, A. R., *Public Finance*, 3rd edition 1967, Weidenfeld & Nicolson.

OTHER

Musgrave, R. A., *The Theory of Public Finance*, 1959, McGraw-Hill. An advanced theoretical text.

Musgrave, R. A. & Peacock, A. T., *Classics in the Theory of Public Finance*, 1958, New York: The Macmillan Company.

Readings in the Economics of Taxation, 1959, Allen & Unwin.

POLICY

Brittan, S., *The Treasury under the Tories 1951-1964*, 1964, Pelican.

Caves, R. E., ed., *Britain's Economic Prospects*, 1968, Allen & Unwin.

Dow, J. C. R., *The Management of the British Economy 1945-60*, 1964, C.U.P.

Index